Hitler's
Stalingrad
Decisions

INTERNATIONAL CRISIS BEHAVIOR SERIES

Edited by Michael Brecher

VOLUME 1   Michael Brecher, with Benjamin Geist, *Decisions in Crisis: Israel, 1967 and 1973* (1980)

VOLUME 2   Avi Shlaim, *The United States and the Berlin Blockade, 1948–1949: A Study in Crisis Decision-Making* (1983)

VOLUME 3   Alan Dowty, *Middle East Crisis: U.S. Decision-Making in 1958, 1970, and 1973* (1984)

VOLUME 4   Karen Dawisha, *The Kremlin and the Prague Spring: Decisions in Crisis* (1984)

VOLUME 5   Geoffrey Jukes, *Hitler's Stalingrad Decisions* (1985)

GEOFFREY JUKES

Hitler's Stalingrad Decisions

University of California Press
BERKELEY · LOS ANGELES · LONDON

University of California Press
Berkeley and Los Angeles, California

University of California Press, Ltd.
London, England

© 1985 by
The Regents of the University of California

Printed in the United States of America

1 2 3 4 5 6 7 8 9

Library of Congress Cataloging in Publication Data

Jukes, Geoffrey.
Hitler's Stalingrad decisions.
(International crisis behavior series; v. 5)
Bibliography: p.
Includes index.
1. Stalingrad, Battle of, 1942–1943.   2. Hitler,
Adolf, 1889–1945.   3. Strategy.   I. Title.   II. Series.
D764.3.S7J79   1985   940.54'21   84-16280
ISBN 0-520-05130-0

Contents

List of Maps vi

Foreword by Michael Brecher vii

Acknowledgments xi

Introduction 1

1. The Pre-crisis Period 21

2. August–September 1942: Failures and Dismissals 49

3. Transition to the Crisis Period 76

4. The Beginning of the Crisis Period: November 1942 95

5. The Crisis Continued: December 1942– 2 February 1943 112

6. The Post-crisis Period 148

7. Overall Conclusions 172

8. Hitler and Stalin Compared 221

Appendix 245

Bibliography 249

Index 253

Maps

1. German Summer Offensive, 1942:
   Basic OKH Plan and
   Hitler's Amendments   25

2. Position at End of the Pre-crisis Period,
   19 November 1942   94

3. The Soviet Counteroffensive,
   19–30 November 1942   106

4. The Relief Attempt,
   12–18 December 1942   119

5. The Finale at Stalingrad,
   10 January–2 February 1943   141

6. The Post-crisis Period:
   The German Counteroffensive,
   19 February–25 March 1943   154

Foreword

MOST INTERNATIONAL CRISES during the half-century 1929–1979 occurred in an environment of negative peace, that is, an absence of collective violence between two or more independent states. Many crises were triggered by violent acts and/or involved violence as a technique of crisis management, including full-scale war. Slightly less than one-fourth of these crises occurred *during* a war and are designated Intra-War Crises (IWCs). They are defined as situational changes which generate among the decision-makers of a state three interrelated perceptions: a high threat to one or more basic values; time constraint in responding to the threat; and an adverse change in the military balance.

IWCs are triggered by several types of acts, events, or developments during a war:

1. Entry of a new major actor into an ongoing war (e.g., the People's Republic of China into the Korean War in October 1950, a crisis for the United States and South Korea).

2. Exit of a major actor (e.g., Germany's attack on Western Europe in May 1940, leading to the fall of France, a crisis for the U.K.).

3. Technological escalation of a war (e.g., the introduction of nuclear weapons with the Hiroshima A-bomb in August 1945, a crisis for Japan in the closing days of the Second World War).

4. A major escalation other than the introduction of a qualitatively advanced technology (e.g., the Tet Offensive by North Vietnam in January–March 1968, as a crisis for the United States and South Vietnam).

5. A perceived high probability that a major actor will enter the war (e.g., Israel's crisis in November 1956 arising from the Soviet threat to intervene directly in the Suez-Sinai War).

6. A perceived high probability that a major actor will withdraw from a war (e.g., the anticipated U.S. withdrawal from the Vietnam War at the time of the Paris Accords, in January 1973, a crisis for South Vietnam).

7. Defeat in a military campaign or significant battle (e.g., the defeat at El Alemain, a crisis for Germany in November 1942).

It is this last type of Intra-War Crisis which Geoffrey Jukes analyzes in depth in the following pages. The literature on the battle of Stalingrad is vast. Mr. Jukes himself has contributed to our knowledge of this turning point in the military history of the Second World War. However, the present work is "a study not of German military history but of Hitler's decision-making in a 'crisis within a crisis.'" The author justifies this focus by noting the centralization of decision-making in Nazi Germany in Hitler's own person, acting through military, party, and governmental agencies under his direct control: the Führer Headquarters (FHQ); the Army Headquarters (OKH); the State Chancellory; and the Presidential Secretariat.

Relying heavily on the multi-volume *War Diary* of the High Command of the Armed Forces, Jukes provides a gripping account of the major decisions, both Führer Directives and Führer Orders, which were made during the twice daily Führer Conferences at FHQ. This is done with care for the three periods of Germany's Stalingrad Intra-War Crisis: *pre-crisis*, a growth of perceived threat from soon after the launching of the German offensive on 28 June 1942—the realization that Soviet forces were withdrawing rather than being destroyed—to the third week of November 1942, a threat perception accentuated by Rommel's defeat at El Alamein and the Allied invasion of North Africa on 7–8 November; *crisis*, a sharp rise in perceived threat, along with an awareness of time pressure and of an adverse change in the military balance, from 19–22 November—when the besiegers at Stalingrad suddenly became the besieged—until 24 January 1943; and *post-crisis*, from 24 January, when Army Group A was successfully evacuated from the Caucasus, to the last week of March.

The narrative in Chapters 1–6 is accompanied by an instructive analysis, for each of the three periods, of the Crisis Components as designated by the framework for comparative case studies designed for the International Crisis Behavior (ICB) Project, namely: the *Environmental Change(s)* which served as the crisis trigger (e.g., the major Soviet counteroffensive north and south of Stalingrad on

19–20 November 1942, as the catalyst to the crisis period); the *Value Threat* (e.g., annihilation of two Army Groups comprising 77 divisions and 1,750,000 men); the *Probability of an Adverse Change in the Military Balance* (e.g., at least eleven requests for permission to withdraw from Stalingrad by German Generals to Hitler from 22 November 1942 to 30 January 1943); and *Time Pressure* (e.g., the awareness of time constraints by the field commanders and most High Command generals—but not by Hitler).

In Chapter 7, Jukes evaluates the Stalingrad Intra-War Crisis in terms of the nine ICB research questions, by testing hypotheses about the effects of escalating and de-escalating crisis-induced stress on patterns of information and consultation, on decisional forums, and on the search for and consideration of alternatives. Illustrative of his findings are the following:

1. The evidence points strongly to increased conceptual rigidity by Hitler under the stress of the peak crisis period.

2. There is no evidence that Hitler's cognitive performance was impaired by fatigue.

3. His receptivity to new information declined as the crisis progressed.

4. The evidence concerning the effects of stress on the search for and evaluation of alternatives is mixed.

5. Increasing stress did lead to a higher value being placed on immediate goals and less attention being paid to the distant future.

6. Most significantly, perhaps, the range of perceived alternatives did not narrow under the impact of greater stress, contrary to the findings from other international crises; the four alternatives open to the besieged German force at Stalingrad were all considered.

Combining the methods of history and political science, Jukes's study of Germany's Stalingrad Crisis makes a valuable contribution at several levels:

1. New light is shed on one of the turning points in twentieth-century world politics.

2. The study enriches our understanding of a crucial case study of state behavior in a hitherto neglected type of international phenomenon, namely, an Intra-War Crisis.

3. Evidence from the behavior of decision-making in a crucial *wartime* crisis is marshaled in order to test hypotheses which

have been generated primarily from crucial *non-war* crises: the Powers in the June–July 1914 Crisis, which occurred prior to a world war; the United States in June 1950, prior to its active entry into the Korean War; and the superpowers in the 1962 Cuban Missile Crisis.

For all of these reasons, and more, this is a welcome addition to the literature on international crisis behavior.

Michael Brecher, Director
International Crisis Behavior Project

Acknowledgments

THE RESEARCH FOR this book was carried out under the auspices of the International Crisis Behavior Research Project. My thanks are due to Professor Michael Brecher for his invitation to participate, his patience, and his help in securing funds from Canada Council resources; the Federal German Bundesarchiv in Koblenz and the Militärarchiv in Freiburg, especially the Reading Room staffs; the Warden and Fellows of Wadham College, Oxford, and the President and Fellows of Clare Hall, Cambridge; Mrs. Robin Ward and Mrs. Shirley Steer for research and secretarial assistance beyond the call of duty; and my wife, Eunice, for forbearance.

Introduction

THIS STUDY IS concerned with the impact of "crisis within crisis" upon the highly centralized decision-making process at the top level of government in Nazi Germany at the end of 1942.

The war itself was a "crisis" of German foreign policy, because Hitler did not expect the British and French to go to war in September 1939, nor did he anticipate that sensational German military successes in the first two years would not persuade the British to respond to peace feelers. In the belief that Britain could do little against Germany, Hitler turned his back and attacked the Soviet Union in June 1941. At first, he appeared as successful as in the previous campaigns in Europe; but a Soviet counteroffensive, launched at Moscow early in December 1941, inflicted on the German army its first major defeat of the war. Although the Soviet offensive eventually petered out, it ensured Russian survival into the next campaigning season, something that many German generals, apprehensive of the wisdom of the invasion, had hoped to avoid. This, coupled with America's entry into the war in the same month, made it clear in hindsight that Hitler's largest single error of the war was his decision to invade the Soviet Union without first subjugating the United Kingdom. It was this that the Chief of the Wehrmacht Operations Staff, Generaloberst Alfred Jodl, undoubtedly had in mind when, in 1946, shortly before he was hanged, he declared that this was the time in which the "God of war" passed from Germany's side to that of her enemies.[1]

1. In Percy E. Schramm, *Hitler: The Man and the Military Leader* (Chicago: Quadrangle Books, 1971), Appendix II, p. 203.

1

But however clear that may have become in hindsight, it was not so at the time. In mid-1942, German troops were again advancing in Soviet territory and in North Africa, while U-boats were scoring impressive successes in the Battle of the Atlantic, and the new Japanese ally was making spectacular progress in the Pacific. Only in the air was there obvious cause for dissatisfaction, in the Luftwaffe's inability to stop nightly British bombing raids on the cities of northwest Germany; but even these were as yet thorns in the flesh rather than daggers at the heart. It was already possible to envisage German troops from North Africa linking up with others south of the Caucasus, and going on to join hands with the Japanese somewhere in India.

From late October 1942 to April 1943, the picture changed radically. The Second Battle of El Alamein (23 October–4 November 1942) put an end to the dream of ousting the British from the Middle East. The Anglo-American landings in French North Africa began on the night of 7/8 November; and on 19 November, the Russians launched a massive counteroffensive at Stalingrad. The catastrophe to which this led Germany was barely mitigated by a local victory at Kharkov and Belgorod before the spring thaw temporarily immobilized the forces of both sides in a sea of mud.

This victory, moreover, was to prove the only significant bright spot in a dark winter for Germany. In March, merchant shipping sinkings in the Atlantic remained high, and U-boat losses low; but in April, a dramatic turnabout was observed, so far-reaching that in May the Commander-in-Chief Submarines, Admiral Dönitz, was forced to concede defeat and withdraw all U-boats from the North Atlantic. Although the Germans remained unaware of the fact for over thirty years,[2] the largest single factor in this also dated to November 1942, when the British "broke" the new U-boat cipher machine system, Triton, and recovered the capacity to read U-boat traffic which they had lost on its introduction in February.[3] November 1942 is therefore the pivotal month of the period, and probably of the entire Second World War.

2. The British Government authorized reference to the activities during the Second World War of the Government Code and Cypher School only after the publication in 1974 of Group Captain Frederick W. Winterbotham's *The Ultra Secret* (London: Weidenfeld and Nicolson, 1974).

3. Patrick Beesly, *Very Special Intelligence* (London: Sphere Books, 1978), pp. 155–160 and 206–213.

Despite the artificially engineered monolithic facade of the one-party National Socialist state, there were deep rifts in the structure, especially between Hitler and many senior Army officers. In 1938, the Chief of General Staff was privy to a plot to overthrow Hitler, which was frustrated by the Führer's success in achieving British, French, and Italian consent at Munich to the acquisition of the Sudetenland from Czechoslovakia. Army plotting against Hitler continued until the unsuccessful assassination attempt of 20 July 1944.[4] The objectives of the plotters were various, but a common factor among the military anti-Nazis was a belief that Hitler's foreign policy objectives were excessive and must eventually bring disaster upon Germany.

Hitler had served in the First World War, rising to the rank of Gefreiter (Private First Class), and receiving the Iron Cross First Class (seldom awarded to enlisted men) for bravery.[5] He therefore had no military training comparable to that of the career professional officers whom politics had made his servants, and he shared the front-line soldier's contempt for "chair-borne" generals such as those with whom he was surrounded at his headquarters. The boldness of his military thinking owed much to his lack of training and therefore of possible stereotyping; and until the defeat at Moscow, he could validly claim to have achieved remarkable results by overruling the professional caution of his generals.

However, the succession of victories between the outbreak of the war and early 1941, marred only by the failure of the German Air Force to win the Battle of Britain and thereby make an invasion possible, fed his belief in his own infallibility, and especially in the superiority of his military judgment over that of his professional military advisers. The invasion of the Soviet Union in June 1941, like those of Norway, Denmark, the Low Countries, and France in 1940, was a subject of deep apprehension among the German military, alleviated or suppressed only by the belief that the Red Army could be defeated west of the River Dnieper, and that the Soviet public's distaste for the Stalin regime would cause it to collapse in the aftermath of initial military defeats.

4. See, for example, Fabian von Schlabrendorff, *Offiziere Gegen Hitler* (Zurich: Europa Verlag, 1946); and Roger Manvell and Heinrich Fraenkel, *The July Plot* (London: Bodley Head, 1964).

5. Konrad Heiden, *Der Fuehrer* (Boston: Houghton Mifflin, 1944), pp. 77–86.

The campaign in the summer of 1941 began with enormous successes: Stalin's insistence on standing fast doomed entire Army Groups to encirclement and virtual annihilation, and Soviet losses in killed or captured alone substantially exceeded four million during the first six months of the Soviet-German war. Nevertheless, the prime military objective of destruction of the Red Army before the winter was not attained; and of the targets of the three major strategic offensives—the capture of Leningrad, Moscow, and the Ukraine—only the latter was achieved. By the beginning of December 1941, the German offensive against Moscow had stalled, and the Russians then instituted a counteroffensive of which Hitler had not considered them capable. The outcome was a near-panic in the German headquarters, leading to the dismissal of the Commanders-in-Chief of the Army, Field Marshal von Brauchitsch, and of all three Army Groups operating on the front between the Baltic and the Black Sea coast. Coinciding as it did with the entry of the United States into the war, this period was defined, after the end of the war, by one of Hitler's principal military advisers, Colonel-General Alfred Jodl, as the one in which Hitler recognized for the first time that the war was lost. There is, however, no indication that Hitler ever acknowledged this, and there is ample evidence that, although discountenanced by the defeat before Moscow, he nevertheless thought that it was not irreversible, while, until very late in the war, he grossly underestimated the capacity of American industrial and manpower resources to influence the final outcome. Whatever private misgivings he may have had, he at once set in motion a planning process for a renewed offensive on the south of the Eastern Front in 1942. The objectives of this offensive were, first, to reach the west bank of the Volga somewhere in the neighborhood of Stalingrad, thereby interrupting Soviet oil supply from the Transcaucasus oil fields to the Soviet armies in Russia and the northern Ukraine, and then, by an offensive across the Caucasus range, to seize the oil fields themselves and make them available for the German war effort.[6]

Although the concentration of main effort in the south, in contrast to the three simultaneous strategic offensives of the previous

6. *Kriegstagebuch des Oberkommandos der Wehrmacht (Wehrmachtführungsstab)*, Vol. II (1942), Part I, ed. Andreas Hillgruber (Frankfurt am Main: Bernard und Graefe Verlag für Wehrwesen, 1963), pp. 46–50. This is the High Command War Diary, and is hereinafter cited as *KTB/OKW*.

year, was an implicit acknowledgment that the strategic balance had tilted somewhat against Germany since 1941, an offensive against Leningrad was also provided for, and its inclusion in the planning caused a certain degree of dispersion of resources until the undertaking was abandoned late in the year.

The 1942 summer offensive attained considerable initial successes in acquisition of territory, but the haul of Soviet prisoners and equipment was not on a scale approaching that of the previous year. Differences of opinion between Hitler and his generals began to arise early in July, barely a week after the start of the offensive, and rose to a major pitch during September, as it gradually became clear that the offensive was not achieving its aims. The city of Stalingrad, which occupied no position of importance in the original German planning, gradually acquired a symbolic significance, derived from its name ("Stalin city") and the stubborn Soviet defense of it, which came to overshadow all other developments on the Eastern Front. The initial aim of reaching the Volga was attained, but the continual pouring of resources into the battle for the city starved the effort to capture the Transcaucasian oil fields, and, even more dangerously for the German Army, led to the creation of a long and vulnerable flank along the Don between Voronezh and Serafimovich, which was manned by the troops of Hitler's satellites, Romania, Italy, and Hungary. Despite misgivings voiced by Field Commanders, by the military at Hitler's headquarters (FHQ), and by Hitler himself, no adequate measures were taken to strengthen the Don front by "corsetting" the ill-armed and, on the whole, ill-motivated satellite forces with a sufficient number of German units. Nor, despite reports that Soviet forces were being massed against the Don front, was adequate account taken of Soviet intentions and capabilities for a winter counteroffensive.

The outcome was the first, and possibly the most devastating to German morale, of a series of disasters that were to befall the German Army on the Eastern Front between the winter of 1942–43 and the end of the war in May 1945. By breaching the satellite front, primarily that of the Italian 8th and Romanian 4th Armies on the Don, and that of the Romanian 3rd Army south of Stalingrad, the Red Army succeeded in encircling and eventually annihilating the entire axis force in the area of Stalingrad and the Don bend, comprising twenty-two German and two Romanian divisions, a regiment of Croats, and a large number of smaller independent

formations. Estimates of the total number of men lost in the encircled force at Stalingrad vary between a minimum of 250,000 and
a maximum of 400,000; the most likely figure is about 300,000. In
addition, a number of other divisions suffered heavy attrition, while
the Italian and Hungarian Armies were so roughly handled that
they had to be withdrawn from the front. Between the surrender of
Stalingrad at the beginning of February and the onset of the spring
thaw in March 1943, a brilliantly conceived and executed counteroffensive under the direction of Field Marshal Erich von Manstein
succeeded in inflicting a severe, though local, defeat upon the pur-
suing Soviet forces north of the Don, while the efforts of the encircled troops at Stalingrad prevented the Soviets from cutting off
and wiping out the German Army Group in the Caucasus, which
for the most part succeeded in withdrawing safely. Nevertheless,
the German summer offensive of 1942 was an almost unmitigated
disaster, which neither a temporary local success nor a successful
withdrawal from an unattained objective could mitigate to any substantial extent.

Although the majority of German military resources were being
consumed in the east during the period covered by this study,
events in other theatres of war occupied a considerable and growing part of Hitler's attention. Most significant among these was the
Mediterranean, where a badly handled British offensive in North
Africa broke down and brought the German-Italian Panzer Army
(DIPA) to within striking distance of Alexandria, Cairo, and the
Suez Canal. The situation here turned sour for the Axis when the
Second battle of El Alamein, which began on 23 October 1942, culminated in a breach of the line and a German withdrawal on the
night of 2 November, to be followed on the night of 7/8 November
by Anglo-American landings in the French North African colonies.

As this is a study not of German military history but of Hitler's
decision-making in "crisis within crisis," specifically the breakdown of the German offensive in the east, the North African situation is referred to here only insofar as Hitler's decisions about it
affected the diffusion of German resources, and has not been followed through to the surrender of German and Italian forces on
that continent at the beginning of May 1943. Nor has much attention been devoted to the Battle of the Atlantic. Although success in
this battle was crucial to continuation of the British war effort, the
German Navy was accorded much greater autonomy, especially in
the handling of the submarine campaign, than was the Army. Dur-

ing the period, a crucial advance was made when the cryptanalysts of the British Government Code and Cypher School at Bletchley Park succeeded in November 1942 in "breaking" the German naval machine cipher "Triton," and thereby regaining an insight into German submarine movements which they had not had since introduction of the cipher early in the year. However, full exploitation of this advantage was not possible until April 1943. In view of this, and because of the small impact of FHQ on German submarine operations, attention to naval decisions has been concentrated here on the aftermath of the unsuccessful attack by German heavy surface warships in the Battle of Bear Island on 31 December 1942, on Hitler's consequent decision to deactivate the major surface ships, and on the resulting resignation of the Commander-in-Chief of the Navy, Grand Admiral Erich Raeder.

In view of the extreme centralization of the German command function under the Third Reich, in which Hitler combined in his own person the posts of Head of State, Head of Government, Commander-in-Chief of the Armed Forces, Commander-in-Chief of the Army, and, at one stage in the period, Commander-in-Chief of an Army Group, this study is essentially concerned with Hitler's personal decisions. Although no attempt has been made at a full-scale comparison between his decision-making and that of Stalin (who, though never occupying the ceremonial position of the Soviet Head of State, in fact possessed as much unchallenged decision-making power as Hitler, being Head of Government, Head of the Communist Party, and Supreme Commander of the Soviet Armed Forces), some comparisons have been drawn between the performance of the German and Soviet decision-making apparatus during 1942.

The study has been terminated at the end of March 1943, so that the "post-crisis" period following the surrender at Stalingrad is somewhat arbitrarily defined at eight weeks. This is partly because the main source for reports of Hitler's day-to-day military decision-making, the High Command War Diary for the second quarter of 1943, disappeared after the Nuremberg War Crimes Trials of 1946, in which it was an exhibit, has never been traced, and is believed to have been burned.[7] But the principal reason is that the pattern of Hitler's decision-making, which, as will be demonstrated, exhib-

---

7. *KTB/OKW*, Vol. III (1943), ed. Walther Hubatsch (Frankfurt am Main: Bernard und Graefe Verlag für Wehrwesen, 1963), contains situation reports from the Fronts for only the period 1 April–30 June 1943.

ited severe disruption between the achievement of an encirclement by the Soviets on 21 November 1942 and the surrender of the
encircled forces on 2 February, had substantially resumed its pre-
November shape by the end of February, suggesting that the "post-
crisis" period selected is not unreasonably short.

THE GERMAN APPARATUS OF DECISION-MAKING

Decision-making in Nazi Germany was highly centralized in Hitler's own person. Appointed to power as Reichskanzler (head of the
executive government) in January 1932, without ever having per-
suaded more than 44 percent of the electorate to vote for him,[8] but
with his opponents failing to form an anti-Nazi coalition, he succeeded to the position of Head of State after the death of President
Hindenburg, on 2 August 1934, by declaring the Presidency merged
with the Chancellorship. On the very day of Hindenburg's death,
the Head of State's constitutional position as titular Supreme Commander of the Armed Forces was made more specific by the device
of having all officers and enlisted men take an oath of unconditional
obedience to Hitler personally as "Führer (Leader, the term that
replaced President) of the German State and People" and "Supreme Commander of the Armed Forces."

From 19 August 1934, on which a plebiscite gave him a 90 percent vote in favor of the steps taken on the 2nd, Hitler consolidated
his position as Head of State, Government, and Armed Forces. The
occasion of an unsuitable marriage by the Minister of Defense, General von Blomberg, was used to force his resignation, whereupon
Hitler abolished his Ministerial post and assumed his function as
executive Commander-in-Chief of the Armed Forces.[9] Simultaneously, the Commander-in-Chief of the Army, Colonel-General von
Fritsch, was coerced into resignation on grounds of "ill health"
after faked evidence of immoral conduct had been produced against
him,[10] and he was replaced by the much more pliant General von
Brauchitsch. The Air Force had already been placed under one of
Hitler's close henchmen, Hermann Göring, and only the Navy re-

---

8. Joachim C. Fest, *Hitler* (New York: Harcourt Brace Jovanovich, 1974), p. 320.

9. Ibid., p. 542.

10. J. A. Graf Kielmansegg, *Der Fritschprozess 1938: Ablauf u. Hintergründe* (Heidelberg: Hoffmann und Campe, 1949); and Alan Bullock, *Hitler: A Study in Tyranny* (Harmondsworth: Penguin Books, 1962), pp. 417–420.

mained relatively free from close Party control, in part because Hitler laid no claim to expertise in naval matters, but mainly because his aims did not at that time include war with the British, and the Navy was therefore of low importance.[11]

In December 1941, after the collapse of the offensive against Moscow, Hitler dismissed the Commander-in-Chief of the Army, Field Marshal von Brauchitsch, and took over his post himself, exercising his functions through the Army Headquarters (OKH), and extending his decision-making function one step further down the chain of command.

The basic decision-making "unit" for this study is therefore Hitler himself, and the apparatus at his disposal was as follows:

1. *The Führer Headquarters* (Führerhauptquartier, FHQ). This initially was located in a camp in a forest near Rastenburg in East Prussia, known by the code name of "Wolfsschanze" (Wolf's Lair). It contained Hitler's Party Chancellory, headed by Martin Bormann, and the Armed Forces High Command (Oberkommando der Wehrmacht, OKW), headed by Generalfeldmarschall (Field Marshal) Wilhelm Keitel, and consisting of a number of sections, the most important of which for the purposes of this study was the Armed Forces Command Staff (Wehrmachtführungsstab, Wfst), headed by Generaloberst (Colonel-General) Alfred Jodl. OKW also contained representatives of the Air Force, Navy, and Foreign Office. On 16 July 1942, the FHQ and Wfst moved to a camp code-named "Werwolf" (Werewolf) near Vinnitsa in the Ukraine.

2. *The Army Headquarters* (Oberkommando des Heeres, OKH), located near Angerburg, a few kilometers from OKW, until 16 July 1942, when it, too, moved to Vinnitsa. The most significant decision-making element of OKH was the Army General Staff, headed until 24 September 1942 by Colonel-General Franz Halder, and thereafter by Colonel-General Kurt Zeitzler. Significant inputs were made by the Intelligence Sections "Fremde Heere Ost" (Foreign Armies East) and "Fremde Heere West" (Foreign Armies West), while the Operations Section (Ia) was the principal transmission belt for orders from Hitler to the Commanders-in-Chief of the Army Groups on the Eastern Front (initially North, Center, and South; in early July, Army Group South was divided into two:

11. Edward P. von der Porten, *The German Navy in World War Two* (London: Pan Books, 1972), pp. 10–11.

Army Group A in the Caucasus and Army Group B on the Don-Volga front, including Stalingrad).

3. *The State Chancellory*. This remained in Berlin throughout the war; it was headed by a senior public servant, State Secretary Dr. Hans Lammers.

4. *The Presidential Secretariat*, under State Secretary Otto Meissner, a survival from the Weimar Republic, in which the offices of President and Chancellor had been separate. It, too, remained in Berlin.

The line of command from Hitler to each of these agencies was clear. His authority over the Party Chancellory derived from his headship of the Party. His control of OKW stemmed from his roles as Head of State and Supreme Commander of the Armed Forces. OKH was subject to him in addition through his position as Commander-in-Chief of the Army since December 1941. The two remaining Secretariats were at his disposal through his tenure of the offices of Head of Government (Chancellor) and Head of State (Führer).

The subordination of all these organs to Hitler is the only clear feature of the administrative apparatus, which embodied a principle aptly described by Fest as "authoritarian anarchy."[12] Overlapping jurisdictions abounded. In the military sphere, for example, OKH broadly bore responsibility for the Eastern Front, and OKW for all other combat theatres, but there were numerous instances of OKW involvement in Eastern Front matters, at least until September 1942, and occasional instances thereafter, while OKH retained considerable noncommand functions in respect of OKW areas, including the provision of intelligence by "Foreign Armies West" which was directly germane to command decision-making in OKW.

The main decision-making sessions were the "Führer conferences" in FHQ, which normally took place twice daily.[13] The morning one, invariably at noon, was the major one; it dealt with events of the previous day and night, and was attended by representatives

12. Fest, *Hitler*, pp. 478–480.
13. Summaries of these appear in *KTB/OKW*, Vol. II, though by no means for all days, and notes on many sessions up to 24 September 1942 are found in Franz Halder's diary, *Kriegstagebuch: tägliche Aufzeichnungen des Chefs des Generalstabes des Heeres 1939–1942* (Stuttgart: Kohlhammer Verlag, 1962–64). Stenographic records of some post-September 1942 conferences also exist.

of all services and the Foreign Ministry from OKW, and by a senior member, usually the Chief of General Staff himself, from OKH. Representatives of other bodies (e.g., the armaments industry or Germany's allies) attended on an ad hoc basis and/or by invitation.[14] While Halder was Chief of General Staff of OKH, it was normal for the Eastern Front to be discussed extensively, and decisions taken in respect of it, but after his replacement by Zeitzler this became uncommon.[15] Partly because of Hitler's growing distrust of Keitel and especially of Jodl, and probably in conformity with Zeitzler's own preference for professional autonomy, it became normal for Zeitzler to open the proceedings with a very brief account of Eastern Front developments, and then leave.[16] This procedure curtailed discussion by OKW personnel almost to the vanishing point, and decisions concerning the Eastern Front were increasingly taken at private meetings between Hitler and Zeitzler, usually during the afternoon.

A second, smaller "conference" took place during the evening, usually at 8:00 or 9:00 P.M., and dealt with events that had taken place during the day.[17]

The term "conference" (Vortrag) is slightly misleading. Although discussion often took place, and sometimes became heated, the normal procedure was for the service representatives to present situation reports for the various combat theatres, and for Hitler to then deliver decisions or accept or reject proposals on the spot.[18] Only in matters of detail, for example in execution of a decision, was initiative left to subordinates, and often even the details were laid down by Hitler.[19]

In military matters, there were two main types of major decision, Führer Directives (Führerweisungen) and Führer Orders (Führerbefehle). A Directive normally related to large operations, on the scale of an Army Group or above, covered a range of operations extending over a considerable area and time period (for

14. Albert Speer, *Inside the Third Reich* (London: Weidenfeld and Nicolson, 1970), pp. 334–340.

15. *KTB/OKW*, Vol. II, Part II, notes for 10–13 October 1942; and Helmuth Greiner, *Die Oberste Wehrmachtführung, 1939–45* (Wiesbaden: Limes Verlag, 1951), pp. 410–425.

16. Walter Warlimont, *Inside Hitler's Headquarters, 1939–45*, trans. R. H. Barry (London: Weidenfeld and Nicolson, 1964), pp. 261–284.

17. Andreas Hillgruber, Introduction to *KTB/OKW*, Vol. II, Part I, p. 13.

18. Speer, *Inside the Third Reich*, pp. 334–340.

19. Noted by, for example, Speer, *Inside the Third Reich*, p. 335.

example, the entire plan for the summer offensive of 1942 was contained in Directive No. 41 of 5 April 1942),[20] and allowed commanders a degree of latitude in deciding how to fulfill their assignments. An Order covered a particular operation such as the capture of a town or city, or the destruction of a particular enemy formation; it was, as Warlimont described it, "summary, imperative and immediate,"[21] and usually more detailed than a Directive. After Hitler delivered his decisions, it was the function of Wfst, normally through its Chief, Jodl, and his Deputy, Warlimont, to translate them into the appropriate orders when they fell within the ambit of OKW, and Halder (later Zeitzler) bore responsibility for the same process in OKH matters.[22]

Hitler occasionally left FHQ for relatively long periods, usually to go to Berlin or to his mountain retreat, the Berghof, near Berchtesgaden in Bavaria. On such journeys he was almost invariably accompanied by Keitel and Jodl, and for his longer absences it was usual for his special train to be followed by another, containing a section of Wfst known as the "Field Squadron" (Feldstaffel), but normally no components of OKH traveled with him. On very rare occasions, he visited the headquarters of an Army Group, as, for example, in July 1942, but more usually he sent an officer from FHQ, not necessarily of senior rank, whose mission was to discuss situations, form impressions, and report back, rather than to issue orders. Senior field commanders would occasionally be summoned to FHQ, or would ask permission to visit Hitler, sometimes by asking his Adjutant to arrange an appointment rather than by attempting to make arrangements through "channels,"[23] as the visits often implied criticism of Keitel, Jodl, or Halder (especially Keitel), who were widely felt among the senior officers to be "chair-borne" soldiers, averse to pointing out to Hitler the difficulties of carrying out his orders or arguing with him about the more ill-conceived

20. Hugh R. Trevor-Roper, ed., *Hitler's War Directives, 1939–1945* (London: Sidgwick and Jackson, 1964), p. 116.

21. Ibid., pp. xviii–xviv.

22. Hillgruber, Introduction to *KTB/OKW*, Vol. II, Part I, pp. 8–10.

23. For example, on 25 February 1943, Field Marshal von Kluge asked Hitler's Army ADC, Major Engel, to arrange for him to meet privately with Hitler. Hildegard von Kotze, ed., *Heeresadjutant bei Hitler, 1938–1943: Aufzeichnungen des Major Engel* (Stuttgart: Deutsche Verlags-Anstalt, 1974), entries of 25–28 February 1943.

ones. (Where Keitel was concerned, their misgivings were fully justified.)[24]

Some problems are involved in any attempt to reconstruct the pattern of German top-level decision-making. The main single source for a record of decisions is the War Diary of the High Command of the Armed Forces (OKW). This was compiled in a series of volumes, each covering three months, and initially was kept by Helmut Greiner. However, after the period of tension between Hitler and his senior military in September 1942, culminating in the dismissal on 24 September of the Chief of the Army General Staff, Colonel-General Halder, pressures arose for the replacement of Greiner, who was neither a Party member nor a soldier.[25] Both Party and Army elements in OKW sought to insert one of their own, to ensure that the War Diary reflected their own views. The Army succeeded in having appointed as Diarist a medieval historian of impeccable scholarly status, who was also a reserve Major, Professor Doctor Percy Ernst Schramm, who was to take over from Greiner as of 1 January 1943. However, he was unable to take up his duties until 8 March; and when he arrived, he had to compile the diary entries retrospectively from the files and from brief notes that Greiner had kept.

Prior to the dismissal of Halder, decisions affecting the Eastern Front were normally taken at the daily Situation Conferences (Lagevortragen) and notified to the OKW Diarist, usually by the Deputy Head of Wfst, General Walter Warlimont, directly after the meeting. The OKW War Diary therefore contained a comprehensive listing of decisions affecting all fronts up to the end of September 1942. However, after Hitler's major dispute with the military in that month, which resulted in his dismissal of Halder and his threat to replace Keitel and Jodl, the division of responsibility between the two organizations was much more strictly maintained. Halder's successor, Colonel-General Zeitzler, thenceforth gave only brief accounts of the situation on the Eastern Front at the OKW Situation Conferences, and decisions affecting the Eastern armies would usually be promulgated by Hitler in subsequent private meetings

24. He was widely known to senior officers as "Lakeitel," a pun on "lackey," and several attempts were made to unseat him. See Halder, *Kriegstagebuch*, Vol. III, p. 475.

25. *KTB/OKW*, Vol. II, Part I, pp. 564–570.

at which no OKW representative was present, and of which no systematic record has survived, though the pattern of decisions can in most cases be pieced together from records of Army Group or Army Headquarters, or from subsequent statements by German generals. Because many of the source materials were destroyed at the end of the war, it cannot be said with certainty that every decision is recorded; but because implementation of major decisions causes them to appear in a multiplicity of sources, it can be said that there is no major body of unrecorded decisions. What is available is therefore sufficiently comprehensive to enable German decision-making at the highest level to be examined in detail. In particular, the complete series of Führer Directives is available both in German and in English translation.[26]

DEFINITIONS OF CRISIS

The definition of crisis employed here is the Brecher definition of an intra-war crisis. This postulates six triggering situational changes:[27]

1. The entry of a new major actor into an ongoing war.
2. The exit of a major actor.
3. Technological escalation during a war.
4. A major escalation other than the introduction of a qualitatively advanced technology.
5. Defeat in battle which decision-makers perceive as significant.
6. A perceived high probability that a major actor will enter a war.

1. In the period covered by this study, no new major actor entered the war. Hitler thought that Turkey and Spain would, but neither did; and though both sides invaded French territories, the circumstances in which France became reinvolved made it impossible for it to play a major role.

2. No major state left the war, though the preconditions were laid for the Italian change of sides which took place in September 1943.

26. Walther Hubatsch, *Hitlers Weisungen für die Kriegführung, 1939–1945* (Frankfurt am Main: Bernard und Graefe Verlag für Wehrwesen, 1962); and Trevor-Roper, ed., *Hitler's War Directives*.
27. Michael Brecher with Benjamin Geist, *Decisions in Crisis* (Berkeley, Los Angeles, and London: University of California Press, 1980), p. 8.

3. No usable weapons system was being held in reserve by either side, and no major new one became available in the period. However, in nonweapons technology, British successes in cryptography at the end of 1942 contributed greatly to a dramatic turnabout, in the Allies' favor, in the Battle of the Atlantic in April–May 1943. The Germans, however, believed this resulted from improvements in Allied radar, to which they expected to develop countermeasures, so they suffered no "actor-crisis."

4. A major territorial escalation occurred during the period, when the Allies invaded French North Africa and the Germans not only sent their own troops there but invaded Unoccupied France, thereby significantly stretching their already strained resources.

5. During the period from mid-1942 to March 1943, Germany was involved in three major campaigns: in southern USSR, in North Africa, and in the Atlantic. All three were ultimately lost, and a case could be made for treating the period as one of multiple intra-war crises. However, apart from the complexity inherent in attempting such a presentation, the crises were not perceived as of equal magnitude by Hitler and the other German decision-makers. The North African theatre was seen as secondary; until the end of 1942, very small resources were allocated to it, and the major contribution in manpower was Italian. Only after the Western Allies invaded French North Africa in November 1942 did Hitler increase the level of German involvement; and by then, given Allied sea and air superiority in the Mediterranean, Germany could not recapture the initiative at any level of force it could deploy.

In the Battle of the Atlantic, it became clear only in retrospect that the events of April–May 1943 defined the outcome. At the time, they were seen by the German Navy as a serious but not irrevocable setback, and Hitler's personal involvement in naval decisions was small.

The outcome of the Stalingrad campaign, however, was universally viewed by the German political and military decision-makers, as well as by the public, as catastrophic. The campaign had been fought on ground and at a time of the Germans' own choosing; it constituted Germany's main military effort of 1942; the forces involved on the Axis side were overwhelmingly German; both the plan of campaign and the amendments to it were the products of Hitler's personal decisions to a very high degree; the military disaster was on a scale unprecedented in modern German history; and the perception of an adverse change in the military balance, though not specifically admitted by Hitler, was widespread among both civilian and military decision-makers in his entourage.

6. As for a perceived high probability that a major actor would enter the war, Hitler expected Turkey to enter the war soon on the Allied side, and Spain to be invaded by the Anglo-Americans. Neither expectation was fulfilled, but the perception caused arms to be sent to Bulgaria and Spain, and preparations were made to deploy German forces to both countries at a time when arms and manpower were in short supply.

Other definitions of crisis which have been examined are those of Buchan, Young, Hermann, and Bell.[28]

The Buchan formulation defines a crisis period as covering the formulation of a challenge, the definition of an issue, the decision on reaction, the impact of reaction on the original challenger, and the clarification of his response. All these elements can be identified within the period studied, but the definition is too general for the Brecher criteria. The Young definition stresses the rapid unfolding of events as characteristic of a crisis; and while these also occurred in the period, the term "rapid" is too vague to make the definition generally useful. Rapidity is relative: the rapid dispatch of a division to a threatened sector may be only a matter of days, while rapid rectification of an arms production problem may require many months. Rapidity is also relative in the sense that if the enemy moves faster still, absolute rapidity may be too slow.

The Hermann definition lays stress on "surprise" as a factor in crisis. Undoubtedly, the Allied landings in North Africa and the Soviet counteroffensive at Stalingrad surprised the German leadership tactically, but they did not constitute a strategic surprise. Hitler had shown almost obsessional concern during the summer of 1942 with the possibility of major Allied landings. The fact of landing was expected, as was the approximate timing, and only the location was a "surprise," in that it was further away from Germany than expected.

---

28. Alistair Buchan, *Crisis Management* (Boulogne sur Seine: Atlantic Institute, 1966), p. 21; Oran R. Young, *The Intermediaries: Third Parties in International Crises* (Princeton: Princeton University Press, 1967), p. 10; Charles F. Hermann, "International Crisis as a Situational Variable," in *International Politics and Foreign Policy*, ed. James N. Rosenau (New York: Free Press, 1969), p. 414; and Coral Bell, "Crisis Diplomacy," in *Strategic Thought in the Nuclear Age*, ed. Laurence W. Martin (London: Heinemann, 1979), pp. 159–160.

Similarly, Hitler's attention had been repeatedly drawn to the vulnerability of the long flank on the south bank of the Don, held by allied troops with inferior equipment and, in some cases, doubtful motivation, and he was well aware that Stalin had played a large part in initiating a successful attack southward from Stalingrad to the mouth of the Don during the Russian Civil War in 1920. Reports had been received of Soviet force concentrations along the north bank of the Don and in bridgeheads on the south bank, and steps had been taken to "corset" the satellite forces with German units. The opening date for the Soviet offensive was not known, but the main factors in the failure to counter it were underestimation of its scale and speed of development and Hitler's refusal to permit the threatened forces to withdraw westwards, out of encirclement. The surprise, therefore, was operational, not conceptual—that is, it arose within the general crisis rather than giving rise to it, and it applied to both sides: the Soviets were surprised by the size of the force they encircled, and had to adjust their plans accordingly. This suggests that "surprise," which can operate at several levels and within different periods before and during a crisis, does not itself define the presence or absence of a crisis. For the purposes of this study, it is merely noted that, especially in relation to the German defeats at Stalingrad and Second Alamein, the factor of surprise was secondary to the inadequacy of German resources to deal with situations that had largely been anticipated, and to errors in the handling of the resources that were available.

Bell defines a crisis as "a tract of time in which the conflicts within a relationship rise to a level which threatens to transform the nature of the relationship."[29] The relationship in this case was one of total war; the "transformation" was of Germany from a power which, till the end of October 1942, was advancing on most fronts and achieving major successes in submarine warfare to one which in November began retreats in Africa and Russia, ending in both cases in the defeat and surrender of large forces for the first time since the outbreak of war, and which was also about to concede defeat in the submarine warfare. In terms of Bell's categorization, it was also a compound crisis, as the transformation in the military position (an "adversary crisis of the central balance") was accompanied by the beginnings of an "intramural crisis of alliance" which

29. Bell, "Crisis Diplomacy," pp. 158–159.

culminated in the overthrow of Mussolini and Italy's change of sides in September 1943.

The Brecher definition of crisis entails subdivision into three periods: pre-crisis, crisis, and post-crisis.[30] While its terminology can be criticized for applying the same term both to the crisis as a whole and to its most acute, central phase, the subdivision establishes a useful framework that enables different crises to be more readily compared than do other definitions, and facilitates construction and testing of hypotheses about state behavior in crises.

In the intra-war crisis constituted by the German campaign in the Soviet Union in 1942–43, the three periods have been divided as follows:

A. *The Pre-crisis Period.* This period lasts from the opening of the German offensive on 28 June 1942 to the beginning of November 1942. A single date cannot be given for it, because the Stalingrad campaign did not take place in a strategic vacuum. The Brecher criterion for a pre-crisis period is a growth in perception of threat, and German decision-making for the Russian front was influenced by happenings elsewhere which constrained German freedom to allocate resources among the various military theatres. The growth in perception of threat begins in July, with the realization that Soviet forces are withdrawing rather than being destroyed in place. During August, it is realized that the attempt to seize the Caucasus oil fields is failing, and that the capture of Stalingrad will be more difficult than expected. However, it is not until the end of October that the perception of mere failure to achieve all objectives changes to one of possible disaster for the forces involved. Objectively, this can be dated to the opening of the British offensive at El Alamein on 23 October, but it did not enter German decision-making perceptions until the evening of 2 November, when Rommel began his withdrawal. The second factor that increased the German perception of threat was the Allied invasion of French North Africa on the night of 7/8 November, and the third was the launching of massive Soviet counteroffensives north and south of Stalingrad on 19 and 20 November, respectively. In all three cases, strategic and tactical surprise was achieved, so that the transition from the pre-crisis to the full crisis phase was abrupt; however, because of the wide-ranging scope of Hitler's responsibilities, it took place in different places at different times.

30. Brecher with Geist, *Decisions in Crisis*, p. 23.

B. *The Crisis Period.* The transition of most direct relevance is, of course, that which took place in southern USSR. The full crisis period is distinguished from pre-crisis by the presence of all three necessary conditions of crisis, rather than merely the first:

1. A sharp rise in perceived threat to basic values.

2. An awareness of time constraints on decisions.

3. An adverse change in the military balance.

1. In the broadest sense, the "basic values" threatened were Hitler's image as a military genius and the Social Darwinist concept of German racial superiority over the Slavs. More specifically, the basic value threatened by the Soviet counteroffensive was the large concentration of German forces in the Stalingrad and Caucasus areas, threatened by action on a scale the Red Army had been considered, right up to the moment of attack, incapable of mounting.

2. The awareness of the constraints on decisions set in among the military leadership at OKH and OKW as soon as the Soviet offensive was launched on 19 November; but Hitler, who had left his headquarters in East Prussia to go to Munich on 7 November, did not decide to return thither until the 22nd, the day the two Soviet pincers met, thus encircling the Axis forces at Stalingrad. It was on that day also that he rejected their commander's request for "freedom of action"—that is, permission to abandon the city and withdraw to the west while the Soviet encirclement was still weak enough to be penetrated. As decisions of this magnitude could only be taken by Hitler personally, it seems advisable to take 22 November as the starting point for this criterion rather than any of the three preceding days.

3. The perception of an adverse change in the military balance derived from the facts that the besiegers at Stalingrad suddenly became the besieged, and that the Soviet counteroffensive threatened in addition to cut off the entire force in the Caucasus. Placed at risk were two Army Groups (A and B), totaling seventy-seven divisions (fifty-three of them German) and about 1,750,000 men. This perception also dates from the period 19–22 November, and became acute for the fifty divisions of Army Group B when the Soviet encirclement closed on 22 November.

C. *The Post-crisis Period.* This period of reduced perception of threat and/or time pressure began with the successful extrication of Army Group A from the Caucasus, which was complete in all essentials by 24 January 1943. The final surrender at Stalingrad on 2 February was followed by a continued Soviet advance westward, but the pressure on the Germans slackened. The movements of remaining German forces were no longer constrained by the requirements of the two threatened Army Groups, and these forces were able to score significant local successes before the spring thaw, during the last ten days of March, imposed immobility on both armies and ended the crisis.

In conclusion, the crisis will be evaluated in terms of the nine specific International Crisis Behavior (ICB) research questions concerning the efforts of escalating and deescalating crisis-induced stress:

on information:	1. cognitive performance.
	2. the perceived need and consequent quest for information.
	3. the receptivity and size of the information-processing group.
on consultation:	4. the type and size of consultative units.
	5. group participation in the consultative process.
on decisional forums:	6. the size and structure of decisional forums.
	7. authority patterns within decisional units.
on alternatives:	8. the search for and evaluation of alternatives.
	9. the perceived range of available alternatives.[31]

31. Ibid., p. 27.

CHAPTER ONE

The Pre-crisis Period

THE GERMAN PLAN FOR 1942

AT EVERY STAGE of the war so far, there had been significant reservations among the German generals—about the initiation of the war itself, the attack on Norway and Denmark, the invasion of France, the planned invasion of Britain, and the invasion of the Soviet Union while the British remained unsubdued.[1] In all cases except the invasion of Britain, quick success had proved Hitler's judgment right and that of his more cautious generals wrong. Like the previous operations, therefore, the German invasion of the Soviet Union on 22 June 1941 gambled on a quick decision; it envisaged destroying the Red Army west of the Dnieper, and capturing Leningrad, Moscow, and the Ukraine before the onset of the winter,[2] thus bringing about the downfall of the Soviet regime, or at the very least, so weakening it that it could be pushed back beyond the Urals and removed from European politics altogether.

For a variety of reasons, the plan failed. Leningrad was besieged, but not captured; and although forward formations reached the outskirts of Moscow, a Soviet counteroffensive, launched just as the impetus of the German offensive was exhausted, flung them back, inflicting on Germany its first major land defeat of the war. In the

---

1. The German generals' reservations about Hitler's military planning are discussed in a number of studies. See, for example, Basil H. Liddell Hart, *The Other Side of the Hill* (London: Panther, 1956); and Field Marshal Erich von Manstein, *Lost Victories* (London: Methuen, 1958).

2. Liddell Hart, *Other Side of the Hill*, pp. 180 and 186–187; and Hugh R. Trevor-Roper, ed., *Hitler's War Directives* (London: Sidgwick and Jackson, 1964), p. 49: Directive No. 21, of 18 December 1940.

south, the major objectives were achieved, but a Soviet counter-offensive in December 1941 forced a retreat from the Rostov to the line of the River Mius, some fifty miles further west.

The onset of winter brought a halt of several months to major offensive operations in the east, and gave a breathing space for building up war production stocks, which was of more use to the Russians than it was to Germany. Failure of the plan to conclude the war in 1941 not only meant that the Russians had to be faced again in 1942, but also threw on to the Allied side the full productive and manpower capacity of America, which had been brought into the war in December 1941. The consequence was that although the military situation of the Axis powers looked good in the first months of 1942, with German armies standing deep inside Soviet territory and advancing in North Africa, significant successes being achieved against vital British maritime supply lines in the Battle of the Atlantic, and Japanese forces sweeping everything before them in the Pacific, the strategic balance nevertheless had tilted against Germany. It was likely to continue to do so as American manpower was mobilized and industry geared up for war production, while newly established Soviet industries in the Urals began to make an increasing contribution to the Russian war effort.

Although there are no indications in surviving materials that Hitler or his closest subordinates fully appreciated American or Soviet productive potential, there was an unacknowledged but nonetheless real appreciation that the military effort in the previous year had been excessively diffused.

At this stage, however, there was no sign of a perception that the "tilt" was significant. In respect to America, Hitler's views reflected a low degree of interest and considerable internal inconsistency. Though aware of American industrial potential, he did not link it to arms production, and on several occasions in 1940 and 1941 derided announced U.S. rearmament targets as exaggerated. Though aware of the possible role of U.S. aid to the British, he did not consider that it could be decisive, and even as late as December 1943 told his generals that it was diminishing and could not make up for Britain's deficiencies. As to America's own participation in the war, he at first (at least up to the end of 1940) considered the United States as incurably isolationist; by early 1941, he had modified this view to the extent of stating a perception that the United States might join in, but would not present a great danger if it did.[3] Contempt for American capabilities was also expressed at various times by Göring, Ribbentrop, Hess, and others.[4]

Because of the contemptuous attitudes of the political leaders, OKW had made no plans for war with the United States; and when, on 8 December 1941, General Jodl, head of Wfst, was asked for information on possible American moves in Europe, his deputy, Warlimont, replied: "We have no data on which to base this exercise."[5]

As to the reverses in Russia and the Ukraine at the end of 1941, there was no disposition to regard them as definitive. Although they constituted Germany's first major land defeats of the war, the limited withdrawals necessitated by them had on the whole been orderly, and the Soviet attempt to launch a general offensive had been a failure. The defeats were attributed to bad weather, problems of supply, deficiencies in training troops for defensive operations, and mistakes by the senior field commanders, most of whom were dismissed.

During the Battle of Moscow, Hitler countermanded the orders of some generals who attempted to make tactical withdrawals, and ordered all troops to stand fast. In the particular circumstances of the battle, in which the attacking Red Army was short of resources,[6] the tactic was generally successful, but it had two effects on Hitler's perceptions which were to condition his approach to the very different circumstances of the Stalingrad battle. First, it confirmed him in the belief that his World War I combat experience as a noncommissioned infantry soldier made him better fitted than his generals to manage and motivate the rank-and-file German soldier; and secondly, it induced a belief that Soviet attacks could be countered merely by standing fast. In the circumstances of December 1941, this riposte turned out more appropriate than it was to prove a year later against better equipped Soviet forces.

German planning for the eastern campaign of summer 1942 was

3. James V. Compton, *The Swastika and the Eagle* (London: Bodley Head, 1968), contains an extensive examination of Hitler's attitudes to the United States, based on an exhaustive study of primary sources, from which the foregoing discussion is summarized.

4. Ibid., pp. 132–136.

5. Walter Warlimont, *Inside Hitler's Headquarters, 1939–45* (London: Weidenfeld and Nicolson, 1964), p. 208.

6. Zhukov's account, in Geoffrey Jukes, *The Defence of Moscow* (New York: Ballantine, 1969), pp. 124–137.

therefore less ambitious than it had been in the previous year. Instead of major offensives on three strategic axes, it comprised a major effort on one axis only, with a smaller one elsewhere on the front. The major axis chosen was the one in the south, the minor one was Leningrad, and the reasons for this were primarily economic.

Although the German attack had deprived Soviet industry of many sources of minerals, most of these could be replaced from unoccupied territory. Oil, however, was an exception. At that time, the only important Soviet oil fields were those of the Caucasus; they lay a substantial distance from the combat front, and the supply routes to the Soviet heartland were few and vulnerable, comprising the River Volga, serving Central Russia, the Don-Donets river system, serving the Ukraine, and railroads that mostly followed the river valleys. A substantial lodgment of German forces on the west bank of the Volga, and the capture of the important rail center of Rostov, at the mouth of the Don, would seal off all major Soviet oil supply routes (see Map 1). The attack toward the Volga would inevitably pass through the Donbass industrial and minerals area, thus depriving the Soviet economy and armed forces of major resources at the same time as it paralyzed the oil traffic, and, by capturing the Eastern Ukraine and Kuban agricultural areas, would add significantly to the difficulties the Soviet regime experienced in feeding its population.

If the offensive succeeded, the important route by which Allied supplies reached the Soviet Union via the Persian Gulf and Caucasus would be sealed off, and the increased supply burden involved in keeping the Soviet Union in the war would fall on two routes only, the Iceland-Murmansk-Archangel convoy route, and the supply line from the U.S. west coast via Soviet Pacific ports and the Trans-Siberian Railway. The first of these was vulnerable to heavy submarine, surface ship, and air attacks from German forces based in Norway, and subject to bad weather, especially in winter, while the second suffered the limitation that U.S. or British-flag ships could not gain access to the major port, Vladivostok, without serious risk of being sunk by the Japanese Navy or Air Force, while Soviet Far Eastern ports outside the Sea of Japan suffered from serious icing problems for over half the year, limited port capacity, and poor or nonexistent rail access. Japan and the Soviet Union were not at war, but the ability to carry supplies to Vladivostok in Soviet-flag ships was constrained by the shortage of shipping and

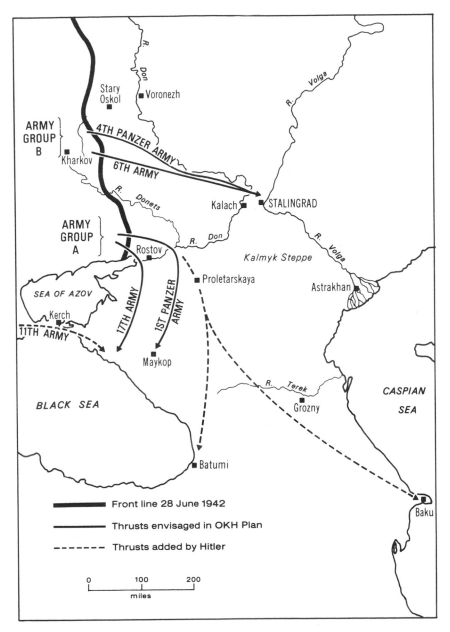

MAP 1.
GERMAN SUMMER OFFENSIVE, 1942:
BASIC OKH PLAN AND HITLER'S AMENDMENTS

crews. Both routes suffered also from the need to transport the cargoes for long distances by rail after they had been landed. The Murmansk-Archangel route suffered from the additional problems that Murmansk, the only ice-free port on the Soviet north coast, was close to the front line and its only rail link, the line southward toward Leningrad, was vulnerable to air interdiction for most of its length, and to physical seizure at several points, given a determined German-Finnish military effort. There was also the consideration that if the offensive in the Caucasus was fully successful, the progress in North Africa continued, and the Japanese advanced westward from Burma, German forces would eventually link up in the Iraq-Iran area, and, either there or in India, would meet up with the Japanese. This was not a close enough possibility to be reflected in the operational planning, but indicated the ultimate value that the success of the operation could involve, in the form of extension into a hitherto British-dominated area of the colonial world, where anti-imperialist nationalist opinion could well work to Axis advantage.[7]

Germany itself was facing critical oil shortages, but in the initial planning for the 1942 offensive the possibility of not merely neutralizing but capturing Soviet oil capacity was not the first priority. The offensive task was to drive eastward, cross the Don, and reach the western bank of the Volga somewhere north of Stalingrad, incidentally capturing the major iron and coal industries of the Donbass, thus further improving Germany's economic position for the prolonged war that the failures of 1941 had made inevitable.

The geography of the southern part of the European USSR virtually dictated the line of advance. A thrust forward in the southern sector of the front would need to be protected against the possibility of a Soviet flank attack from the north. Consequently, the most logical northern limit for the offensive was the line of the river Don, which runs south-southeastward between Voronezh and Serafimovich before making a great bend southward and southwestward toward the Sea of Azov. The attacking forces would therefore have the wide river on their left until past Serafimovich, at

7. The strength of this factor is illustrated by the revolt in Iraq in April–June 1941 and the occupation of Iran by British and Soviet forces in January 1942 to depose the pro-German Shah and his Prime Minister, General Zahedi.

which point their objective, the west bank of the Volga, would be less than fifty miles away. The southern limit of the advance was equally clearly marked by the coastline, at least as far as the mouth of the Don at Rostov.

Despite all its potential advantages, the offensive in the south was not the first choice of the Army General Staff planners in the winter of 1941–42.[8] Their preference was for a more limited offensive, aimed at capturing Leningrad and linking up with the Finns north of the city. Although Hitler rejected this as the main operation, it was not canceled; it remained as a secondary objective through all stages of planning, creating some ambiguities and conflicts throughout the subsequent operations until it was eventually canceled.

The final version of the plan was presented by the Chief of OKH, Colonel-General Franz Halder, at a conference at FHQ on 28 March 1942.[9] It was to be executed by the forces of Army Group South (Field Marshal Fedor von Bock), and comprised two parallel thrusts. The first, along the south bank of the Don, was to be carried out by 4th Panzer Army and 6th Army. The southern thrust toward Rostov would be conducted by 1st Panzer Army and 17th Army, which would be joined by 11th Army once that army had completed the subjugation of the Crimea. Satellite forces would also be involved, comprising the 3rd and 4th Romanian, 8th Italian, and 2nd Hungarian Armies; but as they were not considered the equivalent of German forces in equipment, leadership, or motivation, they were to play only a supporting role, especially in manning the defensive line along the south bank of the Don. The total force available for the operation came to eighty-nine divisions, nine of which were armored,[10] and somewhat outnumbered the Soviet forces (the Southwest and North Caucasus Fronts), which came

8. Liddell Hart, *Other Side of the Hill*, pp. 215–218, indicates that Halder was dubious about the wisdom of *any* offensive, and that Rundstedt and Leeb favored a withdrawal to a defensible position along the Polish-Soviet border.

9. Franz Halder, *Kriegstagebuch: tägliche Aufzeichnungen des Chefs des Generalstabes des Heeres 1939–1942* (Stuttgart: Kohlhammer Verlag, 1962–64), Vol. III, pp. 419–421.

10. "Gliederung der Ostfront am 12 August 1942," in *KTB/OKW*, Vol. II, Part I, p. 571; and "Schematische Kriegs-Gliederung Stand: 1.1.1943," in *KTB/OKW* Vol. III, Part I, pp. 3–5. Halder, *Kriegstagebuch*, Vol. III, p. 457, mentions nine armored and sixty-two and a half other German divisions, but gives no figures for the Italian, Romanian, and Hungarian forces.

to seventy-eight divisions (including fourteen of cavalry), rather
smaller than their German counterparts, and seventeen tank brigades.[11] The Directive for the operation (Führerweisung Nr. 41)
was issued on 5 April 1942.[12] Its language defines it as "fundamentally necessary" to destroy the Soviet forces in the area west of the
Don, "so as subsequently to capture the oil regions in the Caucasus" and to make "an attempt" to reach Stalingrad itself, or at
least to destroy it, by bringing it within range of heavy weapons. In
short, the order of priorities was (1) destruction of enemy forces,
(2) capture of the oil fields, and (3) to take Stalingrad or get close
enough to it to destroy it by gunfire and bombing.

Had these objectives been attained, no crisis for Germany would
have developed out of the summer offensive of 1942. But as will be
shown, realization that they were not being achieved induced in
the ensuing weeks a sense of failure in the subordinate decision-
makers around Hitler. Hitler himself, by resorting to dismissal of a
number of his major field commanders, showed an awareness that
the campaign was going wrong, though he would not as yet admit
the possibility of failure.

However, the time from the launching of the main operation at
the end of June to the middle of November 1942 is a pre-crisis period. There is a conspicuous increase in perceived threat on the
part of German decision-makers, but the threat is simply that of
failure of the offensive. The cluster of events that triggers this perception is diffused over many weeks, ranging from the failure in
early July to capture the city of Voronezh to the virtual halting of
the advances in both the Caucasus and Stalingrad areas after the
end of August. In September, a time constraint begins to be perceived; but it is only that the onset of winter may find the operation uncompleted. At no time is there any perception of a Soviet
ability to strike back on a large scale, or of finite time in the sense
of a need to act quickly to prevent the destruction of major elements of the German or satellite armed forces in the East. The period is therefore one of pre-crisis rather than crisis in terms of the
ICB definitions.

11. *Istoriia Velikoi Otechestvennoi Voiny Sovetskogo Soiuza* [History of the Great Fatherland War of the Soviet Union, hereinafter cited as *IVOVSS*], Vol. II (Moscow: USSR
Ministry of Defense Publishing House, 1963), pp. 411–412.

12. Trevor-Roper, ed., *Hitler's War Directives*, p. 116.

PRELIMINARY OPERATIONS

Two essential preliminaries to the main offensive were the expulsion of Soviet forces from the Crimea and from the Barvenkovo salient, south of Kharkov.

The Soviet forces in the Crimea, confined to the city and naval base at Sevastopol and the Kerch Peninsula, had made an indecisive attempt to expel the Germans from the Crimea during the winter, and had been on the defensive since April. Stavka (the Soviet GHQ) ordered the Commander of the Crimean Front, General D. T. Kozlov, who had three armies totaling twenty-one divisions at his disposal, to clear the Germans out if possible, but at the same time at least to create a stable defense line. This order was not in fact carried out, and the twenty-one divisions were spread out in a single line across the neck of the peninsula.

The three armies had between them 3,580 guns and mortars, 350 tanks, and 400 aircraft,[13] but had not taken steps to organize them properly; in particular, no anti-tank artillery reserve had been created, nor had adequate steps been taken to camouflage positions or to provide anti-aircraft defense for forces and headquarters.[14]

From the German point of view, the capture of the Crimea had two objectives. One was to force the Soviet Black Sea Fleet away to ports on the eastern coast, from which it would have serious difficulties in supporting the ground battle.[15] The other was to free 11th Army so that it could take part in the offensive into the Caucasus.[16] It was decided first to eliminate the armies in the Kerch Peninsula, and to capture Sevastopol afterwards.[17] Forces available for the operation (fifteen divisions, 180 tanks, 2,470 guns and mortars, and 400 aircraft)[18] were less than the Soviets had at their dis-

13. *IVOVSS*, Vol. II, pp. 404–406.

14. Ibid., p. 416.

15. The forced move to the east coast ports not only increased the distance of Soviet fleet bases from the coastal sector of the Front, but it also reduced the effectiveness of the Black Sea Fleet because maintenance, repair, and supply facilities in the east coast ports were limited.

16. Trevor-Roper, ed., *Hitler's War Directives*, pp. 124–127: Directive No. 43, of 11 July 1942.

17. Ibid., p. 118: Section IIB of Directive No. 41, of 5 April 1942.

18. *IVOVSS*, Vol. II, p. 407, credits the Germans with overall superiority, but compares only the forces at Sevastopol, and omits those in the Kerch peninsula.

posal, but their handling by Manstein was much superior. The attack on the Kerch Peninsula was mounted on 8 May with ten divisions, and the Crimean Front very soon lost control of operations. On the night of 11 May, Soviet forces began a disorderly withdrawal to the line of the so-called "Turkish Ditch," a retreat that was not covered from the air and was something of a disaster for the Soviet defenders. By 19 May, the Germans had occupied the city of Kerch itself, and Soviet rear guards were fighting a desperate action to cover the evacuation of the rest of the force on to the Taman Peninsula of the Caucasus. In total, the Crimean Front lost 176,000 men in May alone, including many experienced officers, and almost all its heavy equipment had to be left behind;[19] much of it was later used by the Germans against Sevastopol. Stavka attributed the defeat in the Crimea to the inadequacies of the Front Commander, the Stavka representative (L. Z. Mekhlis, the Head of the Chief Political Directorate of the Red Army, and a Deputy Minister of Defense),[20] and the Member of the Military Council, Divisional Commissar F. A. Shamanin.[21] All three were dismissed from their posts and reduced in rank.

The German victory at Kerch was so complete that only lack of shipping precluded a pursuit of the Soviets across the Kerch Straits to the Taman Peninsula. The 11th Army was now able to turn its full attention to Sevastopol, which had been under siege since the end of October 1941. On 7 June, after five days of artillery and air attacks, the main assault was mounted. It took four weeks to capture the city, and only a few thousand of the defenders escaped. Loss of the Crimea not only worsened the basing situation for the Soviet Black Sea Fleet; it opened a short route to the Caucasus via the Kerch Strait and also influenced Turkey to interpret its neutrality in a somewhat more pro-Axis sense. But though the victory liberated the German 11th Army to join the general offensive, Hitler decided that its experience in the capture of a city would be especially useful against Leningrad, whither he decided to dispatch at least part of it, with Manstein.

The Barvenkovo salient had to be eliminated because Soviet forces could attack from it into the flank and rear of Army Group

19. John Erickson, *The Road to Stalingrad* (London: Weidenfeld and Nicolson, 1975), p. 349.

20. *IVOVSS*, Vol. II, pp. 405–406.

21. Ibid., p. 406; and Erickson, *Road to Stalingrad*, pp. 348–349.

South as it advanced. An operation was therefore planned, under the code name "Fridericus," to precede the major offensive. It entailed nipping off the neck of the salient by 6th Army (Colonel-General Friedrich Paulus) from the north and 1st Panzer Army (Colonel-General Ewald von Kleist) from the South, and was scheduled to begin on 18 May.

But on 12 May the Red Army's Southwestern and Southern Fronts (in Soviet nomenclature a "Front" is an Army Group), under the overall command of Marshal of the Soviet Union S. K. Timoshenko, launched an offensive from the Barvenkovo salient, aimed at recapturing Kharkov, one of the two largest Soviet cities in German hands. The attack put great pressure on the German forces north of the salient, and the plan for "Fridericus" had to be changed, the attack being brought forward by one day to 17 May, and carried out from the south only, by 1st Panzer Army. Thanks largely to Stalin's reluctance to call off the operation, a major German success was achieved, three Soviet armies (each approximately equivalent to a German Army Corps) being wiped out, and twenty-nine Soviet divisions smashed.[22] Between the three battles—Kerch, Kharkov, and Sevastopol—over half a million Soviet troops were lost, along with 1,100–1,200 tanks and 6,000–7,000 guns, well over a month's production of these weapons.[23] The Soviet losses could only be made up in part in the time left before the opening of the main German offensive on 28 June. Manpower and (especially) equipment shortages from this disaster and the only slightly lesser catastrophe in the Crimea were to plague the Red Army throughout the summer, and render the retreat to the Volga almost an inevitability.

THE REICHEL AFFAIR

Preparations for operation "Blue 1," the first phase of the German offensive, were proceeding smoothly, though the starting date had not yet been fixed, when the future of the whole undertaking was threatened.

On 19 June, nine days before the German offensive was due to begin, a light aircraft carrying Major Reichel, the Operations Offi-

22. Paul Carell, *Hitler's War on Russia: The Story of the German Defeat in the East* (London: George G. Harrap, 1964), p. 463.

23. *IVOVSS*, Vol. II, p. 361.

cer of the 23rd Panzer Division, crash-landed just inside the Russian lines near Nezhegol. Reichel was carrying documents that outlined the first phase of the operation and marked the demarcation lines for the Corps (XL Panzer) of which 23rd Panzer Division formed a part.[24] A similar incident had occurred in November 1939, when a German light aircraft, aboard which was a German officer carrying plans for a general offensive in the West, force-landed in Belgium. On that occasion, it had been necessary to postpone the offensive and to make radical changes in the plan.[25] Hitler had therefore issued instructions that strictly forbade such flights, and Reichel's conduct was a serious breach of regulations.

A nearby German unit sent out a patrol, which located the wreck of the aircraft and two graves, one of them empty, but found no sign of Reichel or of his briefcase.[26] It became known after the war that Reichel was killed in the crash, and that the captured documents were sent to the Soviet General Staff on the same day. However, Stalin chose to regard them as a "plant," especially when attacks which, according to the Reichel documents, were to be launched on 22 June failed to materialize. The commander of the Bryansk Front, General F. I. Golikov, was summoned to GHQ, and was seen by Stalin on 26 June. The Reichel documents were on Stalin's desk. Stalin swept them aside, telling Golikov that he did not believe a word of them, denigrating the competence of the intelligence staff for being deceived by them, and ordering Golikov to prepare an offensive, in cooperation with his northerly neighbors (Western Front), to capture the city of Orel. Golikov's staff began to work on this immediately, and completed it at 3:00 A.M. on 28 June, seven hours before the launching of the German offensive made it obsolete.[27]

The Soviet plan for 1942 hinged around discussions that took place in the General Staff and Stavka during the spring.[28] Much of the advantage gained from Zhukov's successful counteroffensive outside Moscow in December 1941 had been wasted through Stalin's attempt to broaden it to a general offensive, for which re-

24. Carell, *Hitler's War on Russia*, p. 481.
25. Liddell Hart, *Other Side of the Hill*, p. 107.
26. Halder, *Kriegstagebuch*, Vol. III, p. 462.
27. Erickson, *Road to Stalingrad*, p. 355.
28. Georgy K. Zhukov, *Vospominaniia i razmyshleniia* (Moscow: Novosti Press Agency Publishing House, 1969), pp. 362 ff.

sources were inadequate. When the General Staff came to consider what the Red Army should do in the summer, its main preoccupation was naturally with the besieged Leningrad and Moscow, the latter of which was still only some sixty miles from the nearest point of the front. The basic decision-making problem that faced Stalin and his military advisers was whether (as the majority opinion of the General Staff favored) to remain on the strategic defensive, thus yielding the initiative to the Germans, but, it was hoped, accumulating reserves for a major strategic offensive at a later date, or whether (as Stalin wanted) to attempt to seize the initiative by smaller offensives of their own. The General Staff position, favoring the strategic defensive, was presented to Stalin in mid-March by its Chief, Marshal Shaposhnikov, and his Deputy, General Vasilevsky, and apparently accepted.[29] But Stalin also approved plans for several local offensives which were prepared at about the same time. Although some of the leading members of the GHQ, notably Zhukov, attempted to reduce these, Shaposhnikov, apparently despairing of changing Stalin's mind, provided no support.[30] The plan that emerged was therefore an uneasy combination of offensives and defensives, beyond the Red Army's resources to execute successfully, and intelligence information indicating a German intention to attack in the south was ignored. Stalin could conceive of no Soviet targets more important to the Germans than Moscow or Leningrad, and therefore regarded all contrary evidence, including the Reichel documents, as planted to deceive.[31] The limited foreknowledge provided by the Reichel affair consequently had no discernible effect on the Soviet riposte to the German offensive. It did, however, result in the first dismissals of the campaign: the commanding Generals of Reichel's Corps and Division, and the Corps Chief of Staff.

THE OFFENSIVE

The starting date was set by Hitler on 23 June. The offensive was to open on the 27th. However, rainy and thundery weather caused a 24-hour postponement. When the offensive opened on 28 June,

29. Erickson, *Road to Stalingrad*, pp. 385–386.

30. Ibid., p. 338; and Zhukov, *Vospominaniia*, p. 367.

31. Geoffrey Jukes, *Stalingrad: The Turning Point* (New York: Ballantine, 1968), pp. 23–24.

the main German blow fell on three rifle divisions of the 13th and 14th Armies of the Bryansk Front, about 60–75 miles east of Kursk. By the end of the day, the Germans had broken through the main defense line and advanced 5–10 miles beyond it. The Soviet GHQ hastily dispatched two tank corps from Southwestern Front and one from GHQ Reserve, and also sent fighters and ground-attack aircraft to reinforce the Bryansk Front.[32] Golikov had decided to try to stop the German advance on the banks of the Kshen river, and for that purpose he dispatched his own front reserve of one tank corps to the Volovo area, at the same time ordering the three that had been sent to reinforce it to concentrate for a counterattack, one at Kastornoye, about fifty miles northwest of Voronezh, and the other two at Stary Oskol, with the aim of counterattacking.[33] However, some of the tank forces did not arrive in time, and those that did were sent into battle piecemeal. Although the Soviets had tank superiority (about 1,000, compared to less than 500 German), mishandling of the tanks led to failure and to an intensified search for scapegoats by Stalin,[34] in which generals were dismissed on a scale so far matched by Hitler only in December of 1941. Among those dismissed were the Chief of Staff of the Southwestern Axis, General Bagramyan, the Commander of the Bryansk Front, General Golikov, the Commander of the 17th Tank Corps, General Feklenko, the Commander of the 60th Army, General Antonyuk, and a number of lower commanders. There was, however, one significant difference between Stalin's and Hitler's practice, in that the majority of the dismissed Red Army officers were reassigned at slightly lower levels of command, rather than simply put on the unemployed list. Golikov, for example, was not even removed from the area; a new Army Group—the Voronezh Front—was set up under the command of General N. F. Vatutin, and Golikov became his deputy.[35]

On 30 June, the German 6th Army broke through the right wing of the Southwestern Front and in three days advanced about fifty miles, surrounding parts of the Bryansk Front's forces in the process. Although many of the encircled forces managed to break out

32. Erickson, *Road to Stalingrad*, p. 356.
33. Ibid., pp. 356–357.
34. Ibid., pp. 357–361.
35. Ibid., p. 359. According to *IVOVSS*, Vol. II, p. 421, Golikov was not demoted. But see Mikhail I. Kazakov, "On the Voronezh Axis in the Summer of 1942" [in Russian], *Voienno-Istoricheskii Zhurnal* (Moscow), No. 10 (1964), pp. 28–37.

to the east, a large gap had been opened in the Soviet defenses, and the road to Voronezh was opened. This was to create a major decision-making problem for both sides.

Shaposhnikov's health had now finally broken down, and on 2 July his deputy, Colonel-General Vasilevsky, succeeded him as Chief of the General Staff. No sooner had he been appointed than Stalin sent him into the field to oversee operations at Voronezh.[36] Additional forces were directed thither from GHQ Reserve in the shape of three "combined arms" armies, which were deployed on the left bank of the Don, and one tank army, which was concentrated south of Yelets with the objective of a counteroffensive into the German flank. At the same time, the Southwestern Front was ordered to organize a solid defense in the Ostrogozhsk area.[37] These measures succeeded in stopping the German attempt to take Voronezh on the run, but German forces nevertheless reached the Don and seized a small bridgehead on its left bank.

From the German angle, the problem was whether or not a major effort to take Voronezh would be justified. It was on the east side of the Don, a river which it was not Hitler's intention to cross until the "Don bend," where it is closest to the Volga. The river was otherwise to be used as a barrier between Soviet and Axis forces, and for this purpose Voronezh lay on the "wrong" side of it. But Bock was influenced by its position as a rail and road center, which made it an obvious gathering point for a possible Soviet counteroffensive into the flank and rear of Army Group South, so he decided to take it. In view of the fact that large Soviet forces were being directed to Voronezh, his apprehensions were reasonable; but they were mistaken, as the Soviet deployment was prompted by the also mistaken belief that Bock intended to thrust north from Voronezh toward Moscow.

Hitler's intention was different. Not knowing that Stalin had ignored the Reichel documents, he was concerned that the Red Army would attempt to avoid destruction by rapid withdrawal to the east. Bock's determination to capture Voronezh was, by this interpretation, the willful loss of an opportunity, especially as Bock, impressed by the Soviet tank strength, planned to use his Panzer and Motorized Infantry divisions to take the city, leaving only the foot soldiers to continue the pursuit along the Don.

36. Aleksandr M. Vasilevsky, *Delo vsei Zhizni* (Moscow: Politizdat, 1974), pp. 197–202.
37. *IVOVSS*, Vol. II, p. 420.

Hitler therefore decided to confront Bock personally, so on 3 July he and Halder flew to Army Group South's headquarters at Poltava. During the three-hour flight, they discussed the situation and agreed that the capture of Voronezh was not necessary.[38] At the conference with Bock, which began at 7:00 A.M and was over by 9:00 A.M., Hitler informed Bock that he need not take Voronezh, but asked him to carry out small attacks, to keep the enemy in doubt as to where the main attacks would come. He emphasized that the Soviets knew the operational plan already and might try to avoid the trap by withdrawing; that loss of the oil areas would bring catastrophe upon the Soviet Union; and that its allies were unlikely to help it by creating a diversion in the West.

When Hitler and Halder left, they thought Bock had been dissuaded from taking Voronezh. Bock, however, thought he had been left with discretion to decide whether or not to do so, and how much effort to expend.[39] On the evening of 5 July, he reported his intention to use mostly his (unmechanized) infantry divisions to attack the retreating Soviets east of Voronezh, and to employ two strong mechanized formations, the 24th Panzer and "Grossdeutschland" divisions, against the city. Hitler thereupon categorically forbade any attack on Voronezh and, through OKW, announced his intention to split Army Group South into two new groups, to be known as Army Groups A and B, with effect from 7 July.[40] Bock would command Army Group B, and Army Group A, to the south of it, would come under the command of Field Marshal List. This should have left Bock in no doubt that Voronezh was not considered important. But by 5 July, when the Don had been reached on a broad front west and south of the city, it was clear that Soviet reinforcements were being poured into the area. Weichs, who had built a northward-facing front as required, reported strong though uncoordinated tank attacks, and that more Soviet forces were moving toward his front and into Voronezh itself.

The midday conference at FHQ on 5 July saw a heated criticism by Hitler of the movements of two of Bock's divisions, 23rd Panzer and 16th Motorized to the Northeast and East respectively, instead of the Southeast to cut off Soviet forces withdrawing eastward to-

38. Halder, *Kriegstagebuch*, Vol. III, pp. 471–472.

39. *KTB/OKW*, Vol. II, Part I, p. 55; and Bock, diary entry for 3 July 1942, Bundesarchiv, Koblenz, Nachlass v. Bock.

40. Halder, *Kriegstagebuch*, Vol. III, p. 474.

ward the Don bend. Bock explained by telephone that he had ordered these movements in order to protect the south flank of the 4th Panzer Army against Soviet tank units that were active in the area. Halder did not feel that these were dangerous; he saw them as units that had become separated from their main body, had no instructions, and so merely attacked targets of opportunity, and thus constituted no serious threat to anybody.[41] Bock's Chief of Staff, General von Sodenstern, agreed with Halder, but Bock was not to be convinced. Halder's opinion was that the Commander-in-Chief of 4th Panzer Army, General Hoth, had accepted Bock's order to take Voronezh only with reluctance, directed all his forces toward it (presumably in order to get it over with as quickly as possible), and demanded that Bock provide him with flank cover.[42]

The consequences of Bock's preoccupation with Voronezh, and his reluctance to make Hoth cover his own flank, were that too much of Army Group South's effort was directed to the capture of the town, and Soviet forces were permitted to slip away eastward. Only after strong representations by Halder did Bock agree to send forces of 6th Army toward the lower course of the Tikhaya Sosna (which joins the Don from the southwest, about fifty miles south of Voronezh), with the aim of catching Soviet forces west of that river. But even then he sent only his nonmotorized infantry, leaving the motorized formations to "mill around," instead of gathering them for a push along the south bank of the Don. At the same time, he was using mobile formations (24th Panzer Division and the elite "Grossdeutschland" Panzer Grenadier Division) against Voronezh, a task for which they were not intended and for which their superior mobility would be of little value, despite having been told by Hitler personally only two days before that the capture of the town was not important.

Bock was killed in an air raid a few days before the end of the war and left no memoirs, so his reasons for persisting with the assault on Voronezh, against the advice of his own Chief of Staff and his superiors at OKH and FHQ, are not known. Whatever they were, he was ordered on 5 July to confine himself to holding the bridgehead on the east bank, withdraw 24th Panzer and "Grossdeutschland" as quickly as possible, and send them off along the

41. Ibid., pp. 474–475.
42. Ibid., pp. 475–476.

Don to the east. The objective was to prevent an orderly Soviet withdrawal, force the Russians away from the south bank of the Don, and cut them off, in a repetition of a maneuver that had been successfully employed several times in 1941. Under this plan, 4th Panzer Army would drive south behind the Soviets, 1st Panzer Army would push north to meet it, and the encircled Soviet forces would be ground down between them and the infantry of 6th and 17th Armies advancing from the West.

However, on the very next day, 6 July, long before the plan could be put into effect, it was discovered that the Soviets had evacuated Voronezh and were hurriedly drawing back their entire line north as well as south of the Don. Hoth was blamed for having painted too dark a picture, and Bock for believing him.[43]

The outcome was another stormy scene at the midday conference that day, with Hitler making loud demands for Bock to coordinate his forces, release mobile elements from the Voronezh operation, and drive over the Tikhaya Sosna to the lower Don as quickly as possible.

Interpretation of the hasty Soviet withdrawal created further dissonances within FHQ. Hitler believed the Soviet commander, Marshal Timoshenko, was trading space for time, while Halder saw the industrial area of the Don as too important to be sacrificed voluntarily, and inclined to the view that the Russian strength was less than expected.[44] Much of the day was spent in frantic telephone conversations between Hitler, Keitel, Halder, Bock, and Sodenstern, a process that Halder described sarcastically in his diary as "painful," since it concerned matters in which "calm consideration should precede the issuing of clear orders."[45]

In the evening, Halder had a conference with Hitler at 6:50 P.M., and another with Keitel at 7:30.[46] Hitler, fearful of Bock's tendency to depart from his orders, laid down a northern limit beyond which main forces were not to go; and Keitel stressed that if Voronezh was cleared of Soviet forces, it was to be occupied solely by unmechanized infantry. Though Hitler was, for the moment, less optimistic than Halder about the implications of the Soviet withdrawal and was insisting on the need for a rapid follow-up, he was unwilling to make available the elite Waffen SS 1st Division (Leib-

43. Ibid., p. 474.   44. Ibid., p. 475.   45. Ibid.
46. Ibid., pp. 475–476.

standarte Adolf Hitler) for 1st Panzer Army, because he had in mind to move it to the West. There seemed no rational grounds for this move, but it was the first sign of a preoccupation with the possibility of Allied action to relieve the pressure on the Russians which was groundlessly to influence decision-making more and more. On 3 July, Hitler had told Halder and Bock that an Allied move to relieve the pressure on the Russians by an attack in the West was unlikely; but on 5 July, he refused to allow SS "Leibstandarte" to be committed to an operation on the Eastern Front in which its high standards of mobility and motivation could have been of the greatest importance, because he had decided it might be needed in the West. But at the same time he rejected Halder's interpretation of the hasty Soviet withdrawal as indicating greater weakness than expected, though it was Halder's argument which, if correct, both reduced the need to keep "Leibstandarte" on the Eastern Front and increased the need for it in the West, where the chances were that Russia's allies would have to act to relieve the pressure on the Red Army. And by 9 July, Hitler's preoccupation with the danger of an Allied invasion had impelled him to issue a very detailed order,[47] referring to the likelihood that the British would be forced by the "quick and great" German successes in the East either to invade or face the loss of the Soviet ally, and therefore there was a "high probability that enemy landings in the area of Commander-in-Chief West will take place shortly." After listing the most probable areas, he ordered a number of steps to be taken. SS Division "Reich," still forming, was to be transferred to the command of the C-in-C West immediately. An SS general command was to be set up to control all SS formations in the West and possibly also the "Göring" brigade. The movement of one regiment of the 23rd Infantry Division to Denmark, which had already been ordered, was to be postponed. Three new divisions in the course of formation were to be moved to the West as quickly as possible; their first units were to be ready to move between 18 and 20 July, and they were to be deployed in southwestern Netherlands and behind the Belgian coast, with precautions against sabotage, which included the taking of hostages from the civilian population living near main railway stations or other vulnerable points. All Dutch, Belgian, and French communities were to be required to seize and hand over strangers

47. OKW/Wfst, Nr. 551213/42.

to the nearest military post. Near especially important and vulnerable targets, personnel and materiel were to be kept ready for quick repairs. The Air Force, in cooperation with the C-in-C West, was to assemble into usable formations all available units of the 7th Air Division and the "Göring" brigade, and to dispatch two combat groups, made up from the C-in-C Air Force's reserve in the east, to France. The Army General Staff, the C-in-C Air Force, the C-in-C West, and the Chiefs of Army Equipment and of Replacement Army were to report to Hitler daily at 0800 hours on the state of progress as of 7:00 P.M. the previous day. If the enemy landed, Hitler would go to the west and lead from there.

No basis has been found for the rapid change between 3 and 9 July in Hitler's assessment of the likelihood of an Allied landing. The daily Air Force reconnaissance reports for the period indicate no unusual activity in southern English ports or waters,[48] and the only mention of British troop movements by Foreign Armies West was a report on 6 July that a convoy was likely to have left for the Middle East on 25 June, while about 40,000 tons of shipping had assembled in Swansea for another troop convoy.[49] Swansea is a Welsh port on the north side of the Bristol Channel; it and ports even further west were to be used for embarcation of the invading forces in June 1944, but only because the forces earmarked for D-day were too large to be handled entirely by the ports on the Channel coast. There would have been no reason in mid-1942 to envisage an invasion mounted solely from one port, and that a remote one using only 40,000 tons of shipping, so Foreign Armies West correctly concluded that what was in question was a further troop convoy destined for Egypt.[50] Hitler's apprehensions were therefore grounded solely in perceptions that his operations against the Russians were actually or potentially so catastrophic for the Soviet Union that its allies would have to do something soon if it was not to be forced out of the war—an interpretation that he himself rejected when even a watered-down form of it was advanced by Halder.[51] Russian pressure on the Allies for a Second Front was in-

48. "Eingegangene Meldungen Generalstab Luftwaffe," in *KTB/OKW*, Vol. II, Part I, pp. 473, 475, 477, 480, 483, 485, 488.

49. Ibid., p. 479.

50. The conclusion was correct that no invasion was contemplated, but the information was probably false, as all German agents in the U.K. were under British control. See John C. Masterman, *The Double-Cross System in the War of 1939 to 1945* (Canberra: Australian National University Press, 1972), p. 6.

51. Halder, *Kriegstagebuch*, Vol. III, pp. 475–476.

deed sustained in this period, as it was to be for many more months, and there was certainly lively concern in the Allied camp at the renewed German advance,[52] but the belief that Russia could be overcome in a few weeks had vanished from Anglo-American thinking at the same time that it disappeared from German thinking, in the winter of 1941. The decision that there could be no Second Front in Europe in 1942 had already been taken,[53] Stalin had reluctantly adjusted to it, and the losses so far in the 1942 campaign, though grievous, did not compare with those which the Red Army had incurred and survived in the previous year. Hitler's apprehensions therefore lacked foundation either in the general situation or in specific British activities. The British were far too concerned with their deteriorating position in the Middle East to spare significant forces for a chancy expedition across the Channel, which could not be mounted on a scale sufficient to affect the much larger conflict on the Eastern Front, and were already far advanced, along with the Americans, in planning a different "relief expedition" against French North Africa (operation "Torch"). However, the fear of a "Second Front" remained an important factor in Hitler's thinking from this time on, and was to be exploited by the Allies in order to encourage dispersal of German forces, especially in the Mediterranean.[54]

Nevertheless, despite the order of 9 July, events on the Eastern Front still claimed most of Hitler's attention. On 11 July, he issued Directive No. 43, for further operations by 11th Army now that the Crimea had been cleared of Soviet forces. The Army was to cross the Kerch Straits to the Taman Peninsula, capture the Soviet Black Sea Fleet's last remaining bases at Anapa and Novorossiysk, and then advance eastward to capture the Maykop oil field. A deception operation was to be mounted, to persuade the Russians that the Army was being moved to the coast north of the Sea of Azov, and there were to be special operations to seize the oil installation at Maykop, and to sabotage railways, bridges, and port installations. On 11 July, an OKH directive was also issued,[55] which envisaged

52. Winston S. Churchill, *The Second World War* (London: Cassell, 1948–1954), Vol. IV, chap. 25.

53. Ibid.

54. For example, "the man who never was" operation of April 1943. See Ewen Montague, "The Man Who Never Was," in *Courage and Achievement: Three Famous Stories* (London: Evans Brothers, 1968).

55. OKH/Gen. St. d. H./op. Abt. (I), Nr. 420499/42.

destruction of the Russians north of the Donets by a joint operation between the inner wings of Army Groups A and B. This was
unsuccessful; the Soviets broke through to the east and southeast.

On 13 July, a Führer order was issued on continuation of operations by Army Groups A and B.[56] It was an expansion of the OKH
order of two days before, and defined the objective as hindering
Soviet withdrawal to the east, in particular preventing a retreat
across the Don. The order took both Panzer Armies toward Rostov,
away from the main eastward line of the operation, because Hitler
believed that the Russians intended to withdraw across the Don in
a southerly direction, toward the Caucasus rather than the Volga.
The main effect of this order was to cause an accumulation of mobile forces at the southern end of the front, in anticipation of a Soviet withdrawal southeast of it, which was not in fact taking place
and does not appear from Soviet records to have been contemplated. The envisaged movement of 11th Army across the Kerch
Straits also appears connected with Hitler's erroneous picture of
the pattern of the Soviet withdrawal.

No explanation of Hitler's erroneous perception of Soviet intentions has been found. However, there are indications that Hitler
was ambivalent about objectives in 1942, as in 1941. "Seizure of
the oil region of the Caucasus" is mentioned among the general objectives of the campaign in the preamble of Order No. 41,[57] but is
not mentioned in the section of it that deals with the plan of operations. And on 1 April, Hitler had confided to Kleist, the commander of 1st Panzer Army of Army Group A, that he and his army
were destined to ensure Germany's oil supplies in perpetuity.[58] So
it is possible that Hitler was unable to choose between alternatives, as in the previous summer when he had defended his preference for capture of the Ukraine against military advocacy of a drive
to Moscow by referring to generals' ignorance of economics.[59] The
choices here were between *denial* of oil to the Soviets, by interrupting supply routes in the Stalingrad area, and *transference* of
Soviet oil to Germany by capture of the oil fields. Both alternatives
had economic implications, both required military action, but the

56. Ibid., Nr. 420538/42.

57. Trevor-Roper, ed., *Hitler's War Directives*, pp. 178–179.

58. Alan Clark, *Barbarossa: The Russian-German Conflict, 1941–45* (London: Hutchinson, 1965), p. 169.

59. Heinz Guderian, *Panzer Leader* (London: Futura, 1974), p. 200.

second alternative subsumed the first, in that it would automatically have denied the oil to the Soviets, and that may be why Hitler erroneously perceived the Soviets as withdrawing their main forces into the Caucasus. The flaw in his perception is that while to him the source of the oil was more important than his adversary's supply route, both were equally important to the Soviets: there would be little point in their retaining the oil fields if they lost the means of supplying the oil to the rest of the Soviet Union.

Also on 13 July, Hitler decided to dismiss Bock from command of Army Group B and replace him with Colonel-General von Weichs. Hitler had been very annoyed at Bock's delay in moving the mobile forces of 4th Panzer Army forward from the Voronezh area, and by Bock's conviction (proved correct) that the OKH directive of 11 July could not be carried out. The removal of an Army Group Commander barely two weeks after the beginning of the major offensive of the year could be held to indicate serious strains in relations between Hitler and the military. In fact, however, unlike some of the later dismissals, this one appears to have been received by the generals with equanimity. There were valid grounds for criticism of Bock's tardiness at Voronezh, which Halder pointed out in the privacy of his diary, and it was Bock's second dismissal in less than eight months: in 1941, he commanded Army Group Center, and was dismissed along with all the other Army Group Commanders after being defeated outside Moscow. His reappointment had been fortuitous, resulting from the death of Field Marshal von Reichenau from a heart attack in January 1942.

Bock's dismissal took effect on 15 July. Possibly more significant that day was a report by Colonel Gehlen of "Foreign Armies East" that the Soviet leadership was contemplating energetic measures to protect Stalingrad. This is the first appearance of any suggestion that the city itself might be fought over. Air Force reconnaissance reported large Soviet troop movements from Stalingrad toward the Don bend east of the river Chir, an indication that Hitler's assumption about a Soviet withdrawal to the southeast was wrong, but the report appears not to have attracted his attention.

The information may have become "submerged" by the preparations to move FHQ and OKH, which took place on the next day, 16 July. FHQ moved to the "Werwolf" camp near Vinnitsa in the Ukraine, and OKH to Vinnitsa itself. However, Halder noted in his diary on 16 July a discussion with Gehlen and Heusinger (Major-

General Adolf Heusinger, Chief of the Operations Department of OKH) that a battle for Stalingrad was planned, and would probably involve entering the city.[60]

Almost unnoticed, the cumulative effects of day-to-day decisions were bringing about a complete change of emphasis in the operations plan. On 17 July, Hitler drafted another set of guidelines for the future operations of Army Groups A and B.[61] These stated that the most important aim was to destroy Timoshenko's armies between the Don and the Donets, and to reach the Volga south of Stalingrad, thereby interrupting all shipping on the Volga, especially the oil traffic from the Caspian. As soon as the Don had been crossed and the Caucasus entered, spare forces of 11th Army were to be transferred to Army Group North and to be used in the capture of Leningrad.

The new set of guidelines caused some lively exchanges between Hitler and Halder at the first daily conference in the new "Werwolf" headquarters. They indicated that the careful phasing of operations insisted on by the Army General Staff and incorporated in Directive No. 41, of 5 April, had been abandoned, and that an attempt was now to be made to achieve all objectives simultaneously.

The guidelines, so hotly debated on 17 July, were issued on the following day,[62] but already Hitler had changed his mind about 11th Army. The earlier decision to move it over the Kerch Straits was rescinded; only the Mountain Divisions were to go that way, and only when the pressure of the Panzer Armies at Rostov had opened the land route to Taman Peninsula. Halder noted with some bitterness that his proposal of the previous day, which had been brusquely rejected in favor of a "senseless clustering" of forces on the north bank of the Don against Rostov, had now been accepted in the shape of an "All-Highest" order to cross the Don on a wide front, which implied the beginning of a battle for Stalingrad.[63]

Rainy weather now intervened to impede operations, and on the 19th an argument took place between Hitler and Halder about the slow buildup of the "assault group Taganrog." There was long and inconclusive discussion about operation "Blücher" (the transfer of part of 11th Army across the Kerch Straits to Taman), as Hitler was torn between the desire to release as many of its divisions as pos-

60. Halder, *Kriegstagebuch*, Vol. III, p. 483.
61. OKW/Wfst, Nr. 55161/42.
62. Halder, *Kriegstagebuch*, Vol. III, pp. 484–485.
63. Ibid., p. 486.

sible for use against Leningrad and his desire to keep the "Blücher" option open until the situation south of Rostov had clarified.

July 21 saw the issuing of Directive No. 44, regarding operations in northern Finland.[64] Its relationship to operations in the south was made clear in its preamble, which stated:

1. That the Soviet Union would soon lose the Caucasus, its most important oil source and an important line of communication for delivery of British and American supplies to it. This, together with the loss of the Donets industrial area, would have "immeasurable consequences."

2. It now remained to cut the northern supply route of the Anglo-Saxon powers to the Soviet Union, by an attack on the Murmansk railway.

3. An offensive for this purpose was therefore to be mounted in the autumn, on the assumption that Leningrad would be captured by September at the latest, and Finnish forces released thereby, and that the 5th Mountain Division would move to Finland by the end of September.

It was emphasized that the main responsibility of 20th Mountain Army remained the protection of the Finnish nickel mines, without which Germany could "probably no longer manufacture" high-grade steel for aircraft and submarine engines.

The directive, with its contingent assumptions which were to prove unwarranted, was followed only two days later by Directive No. 45, of 23 July, which dealt with the continuation of operations against the Caucasus and the Volga.[65] It set Army Group A the task of:

1. Encircling Soviet forces which had escaped across the Don south and southeast of Rostov, and destroying them.

2. After achieving this, to occupy the entire eastern coast of the Black Sea, thereby eliminating all bases of the Soviet Black Sea Fleet.

3. Giving flank cover in the east to the forces engaged on the Black Sea coast, capturing the Groznyy area, and blocking the Osetian military highway. Thereafter, this force was to thrust along the Caspian coast to occupy Baku.

The operations by Army Group B were mentioned almost as an afterthought; it was to push forward to Stalingrad, occupy the city, and maintain the defense against attack from the north between

64. Trevor-Roper, ed., *Hitler's War Directives*, pp. 127–128.
65. Ibid., pp. 129–131.

the Don and the Volga, while mobile forces would advance down the Volga to Astrakhan.

In the expectation that the oil fields of the Caucasus would be captured, and in view of their importance to the German war effort, the Air Force was specifically forbidden to attack refineries, storage tanks, or oil shipment ports, unless this was absolutely essential to army operations. However, shipping, railways, and pipelines were to be attacked as soon as possible, in order to hinder Soviet exploitation of the oil. The Navy's tasks can be summarized as supporting the Army in crossing the Kerch Straits, suppressing Soviet naval action against Army operations along the coast, assisting in supply of the Army across the Don, and preparing to transfer light forces to the Caspian. To maximize the disruption of Soviet operations, Army Groups North and Center were to carry out their local operations in as quick a succession as possible, and Army Group North was to capture Leningrad by the beginning of September.

The conflation of two operations, originally planned as successive, into simultaneous ones aroused Halder's anger. Although Rostov fell on this day, Halder confided to his diary that "the underestimation of the enemy already evident takes ever more grotesque shapes, and is dangerous. It gets ever more unbearable. It is no longer possible to talk of serious work. Morbid reaction to superficial impressions and a complete lack of judgment of the leadership apparatus and its possibilities are the stamp of this so-called leadership."[66] While broadening the commitment of Army Groups A and B, Hitler, over the opposition of Halder and Jodl, ordered that the "Grossdeutschland" division be withdrawn from the front and prepared to move to the west.

The foundations of a major dispute between Hitler and the military were already being laid before the end of the month. The 6th Army, scheduled to attack on 28 July, could not do so because of shortages of fuel and ammunition, and this caused a major outburst on the 29th, in which Hitler flung one insult after another at Halder. On the same day, Hitler's adjutant, Major Engel, visited Weichs and Paulus. He found them both quietly optimistic but worried whether or not Russian reserves were exhausted. They were of the opinion that their forces were too weak for jobs assigned to them,

---

66. Halder, *Kriegstagebuch*, Vol. III, pp. 488–489.

and would be unable to withstand strong counterattacks. Paulus, Weichs, and Weichs's Chief of Staff, Colonel Winter, asked Engel to give their views to Hitler personally, as they did not think Halder was doing so.[67] Already there was uneasiness about the dispatch of so many forces to Rostov, where they were not needed, at the expense of Army Group B; and on 30 July, Jodl said that forces must be urgently transferred from Army Group A to Army Group B, because "the fate of the Caucasus will be decided at Stalingrad." Halder sardonically noted in his diary that this is what he had proposed himself six days earlier.[68] On the following day, 31 July, Hitler, clearly influenced by what Jodl had said, ordered 4th Panzer Army to be transferred back to Army Group B.

On the Soviet side, the permission given to forces that were in danger of encirclement to retreat to the east prevented full realization of German plans during July. Nevertheless, the price the Soviets had to pay for this was a very large one: the highly important industrial region of the Donbass had to be given up; the Germans reached the large bend of the Don, thereby coming within fifty miles of their objectives on the Volga; and the combat capacity of Soviet forces was very adversely affected by their failures and attendant losses. Breakdown of morale and instances of cowardice, panic, and breach of discipline, though not yet threatening the integrity of the forces as a whole, were sufficient to cause Stalin, on 28 July, to issue Order No. 227, which pointed out that further retreats were unacceptable, and that every meter of Soviet ground must in future be defended to the death.

Thus far, Stalin's reaction to defeat was similar to that of Hitler in December 1941: to dismiss generals and order the troops to hold fast.

However, just as dismissals had been followed by reassignment, so the order to stop retreating was accompanied by additional measures. Order No. 227 was the subject of a conference of Members of the Military Council (chief political officers) and heads of political directorates and departments of Fronts (Army Groups) and Armies, held in July.[69] This conference considered steps for improving party political work among the troops, and had a number of

67. Ibid., p. 493; and Hildegard von Kotze, ed., *Heeresadjutant bei Hitler, 1938–1943: Aufzeichnungen des Major Engel* (Stuttgart: Deutsche Verlags-Anstalt, 1974), p. 123.

68. Halder, *Kriegstagebuch*, Vol. III, p. 493.

69. Zhukov, *Vospominaniia*, p. 371.

consequences. In the Main Political Directorate, the Political Directorates of the Fronts, and the Political Departments of Armies, teams of "agitators" (that is, of propagandists concerned especially with short-term issues) were set up, and a Council for Military-Political Propaganda was formed in the Main Political Directorate, with the task of generalizing experience in morale raising and finding ways to improve it even further. The circulation of newspapers and journals for the Red Army and Navy was increased, and a number of senior Communist Party members were sent to talk to the armies in the field. Both political workers and commanding officers gave speeches to their units, explaining the order and its slogan "Not a Step Back." These measures, coupled with the introduction of harsher penalties for indiscipline, prevented the erosion of morale from going disastrously far. The possibly disastrous consequences of the German breakthrough were averted, and though it did not prove possible to stop the retreat immediately, the situation did not degenerate into a rout. Nevertheless, the Red Army entered August considerably weaker than it had been at the beginning of July.

July does not mark the onset of full crisis for Germany, nor even the end of the pre-crisis period. Military operations had not, by any objective standard, been a failure. The preliminaries to the offensive had been well executed, and the offensive itself had gained considerable ground as well as inflicting substantial casualties on the enemy.

But there had been significant misperceptions of Soviet intentions. Bock had misinterpreted their dispatch of troops to Voronezh, and diverted forces there, allowing Soviet forces south of the Don to slip from his clutches. Between 3 July and 9 July, Hitler had switched, for no obvious reason, from discounting the likelihood of an Allied landing in the West to coming to believe it highly probable; and he had directed his armored forces to block a Soviet retreat into the Caucasus which was neither taking place nor planned. By mid-July, it had begun to be realized that Stalingrad would be defended, and discussion again arose between Hitler and Halder over the abandonment of sequential operations in favor of simultaneous ones. Despite the gains in territory and the infliction of casualties, the set objectives were not being attained. It could not, or not yet, be said that operations were unsuccessful, but they were not, or not yet, manifestly successful either.

CHAPTER TWO

August–September 1942:
Failures and Dismissals

AUGUST 1942

THE MONTH OF AUGUST was notable for a gradual loss of impetus by the summer offensive, increasing difficulties elsewhere on the Front, and difficulties caused by the heat of the Ukrainian summer in the new headquarters near Vinnitsa.

On 2 August, General Bodewin Keitel, Field Marshal Keitel's brother and head of the Army Personnel Office (HPA), reported on the personnel situation in the army and drew Halder's attention to the fact that the Officer Corps had no direct representation with Hitler.[1] Since the dismissal of Brauchitsch in December 1941, and Hitler's assumption of his post of Commander-in-Chief of the Army, the Army Personnel Office had come directly under the Chief of OKW (Field Marshal Keitel), whom many officers, his own brother included, felt to be an inadequate representative of the Officer Corps' interests. In any event, Keitel was not the Commander-in-Chief of the Army, and therefore lacked the authority of his predecessors. There is no indication that Halder raised this matter directly with Hitler, but on the following day at the midday conference, an exchange between the two men on the volunteer problem showed the depth of Hitler's basic animosity toward the officer class. He refused to increase the numbers of volunteers which the Army could recruit from men born in 1924–25, on the grounds that the volunteers came from the basically National Socialist circles of the population, did not find what they wanted in the Army be-

---

1. Franz Halder, *Kriegstagebuch: tägliche Aufzeichnungen des Chefs des Generalstabes des Heeres 1939–1942* (Stuttgart: Kohlhammer Verlag, 1962–64), Vol. III, p. 496.

cause of the conservative attitude of broad sections of the Officer Corps, and therefore preferred to go into the Air Force.[2]

In the remainder of the first half of August, the attention of Hitler and the headquarters was taken up predominantly with preparations for offensives in the center and northern parts of the Front. Army Group Center was given the task of liquidating a Soviet salient at Sukhinichi, but its Commander-in-Chief, Field Marshal von Kluge, showed himself very apprehensive about the prospects of success even before the offensive was opened. At a conference with Hitler on 7 August, he drew attention to the problems 9th Army was having, which made it likely to be unable to participate in cutting off the salient in the north. Hitler's response was to order a replay of "Fridericus" by carrying out the operation (code-named "Whirlwind") unilaterally from the south. Kluge issued the operation order for it on 8 August,[3] but the tone of it was strangely ambiguous. It began with the statement "The Führer has decided . . . ," which seemed designed not merely to give it additional force but to indicate reservations on Kluge's part, and it went on to emphasize, somewhat oddly in an order about an offensive, the need for other units of Army Group Center to hold their present positions, implying some doubt that they could.

On the same day, Hitler and the Commander-in-Chief of Army Group North, Field Marshal von Küchler, discussed operation "Northern Light" (the capture and razing of Leningrad). Hitler expressed the desire to raze the city by massed artillery bombardment, on a scale not seen since the battle of Verdun in the First World War, and received support for the city's destruction from Jodl, who believed it would be demanded by the Finns. There seems as yet to have been no readiness to admit that the offensive was losing its momentum, but OKH tacitly admitted that the summer campaign was unlikely to prove decisive when, on 9 August, it issued a directive on the construction of winter positions on the eastern front.[4]

The conference at midday on 12 August dealt with a wide range of subjects and showed its inability to take decisions on several matters. Hitler vetoed Army Group A's plan to use the 1st and 4th Mountain Divisions, in the High Caucasus, east of Mount Elbruz,

2. Ibid.   3. OB H.Gr. Mitte 6200/42.
4. OKH/Gen. St. d. H./op. Abt. (Ia) Nr. 420587/42.

to move down the Ossetian and Georgian military highways toward Baku as an unnecessary dispersion of forces, but he did not actually order them pulled back from the High Caucasus. He ordered the right wing of Army Group A to have priority in fuel allocations, so that it could push through to the Black Sea coast and capture Novorossiysk, after which the Navy would be able to bring in fuel by sea. In Army Group B, he ordered heavy and anti-tank artillery and two divisions under a German corps command to be placed behind the Hungarian 2nd Army on the Don. Halder indicated that two infantry divisions were already being brought in to support the Hungarians,[5] but the question of artillery support was left open. Hitler's apprehensions about the risk of an Allied relieving attack in France were still working on his imagination, so he ordered that one corps of 6th Army should be sent to the west, *after* Stalingrad had been captured.

"Whirlwind" had begun on the previous day, and was going badly. Hitler began to interfere with control of it by noting that he "had the impression" that the 2nd Panzer Army was too strong on its right wing, by indicating that it should attack to the west-north-west, and by telling Halder to order Army Group Center to keep its forces close together on the main line of attack.[6] The 9th Army was still in difficulties; he considered authorizing a withdrawal, but took no decision.

He was also apprehensive that the Soviets might attack Army Group North, and wanted the putative attack repelled without drawing on forces earmarked for "Northern Light." He therefore proposed to move four battalions, which were training in East Prussia, to 18th Army, but when Halder refused,[7] he did not press the point. On this day also, Manstein received a new directive from Hitler,[8] dropping the plan to take his army across the Kerch Straits into the Caucasus, and earmarking most of it for Leningrad, but with one division to remain in the Crimea, one to be sent to Crete, and one moved to Army Group Center to assist Kluge. In the next few days, further difficulties began to be apparent with both Army Groups Center and North. Two projected divisional

5. *KTB/OKW*, Vol. II, Part I, p. 573. Curiously, this is not mentioned by Halder in his diary.

6. Ibid., p. 574.

7. Ibid.

8. Erich von Manstein, *Lost Victories* (London: Methuen, 1958), pp. 260–261.

moves on 13 August in the Army Group North area were canceled: by 14th Motorized Infantry Division, which was refused permission to shorten the line by a withdrawal in the Rzhev area, because Hitler was convinced that the Soviets had no more available reserves with which to attack it; and by the 12th Panzer Division, which was to have moved to Leningrad from the "bottleneck" (the German position south of Lake Ladoga, which cut off Soviet forces in Leningrad from the main front). On the next day, Army Group Center reported that "Whirlwind" was still making only slight progress, and that 9th Army was in serious difficulties at Rzhev. The 14th Division, whose move had been canceled only on the previous day, was now to be withdrawn along with another division, the 256th Infantry Division (ID), into a "hedgehog" position. The Army Group's lines of communication were under heavy attack by partisans, and Hitler ordered troops to be moved from Poland to fight them. At 8:15 that evening, Kluge reported that neither 9th Army nor 3rd Panzer Army could hold their positions. Hasty measures again had to be taken to correct the situation. The 72nd ID, which was on its way to join the 11th Army at Leningrad, was diverted to Army Group Center, and "Grossdeutschland," already in process of moving to France, was diverted to support 9th Army.

On the 15th, Warlimont and Engel were visiting Army Group A in the Caucasus. Engel reported that List and his Chief of Staff (von Gylenfeldt) were optimistic both that they could reach their targets and that the Soviets were incapable of counterattacking. However, he found the attitude of 1st Panzer Army very different. Both Kleist and his Chief of Staff, Faeckenstedt, said that their troops were very near the end of their tether, and that air and ground reconnaissance had shown that access to the Caucasus south of Krasnodar and Maykop was possible only by four mule tracks.[9]

By the following day, 16 August, "Whirlwind" had reached the stage where Kluge reported that it could not be pushed through, and asked for one more additional division, reporting heavy losses and little progress. He also requested permission to withdraw back to the original starting line, but Hitler refused on the grounds that much material would have to be abandoned, and because he felt the Russian attacks would peter out in another four to five days.

9. Hildegard von Kotze, ed., *Heeresadjutant bei Hitler, 1938–1943: Aufzeichnungen des Major Engel* (Stuttgart: Deutsche Verlags-Anstalt, 1974), pp. 123–124.

Army Group B had a more encouraging report. The 6th Army's attack to occupy the Don bend and seize a bridgehead on its eastern bank had begun successfully on the previous day, and was still making good progress. The 4th Panzer Army would also attack toward Stalingrad on the following day, if it could be supplied in time. However, Hitler, worried about the long exposed flank on the Don, indicated for the first time apprehension that Stalin might repeat his attack of 1920, along the Don toward Rostov, and therefore ordered the 22nd Panzer Division to be positioned behind the Italian 8th Army as soon as possible, since he feared that the Italians would not be able to withstand a Soviet attack.

Army Group A reported good progress and few battle casualties, but indicated that it was losing many effectives through sickness and exhaustion on the march. The move by the 298th ID of the 17th Army, ordered two days previously, which would have taken it to join the Western Group of 1st Panzer Army pushing along the coast toward the port of Tuapse, was canceled, over Halder's opposition. Hitler decided to send it back to Millerovo or Stalino "to be used elsewhere." He also ordered formations from 17th Army which were freed by the crossing of the Kuban River to be sent to the *Eastern* Group of 1st Panzer Army, because he expected strong opposition when they attempted to cross the Terek. It was also decided to send Jodl to clarify the situation. In respect of Army Group North, there was no specific development, but Hitler found that, despite his specific order of three days before, 12th Panzer Division had been moved from the bottleneck to the Leningrad Front, and he ordered it moved back at once.

On 17 and 18 August, the only decisions taken dealt with measures to fight partisans behind the Eastern Front, concerning which Directive No. 46 was issued on the 18th.[10] Apart from that, there was discussion at both midday conferences on the question of setting up a Romanian Army Group of two armies on the Don and Volga on either side of Stalingrad, nominally headed by the Romanian dictator, Marshal Antonescu, but actually under the command of the Chief of Staff, General Hauffe, the Chief of the German Military Mission in Romania. No decision was taken on this proposition, but Hauffe discussed the idea further with Halder on the

10. Hugh R. Trevor-Roper, ed., *Hitler's War Directives, 1939–1945* (London: Sidgwick and Jackson, 1964), pp. 132–135.

18th.[11] The 19th, however, brought a number of developments. In Army Group Center, Kluge reported that his forces were "overstrained," and that operation "Whirlwind" had little chance of success because his forces were inadequate, while no reinforcement was possible, as the railroads in his rear area would be fully occupied for the next two weeks bringing up the two divisions ("Grossdeutschland" and the 72nd ID) that had already been allocated to him, and 9th Army needed two additional divisions merely to prop up its existing front. Hitler refused to accept the implied invitation to cancel "Whirlwind," ordering Kluge to continue to use whatever forces he had for it, instructing 3rd Panzer Army and 9th Army to hold their front without reinforcements, and directing the 298th ID (which three days earlier had been the subject of an argument between him and Halder)[12] to be sent from the Army Group A area to reinforce Army Group Center. The signs of overstrain in the German position were beginning to multiply. The argument between Halder and Hitler on the 16th had arisen because Halder did not think Army Group A could spare this division for use elsewhere. On the 19th, Halder was proved right, as Army Group A reported a great increase in Soviet resistance, and doubts as to whether its mountain troops were strong enough to reach Sukhumi, their next objective, while the East Group of 1st Panzer Army was much troubled by Soviet air attacks.

To complicate matters further, this was the day of the Canadian-British landing at Dieppe. The news of this prompted Hitler to consider resuming the move of "Grossdeutschland" to the west, already decided on and canceled once, and it was only when the Commander-in-Chief West reported that he expected to finish the invading forces off by the evening that Hitler decided not to do so.

Later on 20 August, Kluge reported again that "Whirlwind" had no chance of success unless he could get two more divisions, a clear indication that he wanted to abandon the operation, as he had already said on the previous day that there was no railroad capacity available to bring up additional reinforcements for at least two more weeks. Hitler ordered the operation to proceed and told Kluge to come to headquarters for a conference on the 22nd. Army Group A reported that its movements were being much hindered

11. Halder, *Kriegstagebuch*, Vol. III, p. 507.

12. *KTB/OKW*, Vol. II, Part I, p. 596. Halder does not mention the argument in his diary.

by rain and snow, so Hitler, who was very annoyed at the slow progress being made in crossing the Caucasus, ordered a tight concentration of forces and dispatched an officer from the operational section of the High Command Staff to investigate the situation of the 49th Mountain Corps on Jodl's behalf. Finally, the Commander-in-Chief of Army Group North was ordered to come to FHQ on 23 August for a conference on "Northern Light," while Manstein, designated to command the operation but still at this point in the Crimea, was told to report to FHQ a day later. The midday situation conference was the scene of an angry exchange between Halder and Hitler, Halder pointing out that German strength was not sufficient for two such wearing offensives as those of Army Groups A and B to be carried out simultaneously. When he stated that the Russians were producing 1,200 tanks a month, Hitler forbade him to utter "such idiotic nonsense."[13]

The tension between Halder and Hitler became even more apparent on 22 August; Warlimont says, "it could be felt in the room."[14] It was a traumatic day for Hitler also; the outcome of his conference with Kluge was the abandonment of "Whirlwind," with a "small solution" being sought by some juggling of forces, and the purpose being changed from "seeking a decision" to "tying down Soviet forces" so that they could not be moved to other sectors of the Front. Army Group A again incurred Hitler's displeasure, and he emphasized the need for it to reach the coast and capture a port so that supply by sea could begin. Army Group B was short of fuel and ammunition, but was being resupplied and was, in fact, to attack at 4:30 A.M. on the next day. However, Hitler became preoccupied with the possibility of a Soviet attack from Astrakhan against his eastern flank, and ordered the 16th Motorized Division to be deployed to block such a move. This meant a further weakening of Army Group A, and was opposed by Halder,[15] who wanted to keep the Division with 1st Panzer Army. Hitler, however, insisted. His displeasure was further excited when he discovered that the 22nd Panzer Division, which he had ordered to move into position behind the Italian 8th Army, was, except for its grenadier brigade, still fighting in the Don bend northwest of Sirotinskaya. He or-

13. Joachim C. Fest, *Hitler* (New York: Harcourt Brace Jovanovich, 1974), p. 660.

14. *KTB/OKW*, Vol. II, Part I, p. 624. Warlimont attributes the tension in part to the heat of the Ukrainian summer.

15. Halder, *Kriegstagebuch*, Vol. III, p. 509.

dered it yet again to get into position behind the Italians, and additionally ordered German units to be deployed with the Hungarian 2nd Army when the situation permitted it. It would seem that the Soviet resistance was beginning to make an impression on him; in after-dinner conversation that evening, he said that Stalin was a beast, but "a beast on a grand scale."[16]

August 23 was the day on which 4th Panzer Army blasted through to the northern outskirts of Stalingrad and reached the bank of the Volga. As far as FHQ is concerned, however, it was marked by more expressions of apprehension by Hitler. He was worried about an enemy buildup opposite the part of the Front that was held, very thinly, by 9th Army of Army Group Center, and decided to deploy "Grossdeutschland" there, despite his strict injunction of a few days earlier that this division was to be used only for a planned counterattack and not to be tied up in defensive operations. He was further worried that because of the heavy defensive battles they had been fighting, Army Groups Center and North would not have enough troops to spare to build winter positions. After the conference with the Commander-in-Chief of Army Group North, Küchler, the start of "Northern Light" was provisionally scheduled for 14 September, but the meeting was marked by several disagreements and uncertainties. The Air Force was ordered to begin preparatory air attacks on Leningrad on 4 or 6 September, despite the fact that its Chief of Staff, Jeschonnek, who was present, did not think it would be in a position to do so before the 10th or 11th. There was a dispute over the way the battle should be conducted. Küchler wanted to cross the river Narva and join up with the Finns before taking the city, while Halder felt that the city ought to be captured first. Hitler sided with Küchler, emphasizing the need to avoid house-to-house fighting.

August 24 saw heavy Soviet attacks against Army Group Center and a severe clash over evaluation of the situation at Rzhev, a point in Army Group Center's Front relatively close to Moscow, where the Soviets had been making persistent attempts to push the Germans back. Hitler said it reminded him of the winter of 1941; that, as then, every man would have to hold where he stood, and that all operational withdrawals would be refused. The Commander of

16. Adolf Hitler, *Hitler's Table Talk, 1941–1944*, trans. Norman Cameron and R. H. Stevens (London: Weidenfeld and Nicolson, 1973), p. 657.

9th Army, Model, reported that replacements, who had only eight weeks' training, were useless, to which Hitler replied that the Russians were getting even less training. Halder pointed out the possibility that Army Group Center's troops were "burnt out,"[17] and this did nothing to ease the atmosphere between the two men.

The situation conference on 25 August saw no major decisions, except a reversal of the decision, taken two days earlier, to use "Grossdeutschland" in defense. Hitler now ordered it to be used for a counterattack on the east front of 9th Army, and not to be employed in defensive engagements.

On 26 August, there were more signs of spreading insubordination among the generals. Hitler received a report that 2nd Panzer Army of Army Group Center had pulled back its front line near Sukhinichi on its own initiative. In Army Group B, Hitler yet again ordered 22nd Panzer Division "once and for all" to take up its position behind the Italian 8th Army on the Don, where the Russians had made a "deep breach" on its right wing. Army Group A was ordered not to enter the High Caucasus, which would be snowed up by mid-September. And a new cause of disquiet emerged, this time in the sector of Army Group North.

Here maintenance of the siege of Leningrad depended on keeping open the "bottleneck" between the Leningrad Front and the main Soviet forces which had been opened in 1941 by a German drive to the south shore of Lake Ladoga. At its narrowest point, on the shore line of the lake itself, the gap between the main Soviet forces and their besieged brethren was only some seven miles; and on 26 August, the signs that the Russians were about to attack the bottleneck began to multiply. The attack in fact began on the morning of the 27th, and Hitler discovered that 12th Panzer Division, which he had repeatedly ordered moved into the "bottleneck," was still behind the Leningrad Front. The center of the Front remained quiet for the time being, but in the south, Hitler's mounting anxiety about the Italians prompted him to order that two more German divisions be moved onto their sector urgently, using air transport and Italian vehicles, and that the Italian Alpini Corps, which was on its way to the front, be brought up as quickly as possible. Simultaneously, he ordered 6th Army's blocking line between the Volga and the Don to be pushed forward to the northeast, and 4th

17. Halder, *Kriegstagebuch*, Vol. III, p. 510.

Panzer Army to attack to the north to make contact with 6th Army, attacking additionally northeastward into the defenses of Stalingrad only as a secondary mission.

The situation conference of 28 August saw a rare intervention by Göring, who told Hitler that Air Force reconnaissance to the north of the city had had difficulty in finding any Soviet units, despite the bareness of the terrain, so that there could be no question of there being strong Soviet forces in the Stalingrad area. Halder, noting that two Soviet divisions and six tank brigades had been withdrawn from Voronezh to other sectors, asked permission to remove one division from the bridgehead, and Hitler agreed.[18]

After a relatively quiescent period, Kluge surfaced again, asking for permission to use "Grossdeutschland" against the Soviet bridgehead at Rzhev, from which the Rzhev-Vyazma railroad was under threat. Hitler, who only a few days earlier had contemplated employing this elite division for a counterattack at Sychavka, refused permission and said that "Grossdeutschland" was to be used only in very critical situations.

The evening conference was dominated by news from Army Group North that the Soviets had broken into the "bottleneck" south of Lake Ladoga, and the situation there was tense. An indication of the difficulties now facing the German armed forces was that it was necessary for Hitler to order the 3rd Mountain Division, which was on its way by sea from Norway to Finland, to be landed at Tallinn and sent to join 18th Army in the "bottleneck."

By the following day, 29 August, it had already become necessary to divert into the "bottleneck" the 170th ID, which had been sent with 11th Army from the Crimea to take part in "Northern Light," to mount a counterattack in the "bottleneck," and to make ready two Panzer groups to meet a Soviet attack that was expected to be made by the adjacent Volkhov Front. Army Group A again attracted Hitler's displeasure, when he found its advance had come to a halt. The only reinforcement still at hand was the Romanian 3rd Mountain Division in the Crimea, and he ordered it to be sent by land to join the Romanian 3rd Army, rather than across the Kerch Straits. The division had in fact been ready to move since

18. *KTB/OKW*, Vol. II, Part I, p. 650. Göring claimed that the information resulted from "personal reconnaissance" by Colonel-General von Richthofen, Commander-in-Chief of Air Fleet IV.

11 August, but rough seas and the Air Force's inability to provide cover for the crossing had made sea transport impracticable. The discussion about Army Group A was, according to Halder, "very angry."[19]

But on 30 August, Hitler countermanded his order to move the Romanian 3rd Mountain Division by land, and two officers, one Army and one Navy, were sent from OKH to the Crimea to arrange for the division to cross the Straits, regardless of the weather or the availability of air support, if necessary by night. Once again, Hitler expressed acute dissatisfaction with the development of the situation on Army Group A's front, and List was summoned to a conference at FHQ the following day, to discuss a series of detailed complaints. On the sector of Army Group B, 22nd Panzer Division was discovered to be *still* tied up at Serafimovich, despite thrice-repeated orders for it to be sent to the Italian sector (a clear sign of the strain the campaign was imposing on German resources). Army Group Center reported new attacks, and that the situation at Rzhev was again very tense. Kluge asked once more for permission to use "Grossdeutschland," and once more Hitler refused; he did, however, agree to its making a night march to Rzhev. In the afternoon, Kluge reported that Soviet forces had made a deep breach in his front at Zubtsov, and Hitler finally permitted the use of "Grossdeutschland." The situation of Army Group North deteriorated further, as the Russians opened a gap in the east front of the "bottleneck." Use of the first four of the new Tiger tanks proved pointless;[20] two of them were already unserviceable, the terrain was too marshy for off-road movement, their weight made it impossible to use them on the wood-surfaced tracks, and they were too heavy for the bridges. Halder reported renewed diatribes by Hitler against the military leadership, in which he accused it of spiritual haughtiness, unteachability, and incapacity to distinguish the important from the inconsequential.[21]

In Africa, 30 August saw initiation by Rommel of the battle of Alam Halfa, a final attempt to break through to Alexandria, Cairo, and the Suez Canal. Reports from Africa were frequently late in arriving at FHQ, and often sketchy. On this day, for example, the

19. Halder, *Kriegstagebuch*, Vol. III, p. 513.
20. Heinz Guderian, *Panzer Leader* (London: Futura, 1974), p. 280.
21. Halder, *Kriegstagebuch*, Vol. III, p. 513.

situation report from Panzerarmee Afrika refers to no events later than the night of 27–28 August, and there is no mention at all of the African theatre in Greiner's notes of the FHQ conferences. Only on 1 September was it noted that the attack had begun, and it was wrongly ascribed to 31 August. From this, and from the paucity of references to Africa, it can be inferred that in this period Hitler's interest in the African theatre was low.

On 31 August, there were signs of "escapism" in the decision-making process, in the sense that Hitler began to make dispositions that could only be effected after the forces had completed the current tasks which they were finding impossible to fulfill. After Army Group A had cleared the Russians from the Black Sea coast, the two German divisions in the Crimea were to be replaced by "fortress divisions" (that is, static troops), while Army Group B was to make up a mobile formation from its divisions at Stalingrad, when the situation permitted, to provide flank protection in the Don bend. However, the highlight of the day was a conference in the afternoon with the Commander-in-Chief and Chief of Staff of Army Group A, List and Gylenfeldt. According to Warlimont,[22] the conference was cordial, despite Hitler's criticisms of the previous days, and he feels that List went away thinking he had convinced Hitler that his actions were correct. Halder's notes of the discussion do not contradict Warlimont,[23] but Engel says that the atmosphere was very unfriendly, with Hitler often interrupting List and accusing the Army Group of failure to concentrate its forces.[24] A final escapist note of the day was Hitler's order that when Stalingrad had been captured, the female population was to be deported and the male population exterminated.

SEPTEMBER 1942

September was to prove a crucial month in the relations between Hitler and the senior military members of his entourage. It was a month in which Hitler initially dismissed an Army Group Commander and took on his duties himself, and then proceeded to replace the Chief of General Staff, Halder, dismiss (though very soon

---

22. *KTB/OKW*, Vol. II, Part I, pp. 662–663. Comment by Warlimont.
23. Halder, *Kriegstagebuch*, Vol. III, p. 513.
24. Kotze, ed., *Heeresadjutant bei Hitler*, p. 125.

reinstate) the Deputy Head of Wfst, Warlimont, and threaten to replace Keitel and Jodl. Though this last threat was not carried out, relations with the two continued strained for some months, and Jodl, especially, never fully regained Hitler's confidence.

In the military field, the operation at Stalingrad slowed down to advances of a few hundred yards a day, and sometimes to nothing, against a tenacious Soviet defense, while progress in the Caucasus fell far short of objectives. The attempt at a breakthrough in Africa at Alam Halfa, which began on 30 August, had to be abandoned on 2 September, without intervention or even any sign of interest in the outcome on Hitler's part.

Hitler began the month in a fairly optimistic mood. On the 1st, the C-in-C of Army Group Center, Kluge, arrived for a discussion, during which Hitler assessed the Soviet position as one in which about 100 million of a population of between 160 and 175 million lived in areas which Germany had already overrun, and hence had been lost to the Soviet regime. Against German military losses of 1.4 million, he assessed Soviet military losses in killed, wounded, and captured at 8–10 million. No relief for the Russians was likely: there would be no second front in the west, and nothing could happen in Norway. Against this optimistic picture of a destroyed and collapsing Russia, it was perhaps incongruous that Kluge should have to request permission to withdraw part of his front on the sector of 9th Army. Hitler declined to sanction this move, but ordered instead a quick preparation of rearward positions, suggesting that he had doubts about 9th Army's ability to hold its present line. Twelve light battalions would be sent to Army Group Center, to fight partisans—again somewhat at variance with the claim that the 100 million Soviet citizens in German-occupied territory had been removed from Soviet control. The rest of the discussion with Kluge was taken up by detailed points concerning the employment of the new Porsche tanks and operations against Kirov.

On the night of 1–2 September, 11th Army began crossing the Kerch Straits, approximately a month late (Directive No. 43 of 11 July had ordered it to cross not later than the beginning of August).[25] The 16th Motorized Infantry Division was ordered to Elista, to operate in the steppes south of the point where the Stalingrad front petered out. Hitler ordered the entire male population of

25. Trevor-Roper, ed., *Hitler's War Directives*, p. 124.

Stalingrad to be removed after its capture (though this time he did not specify extermination), and use in the artillery preparations for "Northern Light" of "drum fire" (concentration of artillery effort on a small space, with a short but very intensive bombardment immediately preceding the infantry attack), as on 21 March 1918 in the prelude to the last great German offensive of the First World War. He was notified that in North Africa the German-Italian Panzer Army had had to suspend its offensive for lack of fuel, and took this setback unemotionally or without much sign of interest.

September 3 saw a proposal by Army Group A to remove 49th Mountain Corps from the Central Caucasus and deploy it toward the Black Sea port of Tuapse, which Hitler refused. He postponed the release of Directive 47 for operation "Northern Light," on the grounds that Manstein, who had been designated to command it, was due to visit FHQ on 5 September, and his views should first be sought. In the evening, C-in-C West reported his belief that the British would attempt a landing on the Normandy peninsula, so Hitler ordered the 7th Parachute Division, already in Normandy, to be deployed further north. He had already decided some days before (the date is uncertain), on the proposal of Keitel, to send seven replacement divisions from Germany to the West.

September 4 saw a reiterated order to the 1st Mountain Division to leave only a weak guard on the passes and to use its main forces to push on to Sukhumi. An attempt by Kluge to alter the deployment of two of the Panzer divisions was considered, but no decision was taken. The situation at Army Group North caused anxiety because a Soviet force had broken through on the east front of the "bottleneck," and four divisions earmarked for "Northern Light" had to be employed to stop them. Hitler was very annoyed at this redeployment of troops from his intended offensive. Nevertheless, he considered committing further forces, but was assured by Jodl that those already available were sufficient, if adequately led. To provide this leadership, Hitler decided that Manstein should cancel his visit to FHQ and take over the sector. He also ordered Directive 47 to be revised so that it could be transmitted to AG North without subsequent additions.[26] In the west, 7th Parachute Divi-

26. This was the Directive for the capture of Leningrad ("Northern Light"); but as the operation was canceled, it was not issued. Its number was given to a Directive of 28 December 1942 regarding measures for the defense of Southeast Europe against the expected Allied invasion.

sion, ordered to move on the previous day, had already rede-
ployed, and as it had no tanks, Hitler ordered SS "Reich" to move
into the position it had vacated. He also ordered the forces in Africa to be strengthened by the dispatch of modern anti-aircraft
guns, some of the heaviest tanks, an "unlimited" number of mines,
and the 22nd Airborne Division, then in process of reorganization.
Engel noted a high level of tension between Hitler and Halder,
whom the Führer accused of having been in World War I a chair-
borne officer with no knowledge of troops.[27] Engel told Heusinger
that in his opinion the breach between the two men could not be
healed and that Halder should report sick. However, Hitler tried
to mend matters in the evening by being especially friendly to
Halder. The next few days, amid a scatter of minor decisions, saw
Hitler's anxiety about the Caucasus growing, and the tension between him and List increasing. On the 6th, Halder noted for the
first time heavy Soviet counterattacks at Stalingrad.[28] Hitler's reaction that evening was to say that the concentration of effort in defense of the city was "a grave mistake on the part of the Russians,"
a curious observation in the light of his own subsequent actions.[29]

On 7 September, Army Group Center reported that it could
now "clean up" the situation on 3rd Panzer Army's front and south
of Rzhev. Hitler approved the proposed action by 3rd Panzer Army,
but vetoed a counterattack south of Rzhev on the grounds that further enemy attacks were to be expected there and the only High
Command reserve, "Grossdeutschland," could not be spared.

Hitler ordered Jodl to go to Army Group A to discuss with List
further operations in the Caucasus. Jodl returned on the following
day, fully supporting List, and the consequence was a quarrel of
major proportions, Hitler maintaining that List had failed because
he had disobeyed his orders, while Jodl argued that, on the contrary, List had done exactly what Hitler had told him to. Hitler
thereupon became extremely angry, demanded copies of all orders
issued to Army Group A since it had crossed the Don, and ordered
several Reichstag stenographers to FHQ to make verbatim notes of
all future conferences.[30] He ceased to take his meals in the mess
with Jodl and Keitel, ordered Jodl to keep out of his sight until fur-

27. Kotze, ed., *Heeresadjutant bei Hitler*, pp. 125–126.
28. Halder, *Kriegstagebuch*, Vol. III, p. 518.
29. Hitler, *Table Talk*, p. 694.
30. *KTB/OKW*, Vol. II, Part I, p. 697. Comment by Warlimont.

ther notice, and for a long time refused to leave his quarters during daylight, even holding the daily conferences there.[31] Engel formed the opinion that Hitler, having failed in every one of the objectives of the summer offensive, no longer saw an end in Russia, and was expressing his anxiety about the approaching winter in his behavior.[32]

Although the events of 8 September were dominated by the quarrel with Jodl, a number of other decisions were taken. An order was issued concerning measures for resting the troops of the Eastern Army during the coming winter.[33] The west was to be "milked" of eight mobile formations for deployment in the Middle East in early 1943, and of about twelve of its best equipped divisions for the Eastern Front, their place being taken by depleted Eastern divisions brought up to strength with 18-year-olds from the "1924 class" of conscripts. Preoccupation with the safety of Crete, now considered threatened by the forced abandonment of the offensive in Africa, led to an order for its garrison to be restored to its former level of two fortress brigades, while concern with the danger of attack in the west led to an order for English-born inhabitants of the Channel Islands to be evacuated to the continent as soon as possible.[34] An order about the basic principles of defensive fighting was issued,[35] indicating concern about the coming winter and the changing balance of forces.

At the midday conference on the 9th, Halder reported that List, rather than attacking out of his bridgehead across the Terek river, intended to allow the Russians to weaken themselves in an attack and then to mount a counteroffensive.[36] Hitler considered this totally wrong, and in the afternoon sent Keitel to tell Halder that he was dismissing List, taking over the command of Army Group A himself, and was also thinking of replacing Halder with Zeitzler

31. Ibid.

32. Kotze, ed., *Heeresadjutant bei Hitler*, p. 126.

33. OKH/Gen. St. d. H./op. Abt. (I), Nr. 11154/42.

34. The order was published in the Channel Islands on 15 September 1942, but the German military authorities there showed considerable ingenuity in subverting its application, and only a few hundred were deported. See Leslie P. Sinel, *The German Occupation of Jersey* (London: Corgi, 1969), pp. 87–92. This account tends to substantiate Warlimont's claim (*KTB/OKW*, Vol. II, Part I, p. 698) that he and the Commander-in-Chief West had a tacit understanding to subvert the order.

35. *KTB/OKW*, Vol. II, Part I, pp. 704–705; and Warlimont's comments therein, on pp. 705–707.

36. Halder, *Kriegstagebuch*, Vol. III, p. 519.

(Chief of Staff to Commander-in-Chief West), Keitel with Kesselring (the Commander-in-Chief South, an Air Force General), and Jodl with Paulus (Commander-in-Chief of 6th Army). The dismissal of List took effect the same day, and that of Halder a fortnight later. The other changes were never made, but Jodl thereafter lacked Hitler's full confidence; for several months, Hitler would not even shake hands with him.

The unpleasantness in the Supreme Command continued for several days, during which Hitler took no important decisions. The right wing of 4th Panzer Army reached the Volga on 10 September, thereby achieving one of the initial objectives set out in Directive No. 41.[37] On the 11th, Raeder was present at a discussion of a convoy action in the north, during which Hitler expressed the wish for the largest possible number of major surface warships to be kept in Norway during the winter of 1942–43, but reminded Raeder that these ships were not to be committed to action without his prior approval.[38] At 11:30 that evening, Hitler conferred with Weichs, and categorically forbade any voluntary withdrawal from Voronezh. The discussions about the relief of the depleted divisions of the Eastern Army which had taken place on the 8th found detailed expression in an order issued on the 13th.[39] On that day also, a conference was held with the Commander-in-Chief of 9th Army (Model) on the situation in his sector.

An unusual situation was created by the sinking of the British liner *Laconia* on 12 September off the African coast, by U156, one of a group of five German submarines that were heading for the waters off Cape Town. The ship contained about 800 British passengers and crew, 1,800 Italian prisoners-of-war, and their 103 Polish guards. At considerable risk to his vessel, the U-boat commander mounted a rescue operation that lasted five days. Hitler's approval was sought on the 13th, and obtained. However, U156 was subsequently attacked by an American aircraft from Ascension Island, and damaged, and another submarine that had been summoned, U506, was also attacked from the air, unsuccessfully, while carrying 132 survivors. The outcome was the issuing of an order

37. Trevor-Roper, ed., *Hitler's War Directives*, p. 119 (paragraph C7 of Directive No. 41).

38. Edward P. von der Porten, *The German Navy in World War Two* (London: Pan Books, 1972), pp. 225–226.

39. OKW/Wfst, Nr. 551591/42.

that categorically forbade future attempts at rescue except for the purpose of capturing important prisoners.[40]

The dispute with the generals that arose from his distrust of them as a class intensified Hitler's already apparent tendency to interfere in the detailed conduct of operations. On 14 September, for example, he issued orders affecting movements of eight individual divisions, two each in Army Groups A and B, three in Army Group Center, and one in the West. Particularly capricious was that, on receiving an Air Force reconnaissance report from Richthofen, he canceled a proposed move of two divisions to the Stalingrad city area despite the fact that Richthofen's previous reporting of a weakening of enemy resistance at Stalingrad on 28 August had proved unreliable. He also ordered the strengthening of Air Fleet II in the Mediterranean.

On the 15th, the Eastern Front was essentially unchanged; a small offensive in the "bottleneck," planned to begin with the commitment of one division, was postponed by Army Group North to the next day. Hitler therefore devoted further attention to the Mediterranean on the 15th, and, in particular, ordered priorities for the allocation of shipping space, ranking Crete as the highest priority, Africa second, and the Black Sea third. A curious order, given that there were at the time no operational German Army units in Italy, was that German troops in that country should be reduced by two-thirds. The Air Force, which wished to install an anti-aircraft school in Palermo, was overruled and told to put it in Bordeaux instead. Two Führer orders were issued, one by OKH concerning dangers to the Don front,[41] and one by OKW on threats in the Mediterranean.[42]

The 16th saw a reversion of attention to the Russian front, with orders that the Battle of Stalingrad be controlled exclusively by 6th Army, which was simultaneously deprived of two of its divisions (22nd Panzer and 113th Infantry), on their being ordered to take up positions behind the Italian 8th Army on the Don. The attack on the "bottleneck" by one division was judged successful, but otherwise little happened on the Eastern Front that day.

40. Karl Dönitz, *Memoirs: Ten Years and Twenty Days* (London: Weidenfeld and Nicolson, 1959), pp. 256–263.

41. Halder, *Kriegstagebuch*, Vol. III, p. 523.

42. Ibid., p. 524.

The Eastern Front remained relatively quiet on the 17th; Hitler summoned Halder's deputy, General Blumentritt, and appointed him Chief of Staff to Commander-in-Chief West in place of Zeitzler, who was in turn to replace Halder as Chief of General Staff of OKH.

The stalemate on the Eastern Front continued on the 18th, where planned attacks by Army Groups Center and North had to be put off because of bad weather. In his capacity as C-in-C of Army Group A, Hitler ordered an attack on the right wing to begin on 20 September, and the SS "Wiking" division to be attached to the First Panzer Army. He ordered the tank strength of the "Göring" brigade and other mobile formations in the West to be increased. His distrust of his generals came to the fore again, in that though he officially named Zeitzler as Halder's successor, he told his adjutant: "At the moment I have no confidence in any of my generals; I'd put a major up to general and make him CGS if I knew of one."[43]

The bad weather continued for some days. On 20 September, Army Group A's scheduled attack was put off until the 22nd. In Army Group B, Hitler ordered two divisions to be pulled out of the line so that they could begin clearing the northern part of the city on the 22nd, after an air bombardment, which was to begin on the 21st. Some changes in the boundary between Army Group Center and Army Group B placed it further south. Orders affecting seven divisions were issued on this day, including one that forbade the 27th Panzer Division to be used for house-to-house fighting at Voronezh, and a repeated order for the release of "Grossdeutschland." The preoccupation with Crete was still apparent; Hitler ordered personnel and necessary equipment to be moved to the island by air. On being warned by Speer that the tank factories in Friedrichshafen and the ball-bearing factories in Schweinfurt were critical to the war effort, Hitler ordered increased anti-aircraft protection to be provided for these cities. Halder noted on this day that a "gradual burning out of the assault troops" in Stalingrad had become perceptible.[44]

The erosion of 6th Army's strength by decisions taken in previous days was taken in hand on 21 September. Weichs reported that the attack on the north of Stalingrad could not be pursued for the

43. Kotze, ed., *Heeresadjutant bei Hitler*, p. 127.
44. Halder, *Kriegstagebuch*, Vol. III, p. 524.

moment because of the much reduced infantry strength of the army. Hitler therefore countermanded his order of 14 September, directed that the 100th Light Division be moved to the city, and ordered investigations to be made to see whether the 11th Panzer Division could be returned to the control of Army Group B. For the further conduct of the battle, he ordered, first, clearance of the north part of the city; second, clearance of the west bank of the Volga south of the city; and third, an attack to the north inclining toward the Volga bank. Army Group A was set a number of objectives for an attack that was to begin by 23 September, and be followed by an attack on Tuapse by the center of the force on 27 September. Some further indication of the growing shortage of resources could be seen in Hitler's agreement to a proposal by Jodl to employ "special formation Felmy" on the east wing of the Army Group. This formation had been assembled and trained in Greece during the previous year; it was intended to specialize in desert warfare and to be used in the Middle East. The strain on resources was also apparent in the Air Force, which could muster only 112 aircraft to support Army Group A. That a shortage of resources was becoming general was shown by Manstein's report that he lacked one division for "Northern Light," would have to rearrange his front to obtain one, and therefore could not start the operation before 15 October. A proposal by Halder to send two Eastern Front divisions to the west, and replace them by one western division, was accepted.

Despite the growing signs of inadequacy of resources, and the pending appointment of a new Chief of General Staff to OKH, Hitler made preparations to go away for several days. The attack in the "bottleneck" which had begun on 21 September made only slow progress and came to a halt within a few days. Elsewhere on the Eastern Front, the situation was in general unchanged, Army Group Center reporting no major activity, Army Group A reporting only minor progress, and Army Group B reporting slight progress against strong attacks on the front between the Volga and the Don, together with the capture of a few big buildings on the Volga bank. On the 23rd, Hitler met the Romanian Deputy Prime Minister, Mihai Antonescu, and the Croatian State Leader, Pavelic. Halder stepped down after the daily conference on the 24th, with Hitler stating in farewell that Halder's nerves were worn out and his own were no longer fresh. Hitler also referred to the need to educate the General Staff in "fanatical belief," and reiterated his determination to apply his will completely in the Army.[45]

In general, the Navy was subject to far less detailed control by Hitler, presumably because he could claim no naval experience. He had once told Raeder: "On land I am a hero, but at sea I'm a coward."[46] And General Blumentritt aptly remarked after the war that "only the admirals had a happy time," because "Hitler knew nothing about the sea, whereas he felt he knew all about land warfare."[47] In Berlin on 28 September, the submarine situation was completely reviewed at a meeting with Raeder, Dönitz, and Admiral Fuchs, the Chief of Naval Construction. Although the Battle of the Atlantic was going well for the U-boats, problems were already beginning to arise through air attacks on submarines, believed at the time to result from the fitting of superior search radars in Allied aircraft.[48] (Not until 1975 was it disclosed that the principal reason was British success in locating submarines through a combination of direction finding and ability to read some of the German naval cyphers.[49]) Dönitz therefore emphasized the need for air support, and for approval of construction of "true" submarines with a high underwater speed and the ability to remain submerged for long periods. Hitler approved the construction of some experimental prototype submarines. The month ended with the Führer's delivery of the annual "Winter Relief" speech in the Sports Palace, and with yet another harangue to his adjutant about how the General Staff had lost its vision since 1914, had become theoretical, and taken the pen, not the sword, as its weapon.[50]

THE BREAK WITH THE MILITARY ADVISERS

Undoubtedly, the dominant features of the August–September period were, externally, the gradual petering-out of the offensives in Russia and Africa, and, internally, the breach between Hitler and his closest military advisers, not merely the skeptical Halder but

45. Ibid., p. 528.

46. Anthony Martienssen, *Hitler and His Admirals* (London: Secker and Warburg, 1948), p. 2.

47. Basil H. Liddell Hart, *The Other Side of the Hill* (London: Panther, 1956), p. 294.

48. Porten, *The German Navy*, p. 211.

49. Patrick Beesly, *Very Special Intelligence*, revised edition (London: Sphere Books, 1978), pp. 127–144 and 206–220.

50. Kotze, ed., *Heeresadjutant bei Hitler*, p. 128.

the hitherto compliant Keitel and Jodl. This requires a somewhat more detailed treatment than can be given in a strictly chronological account.

The misgivings of German generals about Hitler's strategic ideas are amply documented. Since there was only very limited scope for argument with Hitler, there were only three courses open to officers. One was to conspire against him; but this, apart from being treason by general definition, also required forswearing the specific oath of loyalty to his person which had been sworn in August 1934, and very few officers could bring themselves to do this.

The second option was to resign from command, thereby indicating depth of conviction and obtaining relief from personal responsibility. This course was taken after the failure before Moscow by the Commander-in-Chief of the Army, Field Marshal von Brauchitsch, and two of the three Army Group Commanders, Field Marshal von Leeb (North) and von Rundstedt (South); though of the three, only Rundstedt's resignation was genuinely voluntary and unsought.

The third recourse was to disobey orders and take a chance on dismissal. Despite the authoritarian nature of the regime, it was quite possible to do this on occasion without being found out at all, or without being found out until the object sought by disobedience had been achieved. Rommel, for example, disobeyed orders on a number of occasions, both in advancing further than authorized and in defying the "no withdrawal" order.[51]

But for Eastern Front generals, operating under constant attention from the Führer, the situation was more difficult than for Rommel, who commanded in the remote "sideshow" theatre of war in Africa, at least nominally under the control of the Italian Comando Supremo, and with ample opportunities for exploiting his dual subordination to it and to the German Commander-in-Chief South. At the same time, the disparity between the strategic aims on the Eastern Front and the resources available for achieving them was large and growing. This encouraged harassed field commanders to disobedience, which in turn increased Hitler's distrust of his generals, led to the issuing of orders that further inhibited field commanders' freedom of action, and in turn made their attempts to use their local initiative and discretion acts of disobedience in themselves. When they disobeyed, as they inevitably did

51. Christopher Chant et al., *Hitler's Generals and Their Battles* (London: Salamander Books, 1976), pp. 124 and 127–131.

from time to time, the outcome was more and more interference by Hitler in matters of detail, and an increase in tension between him and those officers at OKW and OKH who had to translate his decisions into detailed operational orders and transmit and justify them to the commanders in the field. These officers, above all Halder, were, on the one hand, victims of Hitler's constant diatribes against the Army in general, and the General Staff in particular, and, on the other, objects of suspicion to the field commanders, many of whom concluded that the reason why they kept on receiving unrealistic orders was the failure of the FHQ officers to explain the difficulties of their situation to Hitler.

The 1942 crisis in Hitler's relations with the military did not arise suddenly. If Hitler's Army Adjutant, Major Engel, is to be believed (and there are problems in doing so, mainly because some of his dates are manifestly wrong, suggesting that the diary was not written up at the time of the events described), the senior officers of Army Group B (Weichs and Paulus) were saying even before the end of July that their forces were too weak for the job assigned to them, and both they and Weichs's Chief of Staff, Colonel August Winter, were insistent that he should report their views back to Hitler, as they did not believe Halder was doing so.[52] Engel also states that when he visited Army Group A and the headquarters of 1st Panzer Army in mid-August, he found the Army Group Commander (List) optimistic, but received a very different account from Kleist and his Chief of Staff, Major-General Faeckenstedt, who claimed that their troops were near the end of their tether.[53]

The OKW War Diary shows that List reported on 2 September that enemy superiority in the area north of Tuapse made a quick breakthrough unlikely. After further exchanges on 5 and 6 September, Hitler ordered Jodl on 7 September to fly to List's headquarters. Jodl returned to FHQ on the same day, and reported to Hitler that evening, endorsing List's position and pointing out that List had obeyed his orders to the letter.[54] At this point, Hitler demanded the production of all orders issued to List since the crossing of the Don, and the interview degenerated into a shouting match, concerning which Engel comments that Jodl yielded nothing to Hitler in volume.[55]

The immediate consequences of the dispute were the dismissal

52. Kotze, ed., *Heeresadjutant bei Hitler*, p. 123.
53. Ibid., pp. 123–124.   54. Ibid., p. 124.   55. Ibid., p. 126.

of List as of 9 September 1942, Hitler taking on the command of Army Group A himself from that date; a decision, communicated to Halder by Keitel on the same day, that Halder was also to be dismissed as soon as a successor was available; the importation into the FHQ of a group of Reichstag stenographers; and a withdrawal by Hitler from all but minimal contact with the members of his entourage. At the daily conferences, he behaved with total hostility toward the OKW representatives, and spoke to them as little as possible. The number of participants at the conferences was reduced, and, from 25 September, when Halder's successor General Zeitzler took over, OKW was almost totally excluded from all aspects of the war in the East, Hitler conducting discussions and reaching decisions on it in private sessions with Zeitzler.[56]

No single event accounts for these dramatic happenings in Hitler's headquarters, but some clues may be found in the various diaries. On 11 August, Army Group Center launched Operation "Whirlwind" against the Soviet salient at Sukhinichi. The operation was a failure from the start, and after the C-in-C of the Army Group, Field Marshal von Kluge, had visited FHQ for a conference on 22 August, it was abandoned. Further north, an operation ("Northern Light") to capture and raze Leningrad, had been planned for mid-September. Preparations for it were disrupted by a Soviet offensive launched on 27–28 August, and it soon became clear that "Northern Light" would have to be postponed, if not canceled altogether. Meanwhile, on the southern sector of the Front, the rapid progress that had been made in the early stages of the summer offensive was proving quite impossible to sustain, as Soviet resistance stiffened. On 6 September, Halder noted for the first time that German forces at Stalingrad had had to beat off heavy Soviet attacks.[57]

Overhanging everything was the realization that winter was not far off. In the High Caucasus, Army Group A recorded that its operations were being hindered by rain and snow as early as 21 August; and on the 23rd, Hitler feared they would become so involved in defensive battles that they would not have enough forces to

56. "[Zeitzler] went further and further in excluding OKW from anything to do with the Eastern Front and, for instance, expressly forbade the officers of the Army Operations Section to give OKW any information whatsoever." Walter Warlimont, *Inside Hitler's Headquarters, 1939–45*, trans. R. H. Barry (London: Weidenfeld and Nicolson, 1964), p. 262.

57. Halder, *Kriegstagebuch*, Vol. III, p. 518.

spare to build positions for the winter. On the 24th, as the Red Army mounted heavy attacks against Army Group Center, Hitler remarked that the situation reminded him of the previous winter, and that every man must hold where he stood, as had been the case then.[58] Two days later, he ordered Army Group A to avoid the High Caucasus, as the roads would be blocked by snow by mid-September. Thus, with the Russians showing no sign of exhaustion, Hitler's references to winter suggest that by the end of August he was having to adjust to the realization that his objectives would not be achieved before the end of good campaigning weather, and, as was his fashion, was looking around for a scapegoat. The most obvious candidates for this role were, of course, the army officers closest to him and the senior field commanders. By 30 August, Halder records serious allegations being made against the military leadership at the highest levels of the Army. On 4 September, Engel recorded that Hitler was extremely rude to Halder, questioning whether Halder, who had "only sat on the same swivel chair," and had not even been wounded in the First World War, could tell him anything about troops. On 8 September, the day after the quarrel with Jodl, Engel recorded the impression that "the Führer can no longer see an end in Russia, since all the objectives of the summer of 1942 have failed to be achieved."[59]

However, the most prominent theme in Hitler's utterances throughout September remains that of diatribes against the senior officers of the Army. On the 9th, the day on which List and Halder were dismissed, Hitler expressed the intention of replacing Keitel with Kesselring, and Jodl with Paulus.[60] On the 14th, he uttered another diatribe against officers, this time including in his strictures the founder of the Reichswehr, General von Seeckt. Four days later, he said that he had no confidence in any of his generals at present.[61] Two days after the sacking of Halder, Engel referred to the coming again of "the old records," aging generals with too little experience of the Front. The month ended with the harangue on 30 September about the General Staff's "loss of vision" since 1914. The threat to replace Keitel and Jodl was never carried out, and Jodl subsequently told Warlimont that he felt he (Jodl) had been

58. *KTB/OKW*, Vol. II, Part I, pp. 761–763.
59. Kotze, ed., *Heeresadjutant bei Hitler*, p. 126.
60. *KTB/OKW*, Vol. II, Part I, pp. 708–709.
61. Kotze, ed., *Heeresadjutant bei Hitler*, p. 127.

wrong to oppose Hitler, since a dictator's strength derives from his self-confidence, which should never be assailed.

The depths of Hitler's antipathy to the officer class can be illustrated from an entry in Goebbels's diary for 10 May 1943.[62] "All generals lie, he says. All generals are disloyal. All generals are opposed to National Socialism. All generals are reactionaries." Hitler also explained that his reason for ceasing to eat in the FHQ mess was that "he just can't bear the sight of generals any longer."[63]

Hitler's army service was the source of his subsequent love of uniforms and the quasi-military spectacle and organization that were to characterize the Nazi Party. But the origin of his antipathy to the officer class is harder to pinpoint. His superiors in the 16th Bavarian regiment regarded him as a model soldier, and there are no reported incidents of antipathy to officers from his war service.

The most likely origin of his hostility to officers, especially senior officers, is the failure of his attempt to disrupt the May Day celebrations of 1923 in Munich. On that occasion, he mustered his Storm Troopers and succeeded in obtaining arms from Army stores by a trick, but was publicly humiliated and forced to capitulate on the demand of the Army Commander in Bavaria, General Otto von Lossow, who had earlier appeared sympathetic to Nazi aims. From this episode, Hitler may well have developed the view of the officer class as untrustworthy.

His view of them as timid and unimaginative is more likely to derive from the ease with which he outwitted them politically after 1933, and their reluctance to support his political use of military power. In the reoccupation of the Rhineland in 1936, and in the invasions of Austria (1938) and Czechoslovakia (1939), he demonstrated that their misgivings were wrong. And in military matters, particularly in adopting new doctrines of tank warfare, in preferring Manstein's plan for the invasion of France to that drawn up by the General Staff in 1940, and in refusing to sanction a general withdrawal on the Moscow front in 1941, his judgment had proved superior to the conventional wisdom of the senior officers.

Warlimont advances an additional speculation for the outburst of hostility which flared up in September 1942, attributing it to the fact that generals had "too often been witnesses of his faults, his

62. Louis P. Lochner, ed., *The Goebbels Diaries* (London: Hamish Hamilton, 1948), p. 289.
    63. Ibid.

errors, his illusions, and his daydreams."[64] This seems unfounded for two reasons: first, that prior to that time Hitler had more often been right on military matters than had his generals; and second, that his "faults, errors, illusions, and daydreams" had frequently been made manifest to civilians such as Goebbels and Speer, to whom he developed no such antipathies (until close to the end of the war in Speer's case, never in that of Goebbels).

The most likely explanation for the violent outbursts of antipathy at this time probably rests on the following considerations. Hitler had enlarged the scope of operations beyond those envisaged in the original General Staff plan, and had attempted to compress the time scale by mounting operations against Stalingrad and the Caucasus simultaneously rather than in sequence. Halder had objected to this, and was being proved correct. It is common enough in such circumstances for higher authority to blame failure not on the impossibility of the task, but on the subordinates' unwillingness or inability to pursue it with adequate determination or competence. All the dismissals of senior officers were attributed by Hitler to one or the other cause. Underlying it all was an erosion of his self-confidence by the fact that for once military caution and conservatism were proving more correct than the bolder course which he had so often prevailed with in the past. It was easier to disguise his waning self-confidence from others (and himself) by believing that he could change the situation by changing the executants. Jodl's remarks to Warlimont show that he, at least, believed his own opposition had eroded Hitler's self-confidence and had, *for that reason*, been mistaken. Engel's observations on Hitler's anxiety about the coming winter also point to the beginnings of erosion of the Führer's self-confidence.

The consequences for decision-making of Hitler's antipathy to the officer class are more important than the reasons for it. It led him with increasing frequency to substitute his judgment for theirs, to dismiss them rather than change plans, to interfere with the detailed execution of operations, and to exploit their professional rivalries with each other.

64. Warlimont, *Inside Hitler's Headquarters*, p. 258.

CHAPTER THREE

Transition to the Crisis Period

During october, manpower problems increasingly came to dominate Hitler's daily conferences. German decisions concerning the Eastern Front became more and more ad hoc and improvised while concern about possible Allied amphibious operations against Western Europe, Norway, and in the Western Mediterranean came to the fore, an especial preoccupation with the defense of islands (the Channel Islands, Crete, Malta, and Norwegian coastal islands) being manifested in the Führer's thought processes. As the Soviet and British plans for major counteroffensives were being finalized, some attention has been devoted to them, especially the Soviet planning for the Stalingrad counteroffensive.

OCTOBER 1942

Hitler was in Berlin until the 5th, and on the 2nd conferred there with Rommel, who expressed little optimism about the prospects of further progress in Africa, pointing out that British air superiority severely hindered German tank movements, and that the British El Alamein position was very strong. On the 2nd, when the 14th Panzer Corps reached the Volga on a broad front, Zeitzler and Jodl attempted to persuade Hitler to give lower priority to the actual capture of Stalingrad, in order to free troops for use elsewhere. Hitler refused absolutely, for nonmilitary (that is, political) reasons. However, he was sufficiently concerned at the shortage of troops to consider, on his return to FHQ on 5 October, whether to allow Army Group B to evacuate its Voronezh bridgehead so that the troops could be used elsewhere; but he reached no decision. He was most worried by the concentration of Soviet forces opposite Army Group Center, so he ordered "parts of" the 11th Panzer Division and the 328th ID to prepare to repulse an attack north of Smolensk, and a group of forces to be assembled to repel an attack westward toward Velikiye Luki. This was to include the first three of the so-called "Air Force Field Divisions" (that is, ground force formations made up of Air Force personnel, yet another instance of "alternative" fighting forces being developed alongside the Army, as the Waffen-SS had been), and preparations were made for part of 11th Army (which was supposed to be designated for use against Leningrad) to be moved into this area also.

A British raid on the Channel Island of Sark was marked by the practice of fettering prisoners until they could be removed; Hitler therefore decided to fetter prisoners taken at Dieppe, including officers, until the British Government formally certified that no German prisoners were fettered. More importantly for the war effort, his expectation that there would be more British landings in the West led him to order a number of countermeasures.[1] These included putting forces on standing alert on likely landing sectors whenever the weather situation was favorable to landings, in the expectation that knowledge of this measure would have a deterrent effect.

The deteriorating manpower situation was further highlighted in Speer's report on a plan to set up five coast defense divisions in the West; these would require between 50,000 and 60,000 men, and "only 12,000–15,000" could be spared from the armaments industry.[2] For armed forces establishments so heavily engaged in so many areas, the release of armaments workers to the forces at all indicated very severe strain on resources.

Under the new Chief of Staff, Zeitzler, OKH succeeded in virtually excluding OKW from anything to do with the Eastern Front, by changing the procedure for the midday conference. Henceforward, Zeitzler opened the reporting, thus excluding the Eastern Front from the OKW report normally given by Jodl. There is no indication whether this procedure was initiated or merely approved by Hitler, but it clearly had his acquiescence, and was presumably a consequence of the efforts Jodl in particular had made to induce him to cut down commitments on the Eastern Front.

1. Greiner's notes of daily conference, 5 October 1942, in *KTB/OKW*, Vol. II, Part II, p. 794; and Warlimont's comments therein, on p. 797.
2. Ibid. On manpower difficulties, see also Albert Speer, *Inside the Third Reich* (London: Weidenfeld and Nicolson, 1970), pp. 215–221.

At the conference on 6 October, the manpower question came very much to the fore. The Army reported that it was one million men short of what it needed. It was decided that this shortage could be made up only by "economizing" six hundred thousand, that is, could not be made up at all, and that four hundred thousand would be provided by ordering economy in personnel and reduction of war establishments of air defense and air warning troops—this at a time when the tempo of Anglo-American attacks on Germany was increasing.

From now on, manpower questions increasingly dominated the daily situation conferences. On 7 October, Hitler agreed to a proposal by Zeitzler that Army Group A should form raiding commandos for small operations against the Soviet eastern Black Sea coast from pioneer units of the 17th Army and from the Navy. Army Group B reported it would be unable to renew its attacks in Stalingrad until 13 October. Hitler simply refused to accept this, and ordered increased activity by the troops and the Air Force to deny the Soviets a breathing space to rebuild their defenses. Army Group North was ordered to be ready to attack toward Toropets on 6 or 8 November. In the west, Hitler again concluded that there was a danger of an Allied landing at Cherbourg, and ordered Commander-in-Chief West to take appropriate countermeasures. More heavy anti-aircraft units were ordered to Crete on the 11th, a measure hardly consistent with the decision of four days before to raise 400,000 troops by reducing anti-aircraft forces.

Between 10 and 13 October, the "power struggle" between OKH and OKW intensified, with Zeitzler making only very brief reports at the midday situation conference, and deciding important operational questions in discussion alone with Hitler during the afternoon and evening. This is considered by Warlimont as widening the split in the High Command, damaging the Army, and "playing right into Hitler's hands."[3]

On the 10th, the Romanian 3rd Army took over complete responsibility for its sector of the Front between Kletskaya and the Don bend southeast of Kazanskaya. Antonescu asked for the proposed transfer of two Romanian Cavalry Divisions to the 4th Panzer Army to be postponed, on the grounds that there were no winter quarters for them, but Hitler nevertheless decided to go ahead with the transfer.

3. *KTB/OKW*, Vol. II, Part II, p. 815. Comment by Warlimont.

At the noon conference on 15 October, a completely new threat emerged, with increasing reports that "Anglo-Saxon" landings in West Africa (that is, the area then usually known as French North Africa) were imminent. Jodl proposed warning the French, so that they could reinforce their African colonies, but Hitler refused on the grounds that the Italians would distrust any reinforcement of the French forces in North Africa. Hitler's increasing and pointless preoccupation with Crete surfaced in a discussion as to whether to re-subordinate it from the Southeastern Command to the Commander-in-Chief South (Marshal Kesselring); a decision on this was left to Göring.

The conference on 17 October indicated that the 1st Panzer Army could not envisage advancing further until the end of the month, which Hitler declared to be much too late, though no decision either to advance earlier or to cancel the operation resulted. The question of the Air Force Field Divisions was raised; OKH, naturally, asked that if the Air Force had surplus men it should transfer them to the Army. This Hitler refused.

On the 18th, the major decision was to issue the so-called "Kommandobefehl," an order that troops captured during British commando raids, even if in uniform, were to be executed on capture.[4] This led to a violent argument with Jodl, who opposed the order very fiercely, but he was not supported by Keitel. Hitler used the occasion to utter a diatribe about the lukewarmness of troops in regard to deterrence measures; he described it as a fault of the higher command, which "wants to make a pulpit out of the military profession." The only other decision recorded was to send an aerial torpedo group to sink the Soviet battleship at Poti, a Soviet Black Sea port from which raiding activities against German coastal positions were expected. Capture of the Red October factory in Stalingrad was reported; in a consequently optimistic mood, Hitler interpreted radio intercept reports of Soviet troop concentrations east of the Volga as an indication of intent to abandon the city and form a new defensive front on the east bank.

October 19 was marked only by more apprehension about the situation in the West. Four batteries of heavy artillery had been installed in Norway, and Hitler ordered one infantry battalion to be allocated for the protection of each, with a special guard placed on

4. Hildegard von Kotze, ed., *Heeresadjutant bei Hitler, 1938–1943: Aufzeichnungen des Major Engel* (Stuttgart: Deutsche Verlags-Anstalt, 1974), p. 130.

the island of Andöy, northwest of Narvik. The evacuation of British-born residents of the Channel Islands had been ordered in September, but Wfst had displayed no urgency in carrying it out. On discovering this, Hitler treated his military to another outburst of anger, and, according to Warlimont, accused them of "sabotage." Warlimont comments that "this order was also sabotaged." Hitler originally ordered the evacuation on 8 September; evacuations were ordered in the Channel Islands on 15, 17, 23, and 28 September, but the evacuation ordered on the 23rd was postponed to the 29th, some of those ordered for evacuation were sent home, ostensibly because of lack of shipping space, and the evacuation ordered for the 23rd was canceled. An account by a Jersey resident indicates that the local German authorities opposed the order, and in some cases German military doctors "suggested minor ailments which did not exist, with a view to the 'sufferer' being classed as medically unfit" for evacuation.[5] The preoccupation with islands continued on the 20th, with Hitler insisting that the Channel and Norwegian Islands should be fortified because of the analogy with the importance of Malta, and the difficulty of recovering them if once lost. On 21 October, the island theme continued, with an order for the further fortification of Crete.

The 22nd was notable for the report that Russian reinforcements had been detected moving against Army Group A, and for a recommendation by Hitler that Army Group Center should counter the new Soviet tactic of attacking on a narrow front from the depths of the defense by a method used by the French in 1918—namely, maintain a large reserve of ammunition and counter the attack with artillery.

On the 23rd, dissent was apparent among Germany's allies. The Italian 8th Army had been placed on the Don between the Hungarian 2nd and the Romanian 3rd Armies, largely because of the possibility that the Hungarians and Romanians would fight each other. The Romanians were ordered to relieve the right wing of the Italian 8th Army, which was felt to be occupying too wide a sector, but in view of their reluctance to do so, Hitler decided to postpone the move. Allegedly as retribution for a British air attack on a military hospital in North Africa, Hitler ordered that British prisoners

5. Leslie P. Sinel, *The German Occupation of Jersey* (London: Corgi, 1969), pp. 87–93, 108–111, 114–117.

taken in a commando raid on the electric power station at Glom-fjord in Norway should be shot immediately. On this day, the British began the Second Battle of El Alamein, but the situation report received from Panzer Army Africa on the following day showed considerable lack of awareness of what was happening. However, Hitler telephoned Rommel, who was on leave in Germany, on the 24th, and asked him to go back to Africa at once.

Also on the 24th, Manstein visited FHQ, where he attempted to dissuade Hitler from allowing the Air Force to form field divisions of ground troops, but was unsuccessful.[6] However, Hitler, who believed a Soviet offensive against Army Group Center was imminent, informed Manstein that he would probably move FHQ to somewhere in the region of Vitebsk, so as to be close to Army Group Center, and that if he did so, Manstein would be put in command of Army Group A.[7] Hitler's adjutant, Major Engel, flew to the Italian 8th Army at Millerovo, where he found General Tippelskirch very depressed about the condition of the Italian troops and the indifference of their commander, General Messe. Tippelskirch was convinced that the Italian Front would be unable to withstand any pressure, and wanted a strong German reserve put behind it. On his return to FHQ, Engel informed Hitler, who took a less pessimistic attitude and defended the idea of a "racially homogeneous" front.[8]

That this attitude was entirely opportunistic was shown on the very next day, 25 October, when Zeitzler reported on his visit to 17th Army, where Romanian formations were being "mixed" with German. Hitler declared that he wanted this done with all allied formations, and ordered *all* allied positions on the Don front to be strengthened by "corsetting" them with German units. The continuation of the British bombardment at El Alamein, indicating that a major offensive was imminent, brought a curious reaction. Hitler saw the greatest danger not in Egypt but in the Western Mediterranean, and his preoccupation with islands surfaced again; he requested a report on the defensibility of Corsica, and said that he was considering occupying it with Italian troops.

In respect to other areas of the Russian Front, he observed again

6. Erich von Manstein, *Lost Victories* (London: Methuen, 1958), p. 267.
7. Ibid., pp. 267–269.
8. Kotze, ed., *Heeresadjutant bei Hitler*, p. 132.

the intensity of Russian supply activity to Leningrad across Lake Ladoga, and complained that this activity was going on unimpeded because, while the Army and Navy were prepared to use captured weapons to a large extent, the Air Force would work only with first-class (German) equipment. They must use everything, he said, including older aircraft. He complained further that Leningrad had not been attacked for some time, thus giving the Russians a chance to restore its industrial activities, and demanded continuing air attacks on Leningrad, the traffic on Lake Ladoga, Moscow, Gorky, Kuibyshev, Saratov, and Baku. He also demanded introduction of the Heinkel-177 four-engine bomber. The introduction of this aircraft had been delayed by research into the possibility of using it as a dive-bomber; Hitler ordered that it should now be brought in as a horizontal bomber because of its large payload.[9]

The volatility of Hitler's opinions was apparent again on 26–27 October. In an attempt to solve two contentious issues—the lack of German formations to stiffen the allied forces along the Don, and the question of the Air Force Field Divisions—Hitler ordered three allied armies to be "corsetted" with the Air Force Field Divisions. As Warlimont comments, this would take some time to bring about, and would be of doubtful effectiveness when done, because the divisions were completely new and totally inexperienced.

The midday conference on 26 October showed considerable anxiety about the possibility of a big Russian attack during the winter against the allied forces on the Don, and south toward Rostov. The grounds for this concern were observations of large-scale Soviet movements and the fact that on many sectors bridges had been built across the river into bridgeheads on the south bank, which had never been cleared out. Further considered were: whether to send five divisions from the west to the east in exchange for five divisions in need of recuperation, or to send fifteen western divisions to the east, or to move two mountain divisions, at present with the 11th Army on the flatland outside Leningrad, to the Caucasus, and to send two light (Jäger) divisions to Norway and Finland. No decisions were taken on any of these, but it was decided to make a large air attack on Kirov, in the middle of Army Group

9. The attempt to use a four-engine aircraft as a dive-bomber was indeed unrealistic, as Hitler complained. This, however, was not the sole reason for the failure of the Heinkel 177 to come into service; it was extremely unreliable, and was known to the forces as "The Flying Firework."

Center's front, and to move all the Army Groups' Panzer Divisions northward to form a mobile reserve in the Kirov area, to beat off the anticipated Soviet attack. On the assumption that Stalingrad would fall soon (though 6th Army notified headquarters that it did not expect to complete the capture of the city before 10 November), 6th and 4th Panzer Armies were ordered to be ready to push north and south along the Volga as soon as the city fell.

But on the 27th, when Zeitzler reported a wave of Soviet propaganda about imminent large-scale offensive operations, Hitler evaluated this as more of a propaganda operation than a real prospect, and Engel reported that "the Führer now has a fixed idea that the Russians won't attack."[10] There was, however, some more discussion of the risk of a Soviet attack across the Don toward Rostov, and Zeitzler suggested putting divisions of limited combat capacity, but equipped with many heavy weapons, behind the allied armies, to improve their static defenses. On 30 October, a spate of detailed orders for reinforcement of Army Group Center in the Sukhinichi area indicate Hitler's preoccupation with the possibility of an attack in this vicinity, and his growing tendency to interfere in matters of detail: the moves he ordered involved units down to battalion size. A report from a captured Soviet company commander stated that the Russians were working on biological warfare, in the first instance the spreading of plague, anthrax, and typhus bacilli, and elicited a definite order from Hitler that Germany was not to do the same. The month ended with a move of FHQ from Vinnitsa back to its permanent quarters at Rastenburg, a move which was carried out by train and put the headquarters out of action for approximately forty-eight hours. That Hitler's penchant for interference in detail was now being institutionalized was shown by an order issued by OKH instructing field commanders to make more detailed reports to him.[11]

THE PLANNING OF THE SOVIET COUNTEROFFENSIVE

In view of the success of the Stalingrad counteroffensive, it is hardly surprising that a number of Soviet generals have laid claim to a role in begetting it. Debate over the genesis of the counteroffensive

10. Kotze, ed., *Heeresadjutant bei Hitler*, pp. 132–133.
11. OKH/Gen. St. d. H./op. Abt. (IIa), Nr. 20753/42 of 31 October 1942.

plan was initially ruled out by the fact that during Stalin's lifetime
no other parentage but his could be claimed for any Soviet victory,
and when debate began after his death, a further complication was
introduced by the fact that Nikita Khrushchev was himself a member of the "Southern Group of Generals," that is, the Front and
Army Commanders in.the Stalingrad area, having been Chief Political Officer of various Army Groups throughout the retreat over
the Don, the defense of Stalingrad, and the counteroffensive. The
basic argument has been between these local commanders and the
representatives of Stavka, and parallels the disputes in many armies between the men on the ground and those at the "center."
But the facts appear to be conclusively established in the writings
of the Deputy Supreme Commander, Marshal Zhukov,[12] and the
Chief of General Staff, Marshal Vasilevsky,[13] both of whom have described their crucial meeting with Stalin on 12 September 1942.

Up to that date, the relief of Stalingrad had been conceived in
terms of a local attack from the north, to wipe out the German formations defending the Don-Volga line and enable the Stalingrad
and Southeastern Fronts to link up. Three armies were being used
for the purpose, and after they had been attacking for a week with
very limited success, Zhukov, who had been personally supervis-
ing the operation, was summoned to Moscow, where he told Stalin
that they could not possibly break through because their supplies
were inadequate and the terrain was unfavorable. Stalin then asked
him what they would need to make the breakthrough effective, and
Zhukov replied that an additional army, a tank corps, three tank
brigades, at least 400 guns, and at least one complete air army
would be needed. Vasilevsky agreed, and Stalin began to study his
own map. While he was doing so, Zhukov and Vasilevsky moved
away and began talking quietly in a corner. At one point, one of
them said that "another solution" would have to be found, at which
Stalin lifted his head suddenly and asked, "and what does 'another
solution' mean? Go over to the General Staff and think very carefully indeed what must be done in the Stalingrad area. Think about
which troops, where from, to reinforce the Stalingrad group, and
don't forget the Caucasus front. We will meet here at 9:00 P.M. to-

12. Georgy K. Zhukov, *Vospominaniia i razmyshleniia* (Moscow: Novosti Press Agency
Publishing House, 1969), pp. 381–385.

13. Aleksandr M. Vasilevsky, *Delo vsei Zhizni* (Moscow: Politizdat, 1974), pp. 190–202.

morrow." After a day of study, Zhukov and Vasilevsky concluded that a much larger-scale operation was feasible, that the main blow must be directed against the Romanian troops on the flanks of the Germans, and that the Soviet forces for the operation ought to include large units equipped with newly produced tanks.

The second meeting with Stalin took place at 10:00 P.M. on the 13th. Stalin asked a number of searching questions, designed to ascertain whether anything so ambitious was possible. No decision was taken, as it was still uncertain whether Stalingrad could be held, but Stalin was sufficiently impressed to order the plan to be studied further in the light of the available resources. Both Zhukov and Vasilevsky were ordered back to Stalingrad, Zhukov to study the situation north of the city, and Vasilevsky that south of it, telling no one anything about the conversation. Zhukov left for Stalingrad that same evening, and Vasilevsky a few days later. There is no suggestion in the memoirs of either that Stalin referred to the 1920 exploit which Hitler thought he might try to repeat. Nor is there any reason why he should: at this stage, what was contemplated was encirclement of Stalingrad from north and south, not a drive along the Don to Rostov. That was to be added later.

Although the situation in Stalingrad remained tense for several more weeks, Halder noted in his diary on 20 September that the "gradual burning out of the German assault troops is perceptible,"[14] and a judicious feeding in of new Soviet divisions enabled the position to be held, though with difficulty, while preparations for the major counteroffensive went ahead.[15] A reorganization of the army groups in the Stalingrad area was undertaken at the end of September, Southeastern Front being renamed Stalingrad Front, and the former Stalingrad Front split into two, entitled Southwestern and Don Fronts. This reorganization facilitated defense of the city, but was also designed to be of use in the counteroffensive, which was accepted by Stavka about the same time, in the form of an operation code-named "Uranus." This would consist of attacks across the Don, north and south of Stalingrad, both aiming to meet in the bend of the Don around Kalach, and aimed at the "weak links," the 3rd and 4th Romanian armies on the German flanks.

14. Franz Halder, *Kriegstagebuch: tägliche Aufzeichnungen des Chefs des Generalstabes des Heeres 1939–1942* (Stuttgart: Kohlhammer Verlag, 1962–64), Vol. III, p. 524.
15. Zhukov, *Vospominaniia*, pp. 386–387 and 398–407.

After more visits by Zhukov and Vasilevsky, a Stavka mission consisting of Vasilevsky, Voronov (the Head of Red Army Artillery), and Ivanov (Chief of the Operations Section of the General Staff) went to Yeremenko's headquarters on the east bank of the Volga and gave him a preliminary outline of the "general intention," with the request for him to "prepare comments" within twenty-four hours.[16] A number of suggestions were made by both Yeremenko and the Commander of the Don Front, Rokossovsky, but none amounted to an attempt at major revision of the plan.[17] On 22 October, Southwestern Front came into existence, and a process of gradual disclosure of intentions to the lower formations then began.

As this is not a study of the Stalingrad battle as such, it is sufficient here to note that the logistical problems involved in preparing the offensive without alerting the Germans were immense. They were solved by a combination of measures: units moving into the area marched only by night, remaining stationary under camouflage from dawn to dusk; vehicles drove at night without headlights; and movements were disguised as much as possible in ways that would cause the Germans to evaluate them as connected with the defensive battle which was still raging in the city.

On 9 October, Stalin gave a sign of confidence in his military by yielding to longstanding pressures for abolition of the control functions of the political officers. On that day, he issued Order No. 307,[18] introducing "unitary command," under which the professional military officers, whether Party members or not, became responsible for all aspects of work among their troops, political officers losing power of veto over orders, and being reduced to "Deputies for Political Affairs." Within a week, Order No. 325, issued on 16 October, specified new functions for all tank and mechanized units, thus bringing tactics up to date.[19]

A process of briefing and war-gaming began early in November, with planning conferences on the 3rd (at the headquarters of the 5th Tank Army) and 4th (with the Commanders of the Don and

---

16. John Erickson, *The Road to Stalingrad* (London: Weidenfeld and Nicolson, 1975), p. 428.

17. Ibid., p. 429.

18. *Istoriia Velikoi Otechestvennoi Voiny Sovetskogo Soiuza* [History of the Great Fatherland War of the Soviet Union, hereinafter cited as *IVOVSS*], Vol. II (Moscow: USSR Ministry of Defense Publishing House, 1963), pp. 489–490 and 632.

19. Erickson, *Road to Stalingrad*, p. 452.

Southwestern Fronts and a number of their army commanders). The date of the offensive was set for 12 November, and the orders for it were signed on the 8th; but on the following day, it was decided to postpone it for a week because movements of troops and supplies had fallen behind schedule. Army commanders made use of the cover. provided by the festival of 7 November, the anniversary of the 1917 Revolution, to assemble their officers at headquarters and run army-level war games, which were repeated at divisional and battalion levels over the next few days. Zhukov returned to Moscow on 11 November to report to Stalin and Stavka; there was almost a final hitch with a furious last effort by the Germans on that day to capture Stalingrad.

A curious feature of the final stages of preparation was that on 17 November, two days before the offensive was to be launched, a letter from one of the commanders, General Volsky (4th Mechanized Corps), was laid before Stalin.[20] Volsky stated that the forces available for the counteroffensive were insufficient, that failure was practically certain, and that the offensive should be called off. The letter was considered at a meeting of the State Defense Committee, and Vasilevsky was summoned back from Stalingrad to attend the meeting, where he pointed out that Volsky had had ample opportunity to express his misgivings during the planning meetings, and had shown neither anxiety nor reservation about the operation as a whole or about that of his own corps. Stalin thereupon telephoned Volsky, and surprised everyone in the room by the mildness with which he treated him. Volsky gave his word that he would do his best to carry out his orders, Stalin told Vasilevsky to keep a special eye on him for the first few days of the operation, and the matter was left at that. Volsky's Corps performed satisfactorily in the counteroffensive, and he appears to have suffered no consequences from his last-minute act of insubordination. Stalin had shown no reluctance in the past to dismiss senior officers, and in the purges of 1938–39 had executed or imprisoned far larger numbers of them than Hitler was ever to do with his own. But this incident reinforces the evidence provided by Order No. 307 of an improved and improving relationship between Stalin and his military at a time when Hitler's relationship with the German generals could hardly have been worse. About two weeks after Stalin had spared

20. Ibid., p. 461.

the nervous and relatively untried Volsky, Hitler dismissed a very experienced and able officer, General Walter Nehring, from command of the Afrika Korps, for a "pessimism" which, unlike Volsky's, proved only too well-founded.[21]

Hitler's apprehension that Stalin might try to repeat his 1920 dash down the Don from Stalingrad to Rostov was to prove premature but not unfounded, as it was added to the "Uranus" plan during October in the shape of an operation code-named "Saturn," designed to cut off Army Group A in the Caucasus. Two Army Groups (the Southwestern and Voronezh Fronts) were allocated to the task and told to work out a plan, which was approved by Stavka on 3 December 1942.[22] "Saturn," however, was secondary to the task, assigned to the Don and Stalingrad Fronts, of wiping out the forces which had been surrounded at Stalingrad. They began an offensive in the first week of December, but soon found that the forces allocated to them were inadequate, because the encircled enemy force was three to four times larger than had been expected. When Manstein mounted an attempt to relieve Stalingrad from the south, this necessitated changes in both the timetable and the scale of "Saturn." Instead of attacking due south toward Rostov and the rear of Army Group A, the Voronezh and Southwestern Fronts were directed to attack southeastward, so as to threaten the rear of Army Group Don and the Stalingrad relief force. The changes in the scale and scope of the operation were such that it was renamed "Little Saturn."[23] The objective of stopping the relief attempt was achieved, but the time and forces required to carry out "Little Saturn" enabled Army Group A to make a successful withdrawal from the Caucasus, partly by way of Rostov, and partly via the Taman Peninsula and Kerch Straits into the Crimea. The Soviet success was therefore limited to the destruction of Army Group B, but this in itself was a very significant success, and Army Group A's abandonment of the Caucasus removed the threat both to the oil fields and to the bases of the Soviet Black Sea Fleet. The priority given to the destruction of the "bird in hand" at Stalingrad over "Saturn" suggests that Stalin was not as dominated by his civil war experience as Hitler had thought he might be.

21. *KTB/OKW*, Vol. II, Part II, p. 1073. Comment by Warlimont.
22. *IVOVSS*, Vol. III, p. 42.
23. Zhukov, *Vospominaniia*, p. 413.

AFRICA

Rommel's advance on the Suez Canal had been stopped by Auchinleck at the First Battle of El Alamein in early July, and his last throw at a breakthrough had been frustrated in three days (30 August–1 September) by Montgomery in the battle of Alam Halfa. During September and October, Montgomery received a steady flow of new weapons (especially American-built tanks) and other supplies, while Rommel received next to nothing because of effective attrition by British naval and air forces against his supply routes from Italy. Such cargoes as survived the dangerous transit of the Mediterranean were subject to further erosion from the totally dominant Royal Air Force during the long road journey from the Libyan ports to the Alamein position. By contrast, the main problem faced by Montgomery and the new British Commander-in-Chief Middle East, General Alexander, was resisting pressures from Churchill to launch an offensive before they felt the time was ripe.

The British planning involved extensive deception measures, including the building and equipping of dummy defensive positions—a counterpart, though on a much smaller scale, to the Soviet concealment of its offensive force north of the Don, and equally successful. In this, the low degree of attention paid by Hitler to Africa undoubtedly helped. Rommel, who was on leave, saw Hitler in Berlin on 1 or 2 October, and was pessimistic about the chance of further progress, but did not foresee an imminent British attack. Apart from that meeting, the OKW diary records only one mention of the Africa theatre before the 24th, the second day of Second Alamein (when Hitler ordered Rommel to return from leave). That mention was on 15 October, and related not to Egypt but to reports of an imminent Anglo-American invasion of French North Africa. The reports were correct—the invasion took place on the night of 7/8 November—but all that happened was that Jodl proposed to warn the French, so that they could reinforce their colonies, and Hitler rejected the proposal on the grounds that the Italians would not favor an increased French military presence in Africa.

Like the Stalingrad operation, the British plan relied heavily on striking at the "weak link" forces of Germany's allies, in this case the Italian divisions that made up the bulk of the German-Italian Panzer Army.

CRISIS COMPONENTS
Environmental Change

The pre-crisis period for Germany was triggered by its launching of a land offensive on the Eastern Front on 28 June 1942. The objectives were to destroy large Soviet forces, interrupt Soviet oil traffic on the Volga, and overrun the oil fields of Soviet Transcaucasia; and throughout the period, inability to achieve these objectives kindled a growing sense of failure among decision-makers in Hitler's headquarters. This in turn led to a growth in dissension among them, a series of dismissals from office by Hitler, and a rift between him and his military advisers. There was, however, no sense in this period of time constraints on decisions; German forces continued to hold the initiative both in Russia and in other theatres of military operations (until late October in Africa, and mid-November in Russia). What made this a period of growing sense of threat was that the Red Army performed much better than Hitler and his closest military advisers expected. But this came in the context of a major Soviet withdrawal, and was not in itself sufficient to create any perception among German decision-makers of a possible adverse change in the military balance.

Threat to Values

The basic values of survival, political independence, territorial integrity, and the societal stability of Germany did not come into question in the pre-crisis period. But the militarist Social Darwinism that formed the philosophical base of Hitler's thinking could not be satisfied by this. It enjoined expansion at the expense of races defined as "inferior," and could be demonstrated only by the successful threat or use of force.[24] Beginning with the remilitarization of the Rhineland in 1936, the use of the military instrument had been overwhelmingly successful; of thirteen countries attacked, eleven had been overrun, and another five countries had effectively become no more than German satellites. But from the outset of the offensive of 1942, it gradually became clearer that the degree of military success enjoyed up to and including the previous sum-

---

24. For example: "This welding together of Europe has not been made possible by the efforts of a number of statesmen devoted to the cause of unification, but by FORCE OF ARMS." Adolf Hitler, *Hitler's Table Talk, 1941–1944*, trans. Norman Cameron and R. H. Stevens (London: Weidenfeld and Nicolson, 1973), p. 541 (29 June 1941).

mer was not being achieved. Initially, rates of advance were almost as high as in 1941, but at no time were large Soviet forces encircled and destroyed, as had happened on several occasions in the previous year.

A difference between Hitler and his senior field commander, Field Marshal von Bock, over the appropriate choice of action in respect to the city of Voronezh led to Bock's dismissal on 13 July. This proved to be but the first of a series of dismissals of field commanders, which implicitly expressed the notion of threat to a basic value of the regime: the belief in its military superiority over its adversaries. Whether the blame lay, as Hitler contended, in military incompetence or, as various generals argued at the time and since, in Hitler's interference, Hitler's basic belief in Soviet racial inferiority and his generals' low opinion of Soviet military competence were equally threatened by the Red Army's successful avoidance of most of the traps that were set for it.

Time Pressure

Perception of time pressure in this period was entirely concerned with degrees of tactical success. When Bock decided to use only his foot soldiers to pursue the Soviets eastward, Hitler's anger was motivated by the fact that this procedure ensured only seizure of territory, not the encirclement and defeat of Soviet forces. Similarly, his interference with dispositions of the mobile forces in late July resulted from a wrong perception of the possibility of cutting off retreating Soviet forces.

The duration of the pre-crisis period was 145 days (28 June–19 November), and it ended abruptly with a perception of the most acute threat to the German armed forces since the outbreak of the war, even without the additional threat perceived from British and American actions in Africa from 23 October onwards.

COPING MECHANISMS

Information Processing

An essential feature of Hitler's method of rule was centralization of decision-making in himself. This entailed also the channeling of information in ways which, as far as possible, kept him alone in possession of the complete picture. Thus, although OKW nominally retained responsibility for overall control of military operations on all fronts, in practice OKH controlled the Eastern Front, subject only to such interventions by individual OKW officers as were ordered by Hitler. The main source of processed information on Soviet field forces and war production was the Intelligence section of OKH, the so-called Foreign Armies East, and its assessments were incorporated into the OKH position at the daily Führer conferences. After the dismissal of Halder on 25 September, the new Head of OKH, Zeitzler, moved to restrict OKW's role in discussion of Eastern Front matters, which thereafter were increasingly dealt with in private sessions with Hitler. This, a consequence of Hitler's personal estrangement from Keitel and Jodl, restricted the interchange of information between OKW and OKH, virtually making conduct of the war in Russia a separate undertaking, and leaving in Hitler's hands decisions over transfers even of small units from OKW to OKH theatres or vice versa. At no time in the pre-crisis period did German decision-makers express dissatisfaction with the flow or processing of information, even though the Soviet counteroffensive was only vaguely perceived—no indication of its scope, objectives, magnitude, or imminence being given by Foreign Armies East or any other source.

Consultations: Persons and Groups

Hitler did not "consult" in the normal sense of the word. From the beginning of the war, he rarely left his headquarters, and he discussed events only with a small number of senior officers there. No Cabinet meetings were held, and even senior Party leaders such as Goebbels and Göring saw him infrequently. This practice did not change in the pre-crisis period, and interchanges with members of FHQ became even more restricted after his quarrel with Jodl and Keitel on 8 September.

Decisional Forums

The decisional forum was Hitler. All decisions affecting operations of forces of one division or larger, and many affecting formations smaller than a division, were taken or approved by him. There were no ad hoc groups of decision-makers. The carrying out of Hitler's decisions was undertaken by the institutional channels of OKW and OKH.

Alternatives: Search and Evaluation

In formulating the plan for the offensive, the only alternative considered had been an attempt to take Leningrad. This was rejected in favor of the southern offensive on the grounds that the latter offered greater prospects of economic gains for Germany (oil, coal, iron ore, and the Donbass industries) and of economic deprivation for the Soviet war effort. The original OKH proposal, for an offensive due eastward to the Volga, was amended by Hitler, who added the capture of the Caucasian oil fields, thus committing his field forces to two widely divergent operations. Arguments about the relative weight to be attached to each operation and about resource allocation between the south and the other sectors of the Eastern Front never amounted to a proposal of alternative plans, and at no time in the pre-crisis period was it suggested that the whole plan should be abandoned or even radically revised. Diary references by Halder to Hitler's "abandonment of reason," or to the possibility that the troops were "burnt out" imply concern that Hitler's decisions amounted to deviations from the plan to an extent that decreased its chances of success, but also imply endorsement of the basic offensive plan as feasible and realistic.

The pre-crisis period of an intra-war crisis in the ICB definition is marked off from the noncrisis period that precedes it by one indicator only—a conspicuous increase in perceived threat; and from the crisis period that follows it by three indicators—a sharp rise in the perceived threat to basic values, an awareness of time constraints on decisions, and a perceived adverse change in the military balance. The Stalingrad pre-crisis period conforms to the ICB definition in that there was a conspicuous increase in perceived threat, but the threat was simply that of failure to achieve the objectives of the offensive. In real terms, the crisis period proper began for Germany when the Red Army moved forces into position for the counteroffensive, the preparations for which were essentially complete by the end of October. But German perception of the turnabout came only with the actual launching of the Soviet counteroffensive, and the transition from pre-crisis to crisis was, for that reason, especially abrupt.

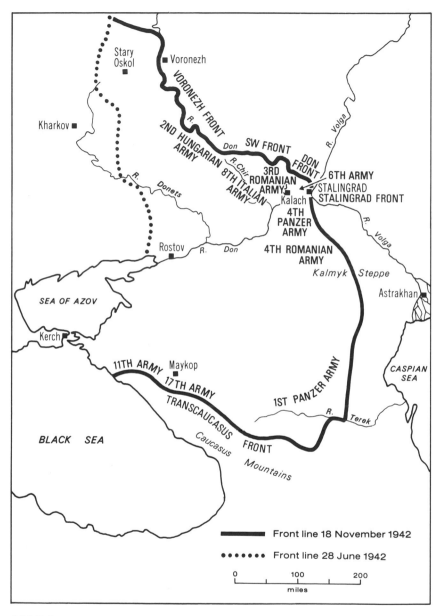

Front line 18 November 1942

•••••• Front line 28 June 1942

0   100   200
      miles

MAP 2.
POSITION AT END OF THE PRE-CRISIS PERIOD,
19 NOVEMBER 1942

CHAPTER FOUR

The Beginning of the Crisis Period: November 1942

THE STALINGRAD OPERATION became an intra-war crisis for Germany because it arose from the failure of the 1942 summer offensive to attain its objectives. It was this increased perception of failure which made the period 28 June to 19 November one of pre-crisis. The crisis period is distinguished from pre-crisis by the presence of all three conditions of crisis: a sharp rise in perceived threat to basic values (in this case, the prospect of a major defeat by a nation considered racially inferior and an army held not only to be professionally inferior but so worn-down as to be incapable of a further major effort in the immediate future, if at all); an awareness of time constraints on decisions (because the unexpected nature, speed, and scope of the Soviet counteroffensive created a perceived need for quick action if German forces on the southern sector of the Eastern Front were not to be cut off and destroyed); and, as this was an intra-war crisis, a perceived adverse change in the military balance (the Soviet attack was totally unexpected by FHQ decision-makers, indications from Intelligence being too fragmentary to carry conviction; the mere fact that the Soviets were able to launch it at all, and on the scale they did, itself showed that the balance was more adverse to Germany than had been previously perceived, and Soviet successes threatened from the outset to make it even more adverse).

NOVEMBER 1942

In hindsight, it can be seen that a general crisis period for Germany began on 23 October 1942, when the British opened the Second Battle of El Alamein with resources that were clearly beyond the capacity of the Axis forces in Africa to match. On 2 November, Rommel, on his own initiative, began a long withdrawal, eventually to Tunisia. A second blow fell on the night of 7/8 November, when Anglo-American forces invaded French North Africa. But the African theatre was regarded as secondary until the Anglo-American invasion, and the entire German commitment there prior to November 1942 comprised only the four divisions (50,000 men) of the Afrika Korps, together with a few squadrons of aircraft. For the Germans, the most important front was that in Russia, and the most telling blow came when the Soviet counteroffensive opened—on the Don northwest of Stalingrad on 19 November, and south of the city on the following day.

It is therefore these dates of 19–20 November which mark the beginning of the period of full crisis at Stalingrad; and the tempo, scale, and geographical scope of the Soviet counteroffensive make the transition from pre-crisis to crisis especially abrupt. But the counteroffensive takes place within a wider framework of setbacks which, as will be shown, impacted upon German decisions in respect to the Eastern Front.

Hitler had long feared an Allied landing somewhere in Western Europe or the Mediterranean, but the actual location and timing of the invasion took him by surprise. His underestimation of Allied capabilities, especially of their ability to control the sea and air routes between Italy and North Africa, led to a series of decisions, the first on 5 November, to reinforce the African theatre on a scale which, if carried out earlier, might have given Rommel control of the Suez Canal and the entire Middle East. Another crucial decision, on 8 November, was to invade unoccupied France; this was prompted by the fear of an Allied landing there, which in fact formed no part of Allied planning at that stage of the war. The effect of this action was to bring French forces in the North African colonies and elsewhere over to the Allied side on a scale that amounted to a partial reentry of France into the war.

Most crucial of all was Hitler's decision on 22 November—in the face of opposition from Zeitzler, Jodl, Manstein, and Paulus, and of deepest misgivings on the part of the Chief of Staff of the Air Force, Jeschonnek—to require 6th Army to withdraw, not westward out of encirclement, but eastward into Stalingrad, and to accept Göring's assurances that all its requirements could be supplied by an airlift.

Apart from these three decisions, the pattern of Hitler's decision-making during the month shows continued interference in matters of detail and an increase in the total number of decisions taken.

A curious feature of the month is Hitler's absence from the FHQ for most of it: he left on the afternoon of the 7th, after it had been reported that a large Anglo-American invasion force was at sea in the Mediterranean. It had become a Nazi tradition that Hitler should deliver a major speech annually at the Bürgerbräukeller in Munich on 8 November, the anniversary of the unsuccessful attempt to seize power in Bavaria in 1923; and it can be argued that in adhering to the custom, he was merely seeking to reassure public opinion, which would undoubtedly have regarded cancellation of the speech as an indication that something serious had happened. That explanation, however, does not account for his subsequent behavior. Instead of returning to FHQ, he went to the Berghof in Berchtesgaden, near the Austrian border, taking with him only his immediate entourage and a part of the Command Staff of OKW. There, several hundred miles from FHQ, with no senior officer of OKH (responsible for the Eastern Front) in attendance, and with even the small part of OKW which had accompanied him located in inconvenient areas twenty to sixty minutes away by road, he remained until 23 November. He was absent from FHQ for sixteen and a half days in all, a period in which the Allies landed in French North Africa, Rommel retreated several hundred miles in Egypt and Libya, unoccupied France was invaded, and the Soviet counteroffensive was launched. November 1942 can be seen in hindsight to have been the major turning point in the Second World War. But even at the time, it was clear that significant events were taking place. Yet, Hitler was, slow to return to his headquarters, and when he belatedly did so, he attempted to put off to the next day consideration of urgent matters pressed upon him by Zeitzler. The probable reasons for this behavior are discussed later in this chapter.

The move of the headquarters was completed by 2 November, and a great many matters were dealt with at the situation conference that day. The central preoccupation was the possibility of a Soviet attack, which Hitler still envisaged as a repeat of the 1920 push across the Don toward Rostov, a clear instance of interpretation of the present in terms of the past. Romanian reports that the number of Soviet bridges across the Don in their 3rd Army sector was still increasing, and the expectation that an offensive would be timed to begin on the anniversary of the Soviet Revolution, 7 November, prompted an order for strong air attacks on the bridges and on the probable troop concentration areas in the wooded country on the north bank of the Don. The 6th Army drew attention to the tiredness of its troops in Stalingrad, asked for permission to postpone its attack for eight days in order to rest them, and was refused. It also asked for the 29th Motorized Infantry Division of 4th Panzer Army to be sent as reinforcement. Hitler refused this also, but agreed to a suggestion by Zeitzler to send its Pioneer Battalion there. The issuance of an order for winter operations was authorized on 5 November; it emphasized the need to defend every strong point to the last. Belated recognition of the problems posed by the Air Force Field Divisions came with a decree to use them only in defense until they were integrated and experienced, Hitler recalling the heavy losses suffered by untrained volunteer divisions in 1914 in Flanders. A request of Manstein's for 30th Army Corps of his 11th Army to be posted to Army Group A was approved.

Severe congestion had been caused on the railroads in the East by partisan activity and the early frosts. To alleviate the consequent supply problems, Hitler intervened in logistics, ordering that loaded trains unable to proceed further should be unloaded, so that the empty wagons could be returned. Preoccupied again with Malta, he ordered the strongest possible Air Force component for action in the Western Mediterranean against supply convoys, and, as far as possible, that only fighter-bombers be used in North Africa, as the only aircraft with any chance of success against British air superiority. More JU-88 groups were therefore ordered to the Mediterranean. As a reprisal for British air attacks on German hospitals in North Africa, he ordered corresponding attacks on British hospitals. Finally, he issued an edict on the need to improve the ammunition supply of blockade runners, and provide radios for their communicating with Air Force units designated to protect them in European waters.

During the evening, Rommel reported that he intended to withdraw from his position at El Alamein during the night. Hitler ordered him to hold his existing position at whatever cost; however, in his "end of day" report, transmitted early in the morning of 3 November, Rommel reported that he had carried out the withdrawal at 10:00 P.M. on the 2nd. It was so unprecedented for a field commander to announce such an important step in a routine report that the Duty Officer, who received it between 5:00 and 6:00 A.M., entirely failed to realize its significance, and did not wake Hitler to give it to him. When Hitler received it at 9:00 A.M., with the rest of the morning reports, he flew into a rage, claiming he could have stopped the withdrawal if he had received the "end of day" report earlier (which, of course, was untrue, since it reported that the withdrawal had already taken place), dismissed and degraded the Duty Officer, refused to receive Warlimont, whom he held responsible, but sent word to him via Keitel that he was dismissed. Warlimont therefore immediately handed over his duties to a subordinate and went on leave from the evening of 4 November (his dismissal was rescinded a few days later). Because of this episode, no officer from Wfst was admitted to the midday conference. Rommel had in fact disobeyed orders from both Hitler and Mussolini, but no action was taken against him.

By 4 November, preoccupation with a possible Russian offensive against the Axis allies on the Don prompted the dispatch of three divisions from the west to Army Group B to "corset" the Romanians and Italians. It was reported that a large number of warships was in Gibraltar; however, the Naval Command (SKL) interpreted it as an escort for a Malta convoy, not an invasion fleet, because very few landing craft and only two passenger ships were present. Given the fears expressed in late October of an imminent Allied landing in French North Africa, the complacency of OKW and SKL is perhaps surprising. The real explanation—that the warships at Gibraltar were intended to cover landings by troops approaching in another convoy from the Atlantic—does not seem to have been considered. Later in the evening, Rommel's ordnance officer, Berndt, a senior Nazi Party figure, arrived, reported on the serious position of the German-Italian Panzer Army, and criticized von Rintelen, a German general at Comando Supremo (the Italian GHQ), for failure to solve its supply difficulties.

On the 5th, Rommel reported that he did not expect to be able to stop the British before the Libyan frontier, and an infantry regiment and two parachute battalions were ordered to Africa at once. There was also inconclusive discussion about the possibility of sending an airborne division from the Eastern Front. The measures ordered reflected Hitler's stress-induced tendency to interfere in details, as well as the strain on German resources, the forces to be dispatched comprising three battalions, twenty-four tanks, ten 88mm guns, and three wings of aircraft, two from the Eastern Front and one from Norway, to provide air support from Sicily. On this day also, FHQ was visited by the Commanders-in-Chief of Army Group North (Küchler) and of 16th Army (Busch), with requests for additional divisions, which could not be met.

On 6 November, the British force at Gibraltar put to sea. SKL now assessed it as intending a landing in North Africa, giving five possible destinations: the Tripoli-Benghazi area, Sicily, Sardinia, the Italian mainland, or French North Africa (which SKL assessed to be *least* likely). The nine U-boats deployed in the Western Mediterranean were ordered out, and Hitler sent them a message saying, "on the destruction of the English formation depends the existence of the African army." Mussolini notified Hitler that he believed the destination to be French North Africa, which contradicted the SKL assessment but was correct.

Nevertheless, at the midday conference on 7 November, when it was reported that the ships from Gibraltar had joined with a strong convoy from the Atlantic, Hitler still accepted the SKL assessment that Tripoli or Benghazi, close behind the German-Italian Panzer Army (DIPA), was the most likely destination. However, he ordered Commander-in-Chief West to prepare to invade unoccupied France. Foreign Armies East reported that a top-level meeting had taken place in Moscow on 4 November, with all the Commanders-in-Chief present, and had decided to mount an offensive "before the end of the year" either on the Don front or in the center. This report was either fabricated by its author, or, more likely, was Soviet disinformation. No such meeting took place on that date. It had already been decided in September that the winter offensive should be mounted north and south of Stalingrad, not on the Don, and certainly not in the center; and two men whose presence would have been indispensable, Marshals Zhukov and Vasilevsky, were out of Moscow (they were both in the Stalingrad area) on 4 November.[1] That credence was given to this report, when the Soviet counteroffensive was a mere twelve days off, shows only that Foreign Armies East had totally failed to appreciate the significance of

1. Georgy K. Zhukov, *Vospominaniia i razmyshleniia* (Moscow: Novosti Press Agency Publishing House, 1969), pp. 402–403.

the information it was receiving from the Romanians and others about Soviet activity on their sectors.

At the end of the midday conference, Hitler and his immediate entourage boarded the Führer's special train, which left at 13:40 for Munich, where Hitler was to make his annual speech at the Bürgerbräukeller, on the anniversary of the unsuccessful putsch of 1923. A situation conference was held in the train at 7:00 P.M., at which Jodl listed the likely destinations of the Allied convoy in the following declining order of probability:

1. A landing in Rommel's rear in Cyrenaican ports.

2. In addition, or instead, a landing in Crete.

3. In combination with either or both of the preceding alternatives, a supply operation to Malta.

4. A landing in Tripolitania or Sicily, which was regarded as possible but less probable.

5. A landing in French North Africa. This was regarded as improbable, on the grounds that it would throw the French into the arms of Germany. The reasoning here is curious, and perhaps a sign of stress. If an Allied invasion of French North Africa was likely to throw the French into the arms of Germany, what effect was the German invasion of unoccupied France, already in preparation, likely to have on the substantial French armed forces in the colonies?

Speer gives a slightly different but sketchy account of discussions during the train journey, saying that the Allied naval operation was evaluated as a supply operation either for the existing offensive in Egypt or for a landing in central Italy.[2]

During the night of 7/8 November, the Allies landed in French North Africa, whereupon Hitler, from Munich, ordered the strengthening of Crete to be given equal priority to Africa. The Italian Foreign Minister, Count Ciano, and the French Prime Minister, Laval, were summoned to meet Hitler in Munich on 9 November; Commander-in-Chief West (Rundstedt) was ordered to get ready for Operation "Anton" (the invasion of unoccupied France), but not to invade until further orders. The Gestapo was instructed to preempt any possibility of anti-German action by French forces in North Africa, by arresting two generals in France, Weygand and

2. Albert Speer, *Inside the Third Reich* (London: Weidenfeld and Nicolson, 1970), pp. 245–246.

Giraud, thought to be capable and willing to lead it. On this day, further reports of Soviet concentrations of troops and tanks north and south of Stalingrad came in from Army Group B, but there is no indication that they were acted on.

The conversation with Ciano took place in Munich on 9 November. Hitler described the military situation as much better than it had been in either of the previous winters, arguing that the American landing in North Africa was less dangerous than the British landings in Norway in 1940, and that the enemy decision to establish a "Second Front" in North Africa would make German and Italian deployments easier because there would no longer be a need to keep large numbers of troops in readiness along a giant front, which might be attacked at any point. The fifty-two divisions he had in France, twenty-two of them of the best class and eight of them elite divisions, could now be dispersed, since there was no longer a threat in that sector. He was preparing to invade unoccupied France, and had asked the Duce to be ready to march into southern France and Corsica. (In fact, the number of German divisions in France was nothing like fifty-two; it was approximately thirty.[3] The idea that an Allied landing in North Africa precluded a later landing in France was, of course, nonsensical, and the reasoning that the situation had been worse in the previous winters is spurious, since Germany had suffered no land defeats at that time, and neither Russia nor America had yet entered the war. Hitler's objective could only be to bolster waning Italian confidence, and perhaps his own, against the beginnings of an "intramural crisis of alliance.") Laval was delayed by fog on his way to Munich, did not arrive there until 4:00 A.M. on the 10th, and met Ciano and Hitler that afternoon. That day the Italians moved to occupy Corsica, and the first Italian and German bombers landed in Tunisia, to a very cool reception from the French. Laval could do no more than agree to German and Italian demands; he was not told that France itself was to be invaded on the following day.[4]

3. The table of deployments "Die Gliederung des deutschen Heeres" as of 15 November 1942 shows forty-one complete divisions (three of which were in process of transfer to the East or Africa) under the command of the Commander-in-Chief West (Holland, Belgium, Luxembourg, France, and the Channel Islands).

4. Andreas Hillgruber, *Staatsmänner und Diplomaten bei Hitler* (Frankfurt am Main: Bernard und Graefe Verlag für Wehrwesen, 1967, 1970), Vol. II, pp. 131–147.

The invasion was launched at 7:00 A.M. on the 11th. Hitler ordered it to be described as requested by the French Government, for protection against further raids by the "Anglo-Saxons." He also ordered a secure bridgehead to be established in Tunis; relations with the French High Command there should be as close and friendly as possible, but if they were uncooperative, their division in Tunis was to be disarmed. Two Italian divisions, three German Air Force wings, and six S-boats (with seven more to follow) were ordered to Tunis at once.

It might have been expected that the rapid developments in North Africa would have prompted Hitler to return to his headquarters; but instead he decided to go to the Berghof at Berchtesgaden, and at midday the staff of Wfst received an order to move to Salzburg. They left Rastenburg at 9:25 P.M. that evening, and arrived in Salzburg at 2:20 A.M. on the 14th. Hitler and his entourage arrived at the Berghof the same morning, with Keitel and Jodl taking up offices in the so-called "Small Chancellory" in Berchtesgaden, about twenty minutes from the Berghof, while the staff of Wfst remained in the special train at Salzburg station, a further forty minutes away, and OKH remained in East Prussia. Hitler clearly felt that while he needed his OKW staff because of the North African landings, no decisive action was imminent on the Eastern Front.[5] But on the 13th, Army Group B again reported that the Russians were probing Romanian positions south of Stalingrad, and those of the Hungarians on the Don; and again no countermeasures were ordered.

Hitler's tendency to withdraw when under stress had appeared before—for example, after the failure of his attempted putsch in 1923, on the death of his favorite niece, Geli Raubal, in 1931, and during the crushing of the SA in 1934. All these withdrawals were brief (two days or less) and were associated with situations in which he had lost the initiative and/or could not decide what to do next.

5. Hitler's operations order (OKH/Gen. St. d. H./op. Abt. [I], Nr. 420817/42 of 14 October 1942) stated: "The Russian himself is seriously weakened by the recent battles, and will not in winter 1942–43 be able to deploy as many forces as in the previous winter." A "short report on the state of the enemy" by Foreign Armies East on 12 November 1942 (*KTB/OKW*, Vol. II, Part II, p. 1306) said only that "an attack against Romanian 3rd Army must be expected soon," but attributed to it only the limited aim of cutting the railroad to Stalingrad, to force a retreat by German forces further east, so that the Volga supply line could be restored.

Speer notes that Hitler had shown signs of overwork before the war, and at such times would appear absentminded, indulge in long monologues, or fall silent, but would recover after a few weeks at the Berghof.[6] Speer also observes that prior to the Russian campaign, Hitler's method of work was "staccato," flurries of activity alternating with spells of indolence. After June 1941, however, he adopted strictly disciplined work methods, which, in Speer's view, ran counter to his nature and affected the quality of his decisions. In short, Speer says that the quality of Hitler's decision-making deteriorated under stress. ("Earlier he had made decisions with almost sportive ease: now, he had to force them out of his exhausted brain.")[7] As Fest points out, referring to the North African invasion, "Instead of consulting and organizing defensive measures, he merely took satisfaction in the fact that it was he against whom this gigantic armada had been assembled."[8] His attempt, when he finally did return, to postpone discussion with Zeitzler may have been prompted by a desire not to appear overcome by events, or it may simply be that he knew that Zeitzler wanted to discuss withdrawal from Stalingrad, had already decided not to permit this, and therefore did not want to discuss it. He had already written on 20 November to Mussolini: "I am one of those men who in adversity simply becomes more determined."[9]

The 14th saw the return of Warlimont to Rastenburg at 6:00 P.M., and the appointment of the head of Air Fleet II, Field Marshal Kesselring, as Commander-in-Chief South. Army Group B yet again reported big enemy concentrations in the Stalingrad area, but no action in response was ordered either that day or the next.

By the 16th, however, some notice again was being taken of the Eastern Front. Hitler decided that Manstein, who was still with the 11th Army, should become Commander-in-Chief of Army Group A (which was still, at least nominally, being commanded by Hitler since the dismissal of List in September), but only after 11th Army had carried out an operation in the northern sector of the Front at

6. Hildegard von Kotze, ed., *Heeresadjutant bei Hitler, 1938–1943: Aufzeichnungen des Major Engel* (Stuttgart: Deutsche Verlags-Anstalt, 1974), p. 136.

7. Speer, *Inside the Third Reich*, pp. 400–402.

8. Joachim C. Fest, *Hitler* (New York: Harcourt Brace Jovanovich, 1974), p. 663.

9. Walter Warlimont, *Inside Hitler's Headquarters, 1939–45*, trans. R. H. Barry (London: Weidenfeld and Nicolson, 1964), p. 277.

Toropets. A number of detailed decisions about movements of divisions were taken on this day, but none of them affected what was in fact the most threatened sector of the Front, namely Army Group B. In contradiction of his confident statement to Ciano on the 9th, that the opening of a "Second Front" in North Africa removed the threat to other areas, Hitler now declared that it was more important to secure the north than to mount a spring offensive in the east, and ordered the strengthening of forces in Norway and Finland, clearly fearing some action by the Swedes, who were said to have been "very impressed" by the North African landings. At the same time, his apprehensions about Crete and the Balkans caused him to order one of the new Air Force field divisions to be sent to Crete, and the Peloponnese to be strengthened.

Engel records that the atmosphere of the situation conference was very bitter, and that Hitler, who had just held a prolonged discussion with Himmler, complained at length about his deteriorating endurance, the strengthening of his enemies as the war went on, and the attempts to destroy his work which were being made by groups drawn from the intelligentsia, the churches, and high-ranking officers.[10] He received a present of caviar and confectionery from Marshal Antonescu, and ordered it to be destroyed at once, presumably for fear that it was poisoned. On the following day, 17 November, before leaving the Berghof, he ordered 6th Army to capture the remainder of Stalingrad as quickly as possible.[11]

The 18th was spent in preparations for disarming the French Army and seizing the French Fleet in its base at Toulon; an order to do so was issued at 1:54 A.M. on the 19th. Four and a half hours later, at 6:30 A.M. (7:30 Moscow time), Voronov heralded the beginning of the Soviet counteroffensive with an 80-minute bombardment of Romanian 3rd Army by 3,500 guns.[12] Engel noted "a bad evening conference."[13]

By the next day, 20 November, Zeitzler was reporting deep Soviet penetrations of the Romanian positions. In the afternoon, Hitler ordered the attack group of 11th Army to be disbanded, and

10. Kotze, ed., *Heeresadjutant bei Hitler*, pp. 136–137.
11. This order was transmitted by Paulus to his subordinate commanders as AOK6 Ia Nr. 4640/42 of 17 November 1942.
12. Zhukov, *Vospominaniia*, p. 407.
13. Kotze, ed., *Heeresadjutant bei Hitler*, p. 137.

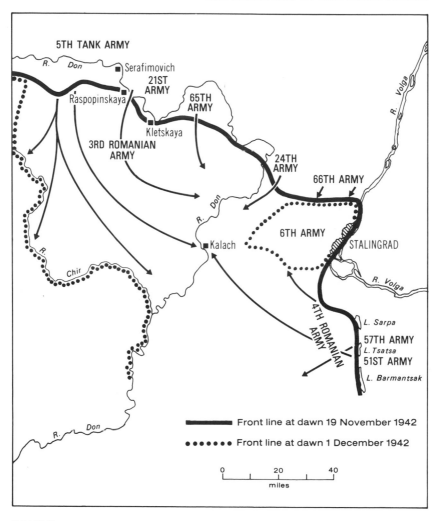

MAP 3.
THE SOVIET COUNTEROFFENSIVE,
19–30 NOVEMBER 1942

its Commander, Manstein, to take command of Army Group B's forces at Stalingrad (6th Army, 4th Panzer Army, and the Romanian 3rd Army), under the new title of Army Group Don. Apart from this, no decisions were reported, and Engel wrote in his diary: "The Führer himself is completely uncertain what to do." [14] Also on

14. Ibid.

the 20th, the second pincer of the Soviet attack was activated from south of Stalingrad, against 4th Panzer Army and the Romanian 4th Army.[15] In the evening, Hitler ordered 6th Army to hold the western and southern corners of its position in all circumstances. Various units were ordered to the area to reinforce it; they comprised two Panzer divisions and one Mountain division immediately, with two Infantry divisions to come later. These were far from adequate to plug the gaping holes in the front, but all that could be found.

Part of the 21st was occupied with moving the field squadron of Wfst from Salzburg railway station to the Jäger barracks in Strub, near Berchtesgaden, where it would be closer to the Berghof and the "Small Chancellory." Ironically, the especially strong and well-equipped 22nd Airborne Division arrived in Crete, where there would be no one for it to fight. Jodl suggested evacuation of the Volga front, but Hitler refused.

On the 22nd, troops of the Soviet Stalingrad and Southeastern Fronts joined up at Kalach, thereby encircling 6th Army in the land bridge between the Volga and the Don. At midday, Hitler ordered everyone to return to the FHQ in Rastenburg. Considering how the situation was developing, the arrangements were strangely leisurely, the main body of Wfst not leaving until the afternoon of the 23rd, and not arriving till the early morning of the 25th. Paulus was ordered to move his headquarters into Stalingrad, and as Manstein had taken over the newly created Army Group Don, Colonel-General von Kleist (C-in-C of 1st Panzer Army) was appointed in his stead to command Army Group A. In the afternoon, Paulus received a Führer order to hold his position; the order contained a reference to the possibility that the Army would be supplied from the air. At 7:00 P.M., Paulus requested freedom of action, stating that the situation might compel him to abandon Stalingrad and his northern front, that is, to retreat westward. Hitler replied to the effect that "6th Army must know that I'm doing everything to help and relieve it," and therefore tied Paulus tightly to Stalingrad city.

The essential problem here concerned the airlift. Supply of troops by air was not in itself a novelty, and both Germans and Russians had practiced it successfully, but the size of the encircled force created a problem of unprecedented scale.[16] Hitler arrived

---

15. Zhukov, *Vospominaniia*, pp. 410–411.

16. Cajus Bekker, *The Luftwaffe War Diaries*, trans. and ed. Frank Ziegler (London: Corgi, 1969), pp. 351–354.

back at Rastenburg late on the evening of 23 November, to find Zeitzler waiting for him with a list of matters on which decisions were overdue, and attempted to put him off to the next day, but was unsuccessful. No reports had been received from either 4th Panzer Army or 6th Army, as their telephone communications were cut, but radio contact was established with Paulus, and Hitler spoke to him at 9:30 P.M., reiterating the standfast order, and ending his message with more references to an airlift. Both Zeitzler and the Chief of Staff of the Air Force, Jeschonnek, had the deepest misgivings about the possibility of a successful airlift, because of the shortage of suitable aircraft, the limited capacity of the airfields in the Stalingrad area, and the bad weather. However, Göring, who arrived at FHQ on the 24th, insisted (during a stormy meeting in which he and Zeitzler almost came to blows) that the Air Force could do it.

Göring was still nominally Hitler's successor, but the Air Force's failure to win the Battle of Britain and to stop the Allied bombing over Germany had considerably reduced his status within the hierarchy. He undoubtedly saw the Stalingrad airlift as an opportunity to regain some of his lost standing, and insisted that it could be done, over the protests of Jeschonnek and the violently expressed skepticism of Zeitzler, both of whom were to be proved right.

The airlift requirement was from a minimum of 500 tons a day to a desirable 700 tons. On no occasion was even the minimum figure remotely approached; the maximum in one day was 289 tons, and the average under 100 tons a day.[17]

The 25th of November saw Hitler expressing confidence about the situation of 6th Army. Two Infantry divisions of reinforcements had arrived, another was on its way, and it was hoped that two more Panzer divisions would arrive soon. The Chief of the German Military Mission in Romania, General Hauffe, asked Marshal Antonescu for fresh forces.

The situation in fact did not justify much confidence: 6th Army had managed to hold on all fronts, but its supply situation was critical, and the weather, plus Soviet superiority in fighters and the large numbers of anti-aircraft guns which they were beginning to install in regained territory along the flight path,[18] made it doubtful

17. The figures are taken from a graph in Bekker, ibid., p. 371.
18. Alexander M. Samsonov, "Stalingrad: The Relief," in *History of the Second World War*, ed. Barrie Pitt (London: Purnell, 1967), Vol. III, p. 1302.

that the required 700 tons a day could be supplied, especially as Air Fleet IV needed 500 aircraft for the airlift, and had only 298. The General commanding 8th Air Corps, Fiebig, proposed to Hitler that 6th Army should disengage westward, to attack again at a later date. This was refused. So was Manstein's proposal that, rather than attempting to push a relief force through from the southwest, 6th Army should break out in that direction, while he safeguarded its rear by holding down the Russians northeast of it.[19]

However, on 26 November, 6th Army evacuated its western bridgehead, on the Don, in order to shorten its line and make forces available for an attack to the southwest to link up with the expected relieving force. To strengthen the arm of the advocates of evacuation, an Air Force officer, Major Christian, was brought to FHQ in an attempt to convince Hitler that the airlift could not work. He told the Führer, correctly as it turned out, that the most that could be expected would be an average of 100–150 tons a day; but Hitler contradicted him ex cathedra.[20]

On the 28th, a new factor of alarm was introduced into the situation: OKH reported, wrongly, that the Russians were now about to cross the Kerch Straits and seize the Crimea. Zeitzler proposed to send some SS and "alarm units" belonging to Army Commander Ukraine thither. Army Group Don reported that only thirty JU-52's had succeeded in reaching Stalingrad that day (as a JU-52 could carry a payload of only two and a half tons, this means that the supply for that day was only about seventy-five tons). The confusion reigning about the state of affairs on the battlefield was shown by the statement that the German and Romanian forces encircled at Stalingrad totaled about 400,000, whereas in fact they were actually about 100,000 fewer. (The Russians have claimed 330,000, but this appears to be based on a rule of thumb calculation of twenty-two divisions multiplied by 15,000 men.) It was also reported, more correctly, that strong Soviet forces were preparing to attack the Italian 8th and Hungarian 2nd Armies, on the Don between Voronezh and the broken sector formerly held by the Romanian 3rd Army. The only riposte that could be made to this was for Hitler to accept Zeitzler's proposal to bring one division from the West to this sector. At 4:30 P.M., Rommel arrived at FHQ to report on the situation in Libya. He told Hitler that Africa was lost, and that the

19. Erich von Manstein, *Lost Victories* (London: Methuen, 1958), pp. 304–309.
20. Kotze, ed., *Heeresadjutant bei Hitler*, p. 140.

only course possible was to extract the Afrika Korps. This led to a shouting match, after which Rommel left for Rome with Göring in the evening.

November 29 passed fairly quietly, except for a request by Kluge, which was refused, for permission to make a minor withdrawal on the front of Army Group Center. The military commander in France (Stülpnagel) pointed out that some of Hitler's orders were violations of French sovereignty; but Hitler made it clear that he wanted newly-occupied France exploited for war materials as much as possible, and was not overly concerned with legal niceties.

The month ended with increasing reports of an imminent Soviet attack against the Italians and Hungarians, and a spate of decisions by Hitler, most of them concerned not with the Eastern Front but the Mediterranean. He criticized the Army strongly for failing to supply the Italians and Romanians with adequate numbers of anti-tank guns, and ordered these to be provided from captured French stocks. He also remarked that the German formations behind the two satellite armies needed more heavy weapons, and he decided, belatedly, to reinforce the threatened fronts. He then turned to the Mediterranean. He felt that the French Mediterranean coast was not threatened, except perhaps for the Italian-held sectors, so that three divisions could be withdrawn to prepare for "Operation Gisela" (intervention in Spain and Portugal if the British landed there). He ordered the SD (Security Service) to find hidden French arms stocks as soon as possible, and that French officers were no longer to be released on parole. Four additional batteries of 88-mm guns were ordered to Tunis and Bizerte, bringing the total ordered to Africa to 560 guns, an entire month's production. In addition, he ordered one hundred 88-mm anti-aircraft batteries with German crews to be sent to northern Italy, which had suffered heavy air attacks. Commander-in-Chief South was ordered to disarm the French forces and warships in Tunis, and hand over the coastal batteries and ships to the German Navy. One regiment of infantry was released to him for immediate dispatch to Tunis, and a second regiment was ordered to Italy by air for subsequent transit to Tunis.

The detailed pattern of decision-making is dealt with in Chapter Seven, but at this point two features may be noted. One is that tabulating the number of decisions taken (without discriminating between major and minor ones, or attempting to assess "quality") shows a "diffusion" into areas other than those of the main offensive. The second is that this occurred in a context of increased decision-making in respect to some areas even as a perceived need arose for decisions in respect to others. The pattern may be seen in the following table:

Area of decision	No. of decisions		
	28 June–31 July	1–31 August	1 September–19 November
1. Southern sector of Eastern front	14	28	42
2. Other sectors of Eastern Front	2	33	27
3. Other areas	2	4	73
Total	18	65	142
Daily average decisions taken	0.53	2.1	1.8

The reasons for this are discussed in Chapter Seven, but it is sufficient to note here that the decision-making load more than trebled as the pre-crisis period progressed, thereby increasing the stress on the dominant decision-maker, and that he was required (or imposed the requirement on himself) to devote increasing attention first to other areas of the Eastern Front and then to other parts of Germany's defense perimeter, without any diminution in the perceived decision-making requirement for the area of primary initial concern, the summer offensive in Southwestern USSR. Hitler was, in fact, becoming involved in multiple crises.

CHAPTER FIVE

The Crisis Continued:
December 1942–2 February 1943

BY THE END of November, the range of alternatives available to German decision-making for saving the situation at Stalingrad had been narrowed, in that one option—an unaided breakout by the forces surrounded there toward the main German forces—had been closed off. Initially, the closure was volitional, because Hitler refused to countenance the abandonment of Stalingrad which it would have entailed; but within a few days, the strengthening of Soviet forces in the Don-Volga corridor put it beyond resurrection, so OKH and OKW ceased to urge it upon Hitler. Thereafter, their efforts centered on an attempt by Manstein in December to open a passage to Stalingrad from the southwest. On the purpose of this passage there was never clear agreement between Hitler, Manstein, and Paulus. Hitler saw it as intended to enable additional forces to be introduced to hold the city, while Manstein's intention was to withdraw the trapped forces through the corridor. But when the Russians halted the relief expedition, about twenty miles from its objective, Hitler refused to reply to Manstein's request for the trapped forces to be given freedom of action to fight their way out toward him; and when Manstein, taking Hitler's silence for consent, himself ordered Paulus to do so, Paulus refused, claiming lack of fuel. After this failure, the number of Stalingrad-related decisions taken at FHQ fell to a very low level, indicating that the decision-makers there had at least tacitly reconciled themselves to loss of the besieged forces.

By contrast, Zeitzler and Jodl maintained pressure on Hitler to save Army Group A by withdrawing it from the Caucasus to west of the Don, and finally wrung a decision from him to that effect near the end of December. Characteristic features of December and January were: (1) a marked increase in the number of matters discussed but left undecided; and (2) diffusion of decision-making, in terms both of geographical expansion and of descent often into trivia. In particular, Hitler showed an increasing preoccupation with the fear of Turkish entry into the war, an Allied attack on the Balkans, and the need to arm Bulgaria to resist it. But he twice rejected Mussolini's advice to give up the war in Russia.

On the very last day of December, an attack by German heavy warships on a convoy bound for Murmansk was repelled by the inferior British escort; as a result, Hitler decided to scrap all the large surface warships. This decision was partially rescinded, but only after several weeks of argument by the Naval Commander-in-Chief, Raeder, and his successor, Dönitz. These aspects of Hitler's decision-making activity are discussed in detail at the end of this chapter.

December opened with one of Mussolini's increasingly infrequent assertions of independence. When he met Göring in Rome on 1 December, he told him bluntly that the war in Russia now no longer had any point, and should be wound up as soon as possible so that troops could be brought back to the West and the Mediterranean to face the expected Anglo-American invasion. There is no record of Hitler's reaction to Göring's report of the conversation. On 18 December, when Ciano met Hitler at Rastenburg, the Italian Foreign Minister put the same proposition to him again, and was told at length that it was impossible.

On 2 December, 1st Panzer Army was permitted to withdraw from east of Mozdok, in order to free forces for mobile fighting, while it was decided to mount Manstein's relief operation toward Stalingrad on 9 December. As if to counterbalance 1st Panzer Army's permission to withdraw, Army Group Center was ordered to undertake an offensive with four Panzer divisions to reestablish contact with its isolated "hedgehog" position at Velikiye Luki. A proposal by Army Group North to replace one infantry division with an Air Force Field Division was accepted.

The new "Tiger" tanks, from which Hitler expected a great deal, were scheduled to be sent to Tunis, but Hitler decided to try them out first in the so-called "land bridge" of Army Group North. He decided that the coastal artillery in the West was paying insufficient attention to firing at sea targets, and ordered its Army units to be

subordinated to the Naval Coast Artillery. He expressed dissatisfaction with the growing losses of the transport ships in the Mediterranean, but did not order any specific action to be taken, and he
deferred a decision on the command of forces in Tunisia pending
negotiations with the Italians.

On 3 December, the only decision reported was to set up an
Army headquarters (5th Panzer Army) in Tunis, and nominate
Colonel-General von Arnim to command it. As an indication of the
confusion prevailing in the Stalingrad area, it was reported on this
day that the encircled units of 6th Army had a comprised strength
not of 400,000 men, as previously thought, but "about 300,000."

Consideration was given on the 4th to economizing in forces by
giving up the bridgehead at Voronezh, but 2nd Army reported that
its present position was better than the one it would have to take
up if withdrawn, so it was left where it was. Hitler ordered all Tiger
tanks in Italy to be sent not to the German-Italian Panzer Army
(DIPA) in Libya but to the new 5th Panzer Army in Tunisia. During
the evening, he agreed to the withdrawal of the extreme southern
units of 3rd Panzer Corps of Army Group A, and ordered the 7th
Panzer Division from France to Army Group Don.

On 7 December, Hitler outlined how he thought the situation
would develop. The "Anglo-Saxons" would make for the Balkans,
and possibly put naval forces into the Adriatic. Crete was safe, but
Rhodes and the Peloponnese were threatened. Turkey's attitude
was unclear, and Bulgaria must stay prepared against a possible
Turkish attack. Hungarian troops were not to be deployed in Croatia, for fear of Hungarian expansionist aims. Above all, a group of
light (Jäger) and Mountain divisions, recruited from Army Group
North and the (Austrian) SS Prinz Eugen Division, must be formed
in the Balkans, with the ultimate aim of producing a mixed operational reserve with a strong German nucleus.

This analysis was wrong in most respects. The "Anglo-Saxons"
were not contemplating invading the Balkans, and naval forces did
not enter the Adriatic until Allied armies were installed in Italy late
in the following year. And while Hitler's preoccupation with Turkey
was shared by Churchill, there was at that time no likelihood that
Turkey would enter the war soon or at all. The decision to form an
operational reserve for the Balkans was therefore erroneous.

No attempt to explain why Hitler's analysis took this form can be
more than speculative. As a citizen of the former Austro-Hungarian

Empire, which included most of the subsequent Yugoslav state and large areas later ceded to Romania, Hitler would have been well aware of Balkan issues. His reluctance to allow Hungarian troops into Croatia (which under Austro-Hungary had been administered from Budapest) suggests that this factor was in his mind. As for Turkey, he was certainly aware of the attempt made in 1915 to remove Turkey from the Central Powers by the unsuccessful Gallipoli invasion. He may have known also of Churchill's personal role in initiating it, and of its secondary purpose of opening a supply route to Russia. As for Greece and Bulgaria, he was aware that in the First World War the Allies had occupied northern Greece and had succeeded, after initial setbacks, in forcing Bulgaria into becoming the first German ally to capitulate. Hitler's analysis would therefore seem to have been based more on interpretation of the present in terms of the past than on the realities of the situation at the time. In respect to Greece, however, his belief that Crete was safe while Rhodes and the Peloponnese were not probably had its basis in the fact that Crete had a German garrison, whereas the other places were wholly or mainly garrisoned by Italians. While at this stage of the war it was not customary to refer to the shortcomings of Germany's allies, the inferior equipment and lower motivation of Italian troops had been demonstrated in Albania, Greece, Russia, and North Africa; and only a few days before, Mussolini had given further cause to doubt Italian commitment by urging Hitler to end the war in Russia.

In respect to North Africa, there was a difference of opinion between Hitler, who wanted to hold on to the Mersa Brega position, and Mussolini and Rommel, who wanted to abandon it. The dispute was solved by the DIPA's lack of fuel for a withdrawal. Hitler also ordered the Air Force to attack only enemy-held harbors, when not engaged in local support of the Army.

Sexual intercourse between German women and prisoners-of-war was punishable by death for the prisoner and a long prison sentence for the woman. With large numbers of prisoners-of-war working unsupervised on farms, and so many German men away in the forces, the law had been frequently broken, and the heavy penalty caused much resentment, especially among troops who arrived home on leave to find their wives in prison and their children in orphanages. The existence of strong public sentiment in favor of a lesser penalty was mentioned by the Security Service in a number of its bi-weekly reports on public opinion,[1] and was reinforced by materials[2] from most of the district courts (which were required to submit monthly reports on public opinion as well as on trends in crime). Goebbels raised the issue on 8 December, but Hitler refused to allow any amendment. At the midday situation conference, he received without comment a report of Manstein's impression of the military situation, denied Kluge's request for permission to make a tactical withdrawal at Velikiye Luki, ordered the French police and mobile guard to be strengthened and the French to take responsibility for their own anti-aircraft defense, agreed with Rommel's diplomatically expressed intention to hold the Mersa Brega position "as long as possible," and ordered a light division with 18th Army in Russia to be relieved by an Air Force Field Division from 18 December and sent to northern Greece. In the evening, he drew the attention of Commander-in-Chief South to the large differences between enemy and Axis sea transport capabilities to North Africa and sought information on Axis carrying capacity, on which "far-reaching decisions depend."

On 9 December, having spent half the previous month at the Berghof, Hitler expressed the desire to go there again "for a longish time," in order to "clear his head for new decisions." Zeitzler asked him to stay at FHQ while the situation on the southern part of the Eastern Front was so critical, but Hitler did not finally abandon the idea of leaving until the 15th.

It was decided on the 9th that the attempt to relieve 6th Army should begin on the 11th or 12th if the weather was good. Hitler expressed high confidence that the old position on the Don would be regained, and that the first phase of the Russian winter offensive had ended indecisively. For the Mediterranean theatre, he ordered Air Fleet II to be strengthened for use mainly against Algerian harbors; and its range increased by stockpiling fuel in Sardinia. He expressed the intention to reinforce Tunis, on the grounds that Allied forces moving up from southern Tunisia were not very strong.

This decision was correct in terms of the immediate situation, but indicates continued conceptual rigidity. There was in fact an alternative, which was to abandon North Africa altogether. Rom-

---

1. Bundesarchiv, Koblenz, Series R58, passim, especially R68/176/93–95; and Louis P. Lochner, ed., *The Goebbels Diaries* (London: Hamish Hamilton, 1948), p. 177.

2. Bundesarchiv, Koblenz, Series R22, passim.

mel had urged this in the previous month and been abused for suggesting it. Since then, the scale of the Anglo-American effort, and especially of their domination of Mediterranean sea and air routes, had become sufficiently apparent for Hitler to express concern at losses of transports and inadequacy of Axis resources (on 2 and 9 December) and to order (on 9 December) arrangements to increase the strength and range of Air Fleet II. At no point is there any evidence that the pros and cons of attempting to retain North Africa in the face of Allied sea and air superiority were considered anywhere within FHQ, despite the difficulties that were being experienced in finding forces for the Eastern Front (where the attempt to relieve Stalingrad was about to be launched), to say nothing of Hitler's perception that the Balkans also needed reinforcement. Hitler reiterated this on 9 December, wanting special attention paid to Southeastern Europe, where his distrust of Turkey had grown to the extent that he began to perceive the arming of Bulgaria as urgent.

December 10 saw the finalizing of the plan for the relief of 6th Army. It was to begin on 12 December, Phase One comprising an attack from Kotelnikovo northeastwards, Phase Two an attack out of the Chir bridgehead, and Phase Three a breakout to the southwest by 6th Army itself. Hitler ordered two divisions to be brought to Kotelnikovo, and a further attack group of two Panzer divisions formed for Phase Two of the operation. One of these latter two was still in France, and, as Warlimont points out, its first unit could not possibly arrive in the east before 26 December.[3] An attempt by Commander-in-Chief West to remove the German plenipotentiary-general in Vichy, General Neubronn, was vetoed, but Hitler did agree to release all French railway personnel from prisoner-of-war camps, to improve the operation of the French railways. A further indication of the shortage of German reserves was his order to send the so-called Afrika Brigade 999 (a penal unit consisting entirely of military offenders) not, as originally intended, to Crete but to Tunis.

The Italians had asked for the French destroyers captured at Tunis, so the original intention to man them with Germans was abandoned, and the Italian Navy was told it could have them.

On the 11th, still preoccupied with sea transport in the Mediterranean, Hitler ordered landing craft to be built in the French Mediterranean ports. He also ordered 11th Panzer Division, which was

3. *KTB/OKW*, Vol. II, Part II, pp. 1110–1111.

situated at the Chir bridgehead in readiness for use in Phase Two of Manstein's relief operation, to be moved at once to the Kotelnikovo area, so that it could be used instead in Phase One on the next day.

The attempt to relieve 6th Army began on the 12th and made good initial progress. But before the end of the first day, Manstein had already asked for two additional divisions to protect the flank of the breakthrough force, and been refused. More than that, Hitler began tampering with the deployments of 1st Panzer Army in Army Group A, by proposing to detach the SS "Wiking" division, in order to form a strong motorized breakthrough group with another Panzer division. In Libya, the British 8th Army began another offensive, but no steps to counter it were ordered. According to the surviving fragments of the stenographic record of the midday conference, Hitler was more worried about the Eastern Front, asking, a few hours after the beginning of Hoth's operation toward Stalingrad, "has anything catastrophic happened?"[4] Decisions to arrange, in the near future, meetings with the Spanish Chief of Staff, and with Antonescu, Mussolini, and the Bulgarians, indicated the diffusion of Hitler's attention between the various possible threats that he perceived.

On the 13th, he considered withdrawing the 1st Panzer Army from the Caucasus altogether, and took no action on a report by Manstein that the forces he had were insufficient either to break through to Stalingrad or even to protect his lengthening flanks. All that Manstein gained was a decision by Hitler not to move the 11th Panzer Division from the Chir bridgehead, but instead to give him 17th Panzer Division. On 15 December, Hoth's attempt to break through to Stalingrad came temporarily to a halt. The expected major attack on the Italian 8th Army had not yet occurred, and Hitler concluded optimistically that it appeared to be designed only to pin down reserves.

On 16 December, attention moved to problems of partisan warfare, and Commander-in-Chief Southeast was ordered to begin operations against the partisans in Croatia. On the 17th, there began a shuffling of coastal batteries from France to Crete, Lemnos, and Norway. The expected Soviet attack on the Italian 8th Army began,

---

4. Fragment No. 8 of transcripts of midday situation conferences, cited by Warlimont in *KTB/OKW*, Vol. II, Part II, p. 1121.

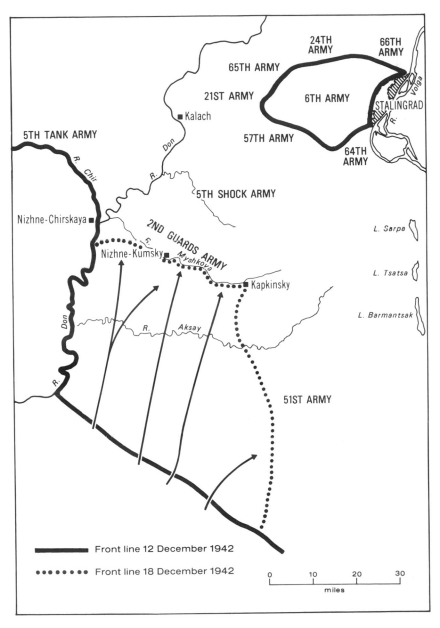

MAP 4.
THE RELIEF ATTEMPT, 12–18 DECEMBER 1942

and a large breakthrough was achieved at once. The Chir line was also breached, and Hitler ordered withdrawals in both sectors. However, he yet again declined to allow 6th Army to attempt to break out from Stalingrad toward the stalled relieving force. In the Mediterranean, Rommel disengaged from Mersa Brega and continued his retreat. Hitler ordered Speer to surrender 200,000 industrial workers to the Army, receiving 150,000 overage soldiers in exchange. Ciano and Cavallero, the Italian Chief of Staff, arrived at FHQ for talks, in the course of which Ciano reiterated Mussolini's argument of 1 December on the need to end the war in Russia. He was given a long list of reasons why this could not be done.

In the memorandum that Ciano wrote for Mussolini,[5] Hitler is reported as having said that in the winter of 1940–41, particularly during the visit by Foreign Minister Molotov to Berlin, every effort had been made to direct Soviet ambitions toward "Central Asia," but the Russians had instead brought up their historic claims on Finland, the Dardanelles, and the Balkans. The Russia of Stalin followed the path chosen by Peter the Great, of expansion toward the North and Southwest, and had not been prepared to follow German proposals directing her toward India and the Persian Gulf, because those were secondary to, and would follow from, attainment of hegemony over Europe. Rumors some months previously of Soviet interest in a separate peace had been spread by the Russians themselves in order to spur their allies on to give them more armaments and secure the opening of a Second Front.

If an agreement were reached, the Russians would break it as soon as they had six months to build up their strength, and Germany could not retreat to a shorter defense line because that would mean transferring indispensable sources of food and raw materials from German to Soviet control. There would be no saving in demands on the air force, because it would take at least six months to redeploy. For that reason, it would be too dangerous to withdraw air strength from the Russian front, as it would be needed there in case the Russians broke the agreement. The only advantage, reduction in manpower losses, was not sufficient to outweigh the disadvantages. In any event, an "understanding" with Russia would

5. Frederick W. D. Deakin, *The Brutal Friendship: Mussolini, Hitler and the Fall of Italian Fascism* (London: Weidenfeld and Nicolson, 1962), pp. 116–117.

not enable the African front to be strengthened, as the constraint there was not lack of troops or material but the difficulties entailed in transporting them across the Mediterranean.

Of the reasons given, most are specious. It is true that in the November 1940 meeting, Molotov had shown little interest in the Asian baits that were dangled before him, and had persisted in detailed questioning about German activities in Finland and the Balkans[6] (which were, of course, part of the preparations for the invasion of the Soviet Union in June 1941), but the "food and raw materials" argument has to be viewed in the light of German ability to attack the Soviet Union in 1941, and come closer to victory without them than at any time after it secured them, and to maintain war production, which peaked in July 1944,[7] a year after they had all been lost. The argument that air forces could not be moved from one front to another in less than six months was nonsensical; in the four weeks since the launching of the Soviet counteroffensive, many hundreds of transport aircraft had been brought east for the Stalingrad airlift, whose failure resulted from inadequate payloads for the sheer size of the beleaguered force, enemy activities in the air corridor, and the short daylight hours of the Russian winter; the ability of the Luftwaffe to move and maintain a large number of aircraft was not in question, and was the most successful aspect of the ill-fated operation.

Most specious of all was the argument that the major constraint was not shortage of manpower or material, but of transport. Shortages of both manpower and weaponry have already been seen to figure prominently both in FHQ conferences and in requests from the field commanders. And granted the difficulties of crossing the Mediterranean in the face of Allied sea and air power, the most obvious consequence of an "understanding" with the Soviets (or even a more modest decision, to allow the force at Stalingrad to attempt to fight its way out through the "corridor" which Manstein was at that very time essaying to open) would have been the freeing of the large force of transport aircraft then engaged in the Stalingrad airlift, and the fighter aircraft which were attempting to protect them,

6. Alan Bullock, *Hitler: A Study in Tyranny* (Harmondsworth: Penguin Books, 1962), pp. 617–619.

7. Albert Speer, *Inside the Third Reich* (London: Weidenfeld and Nicolson, 1970), pp. 295–296.

to supplement those already flying troops to Africa. The conclusion is inescapable that for Hitler the war in the East was beyond arguments, and all else secondary. This, as will be seen, was to change somewhat, but only after the failure of the relief attempt.

As the Russian breakthrough on the Italian front along the Don deepened and widened on the 19th, three more divisions were ordered from the west to the east, and one was ordered from Russia to France for "recuperation." Two new SS divisions were ordered to be deployed in the west, two divisions were ordered to Tunisia, and the calling up of conscripts previously rejected as unfit was decreed. Manstein sent an urgent message asking for full discretion to free 6th Army by allowing it to break out to the southwest toward the relieving force, received no reply, and finally, on his own initiative, ordered 6th Army to commence breaking through to the southwest at once. This brought a violent diatribe from Hitler against Manstein, but had no other result, as Paulus, reluctant to disobey his previous orders from Hitler, claimed that 6th Army had insufficient fuel to move. The Commander of the Replacement Army (Fromm) and Speer complained to Hitler about difficulties in armament supply, and received a calm hearing, but no decision.

On the 20th, a belated decision was taken to replace the Italian 8th Army with a German group of army size, and to deploy the three divisions ordered from the west, as well as two others from elsewhere on the Eastern Front, to Army Group B. The 16th Motorized Division, which had been "floating" in the Kalmyk steppe, received belated permission to pull back, and the SS "Wiking" Division from Army Group B was ordered to replace it, a contradictory decision, as SS "Wiking" was scheduled on the same day to be transferred to the 4th Panzer Army. Hitler discussed the idea that 6th Army should withdraw from Stalingrad, but probably only so as to reject it. Certainly no withdrawal was ordered, then or later.

The situation conference on the 21st was dominated by Manstein's reports that 4th Panzer Army could not make any further progress toward Stalingrad, about thirty miles away, and that 6th Army had fuel sufficient to move only twenty miles. Zeitzler, after a long and stormy session with Hitler and the Chief of Staff of the Air Force (Jeschonnek), managed only to extract a decision from Hitler that 6th Army could break out provided that it could also hold on to Stalingrad, a nonsensical decision which led Greiner to write in his notes on the meetings that "it seems as if the Führer is no longer capable of decisions."[8] However, a decision was made that thirty to sixty "storm brigades," each with a strength of one reinforced battalion, should be set up as mobile defense forces, though what function they could fulfill in the short term is unclear.

Greiner's comment highlights the problem of the deterioration under stress of the decision-making capacity of Hitler, and therefore of the whole highly centralized High Command machine. The relief attempt forms a self-contained "episode" twelve days in duration (12–23 December), and it is worth considering at this point Hitler's decisions regarding it.

On 9 December, he had authorized it to begin on the 11th or 12th, weather permitting. On the 10th, the plan had been finalized: it was to consist of sequenced attacks from outside the pocket, followed by a breakout from the inside. Clearly, the operation had to be a fast one, as the longer it lasted, the more time there would be for the Red Army to bring up reinforcements and frustrate it. But Hitler ordered a Panzer division to be brought from France to join one already in Russia for the second sequenced attack, rather than using one of the many Panzer divisions that were already in Russia on other, quieter sections of the front. The division from France would not even begin to arrive until 26 December, a fortnight after the first attack had begun, and the second attack could not be launched without it.

The sources are not clear as to why Hitler, on 10 December, attempted to detach the Panzer division SS "Wiking" from Army Group A, in order to team it with another (unidentified) Panzer division to form a breakthrough group. This could have been either an attempt to find a substitute for the division from France, the result of belated realization that the latter could not reach Russia in time, or the reconsideration of an already rejected request from Manstein that same day for two additional divisions. In either case, the change of mind shows Hitler reacting adversely to time constraints, and, in addition, suggests that he had difficulty in choosing between alternatives, namely the breakthrough and the future of Army Group A. SS "Wiking" was the strongest division in 1st Panzer Army, which was itself in danger of being cut off in the Cau-

---

8. *KTB/OKW*, Vol. II, Part II, p. 1168.

casus if the attempt to relieve the encircled forces at Stalingrad was a failure. Though close enough to be moved fairly quickly to the breakthrough area, it was not significantly closer than some of the divisions of Army Group Center, which could the more easily have been moved because the front there was relatively quiescent. Hitler's question "has anything catastrophic happened?" which he asked on the 12th only a few hours after the relief operation began, indicates that he was apprehensive.

During the next few days, the following pattern emerges in respect to the relief operation:

Date	Subject	Outcome
13th	Withdrawal of Army Group A from the Caucasus	No decision
	Request from Manstein for reinforcements	No decision
15th	Relief force comes to a halt	No decision
17th	Request for 6th Army to be allowed to break out	Refused
19th	Request of the 17th repeated as matter of urgency	Refused
20th	Contradictory orders on movement of SS "Wiking"	Confusion
	Withdrawal of 6th Army discussed	No decision
21st	6th Army authorized to break out, if it can also hold Stalingrad	Confusion
22nd	Further request for breakout by 6th Army	Refused
23rd	Relief attempt abandoned	

To construct a more complete picture of Hitler's reactions to stress, it is important to look at the other decisions taken by him while the relief attempt was in progress. They can be divided by area ("Eastern Front" and "Other"), and by category of decision (Action initiated, Action refused, No decision, Contradictory decision).

The decision-making pattern for 12–23 December comes out as follows:

	Eastern Front	*Other*
Action initiated	4	7
Action refused	4	1
No decision	3	1
Contradictory decision	3	0

There is a clear difference between the "Eastern Front" and "Other" categories: time constraints were operative to a greater extent on the Eastern Front than elsewhere, but it is precisely in Eastern Front decisions that the greater negativity is found, indicating a serious deterioration in Hitler's decision-making capacity under stress. It is also relevant that the desire to withdraw from a situation in which he had lost the initiative (and which may have accounted for his long absence at the Berghof in November) was again in evidence. On 9 December, he expressed the desire to return to Berchtesgaden to "clear his head for new decisions," and did not abandon the idea until the 15th. A further feature of this period is that decisions on minor or non-urgent matters predominate. (On 12 December, for example, decisions are taken about a single SS division and the dates for various meetings, but not about the renewed British offensive in Libya; on the 17th, to shuttle minor units from France to the Mediterranean and Norway, but not to permit 6th Army to attack to try to link up with the stalled relieving force; and on the 21st, to form various units of battalion size, but not to permit 6th Army to break out unless it can also hold its existing positions.)

Manstein continued on the 22nd to press for a breakout by 6th Army, but Zeitzler again failed to persuade Hitler to authorize the abandonment of Stalingrad. Engel noted that "almost everybody," including Jodl, Zeitzler, and Manstein, now hoped that Paulus would break out on his own initiative.[9] On this day, the prospects of the airlift, which had grossly failed to meet its targets so far, were further worsened by the loss of the major western terminal airfield at Tatsinskaya. Manstein apparently gave up hope for Stalingrad on the 23rd, and ordered Hoth to abandon his attempts to reach the city, to hold on to his existing position thirty miles south of it with

9. Hildegard von Kotze, ed., *Heeresadjutant bei Hitler, 1938–1943: Aufzeichnungen des Major Engel* (Stuttgart: Deutsche Verlags-Anstalt, 1974), p. 141.

two of his three Panzer divisions, and to dispatch the third one to the Don, where the danger of a Soviet breakthrough to Rostov, which would cut off Army Group A in the Caucasus, was now being taken very seriously.[10]

The remainder of the month was dominated by plans to scrape up reinforcements. On the 24th, it was decided to convert the Croat mountain divisions into a "legion," with German officers and NCOs, two divisions to be ready as soon as possible, and four by the autumn of 1943. Four anti-tank companies were ordered to be released from the West for transfer to the Eastern Front, each to have eighteen heavy anti-tank guns, and movement to begin on 3 January 1943. The anticipated arrival of the new Tiger heavy tanks prompted orders for three Tiger detachments to be established: one, of the Waffen-SS, in January, and two of the Army, one each in February and March. In addition, it was planned to set up about one unit of "Panthers" (the new medium tanks) from personnel of Panzer divisions of the Army each month. Uncertainty about the strength of units prompted the issuing of an order to Army Groups and below for special "counting" parades to be held.

A Führer order for further conduct of the battles on the southern wing of the Eastern Front was drafted on the 26th and released at 3:00 A.M. on the 27th. It emphasized that the main objective for the near future remained the relief of 6th Army. Responsibility for this, as before, was laid on Army Group Don, with the much reduced Army Group B instructed to hold its line so as to prevent the extension of Army Group Don's northern flank, and to protect its rear. Army Group A was ordered to release its railway supply line through Rostov for use by Army Group Don, and to rely entirely on supply by sea across the Kerch Straits. It was also ordered to repel all enemy attacks on its existing positions. Army Group Don was enjoined to hold on to the Kotelnikovo area in all circumstances, and Army Group B either to hold or, where necessary, to win back a line running from Kalitva to the Don. A number of movements of units varying in size from divisions down to battalions were also ordered.

But on the very next day, 28 December, Hitler issued Operations Order No. 2, which made significant alterations. First, it spoke not of relieving 6th Army but of "maintaining it in its for-

10. Erich von Manstein, *Lost Victories* (London: Methuen, 1958), p. 345.

tress," and creating the "preconditions" for its relief. Army Group A, which had been ordered to hold on to its positions, was now told to make a gradual withdrawal into a shortened line. Army Group Don was permitted to make withdrawals westwards, though only when absolutely necessary. Command arrangements were altered, in that Army Group A was subordinated to Army Group Don. A supplement to this order, issued on 31 December, announced the drafting from the West of three elite SS divisions (Leibstandarte, Reich, and Totenkopf) and of the elite Army division "Grossdeutschland" from Army Group Center, to form a strong armored group southeast of Kharkov by the middle of February, for the purpose of relieving 6th Army. In addition, also by mid-February, three infantry divisions from the West were to be assembled south of Kiev. It was envisaged that from the middle of February, if the weather permitted, this group, together with other mobile formations, from Army Groups A and Don, would attack toward Stalingrad north of the Don. Engel indicates that the withdrawal of Army Group A to a narrow bridgehead in the Kuban was approved by Hitler only after a very heated discussion with Zeitzler and Jodl.[11] Other decisions, taken by Hitler on the 29th, demanded the taking of steps against the Soviet truck convoys that were supplying Leningrad across the ice of Lake Ladoga, and the deployment of heavy mortars against the city. The order to transfer three SS divisions to the East was qualified by Hitler's insistence that "Totenkopf" be left in the West to "recuperate" as long as possible. Antiaircraft defenses along the Salonica-Athens railroad were also ordered to be strengthened.

Preoccupation with southeastern Europe was also shown in the issue on 28 December of Directive No. 47, concerning command and defense measures in the southeast. The directive referred to the possibility of attacks in the foreseeable future on Crete and on German and Italian bases in the Aegean Sea and the Balkan Peninsula, with the expectation that these attacks would be supported by risings in the western Balkan countries. Vigilance was also required in respect to Turkey, because of "the increasing influence of the Anglo-Saxon powers" on its attitude. On the 30th, reference was made to the need to fulfill Bulgarian demands for arms broadly and speedily.

11. Kotze, ed., *Heeresadjutant bei Hitler*, p. 143.

The final day of the year saw a temporary shift of attention to naval warfare, in which Hitler interfered only sporadically.[12] The origin of this episode was the sailing from Scotland on 22 December of convoy JW-51B. By 28 December, this convoy, then well to the north of the North Cape of Norway, ran into heavy weather which drove it south, so·that by 30 December it was less than two hundred miles from a group of heavy German warships based in Altenfjord.[13]

On 30 December, at a conference at FHQ, Hitler was adjudicating on a jurisdictional dispute between the Commanders-in-Chief of the Navy, Raeder, and Air Force, Göring, over the control of transport ships in the Mediterranean, and punctuating the proceedings with angry monologues about the deficiencies of the German Navy compared to the British. According to the naval representative at OKW, Admiral Krancke, Hitler said: "Our own Navy is only a copy of the British—and a poor one at that. The warships are not in operational readiness; they are lying idle in the fjords, utterly useless like so much old iron."[14] One of the participants attempted to defend the Navy's inactivity by pointing out that there were no British convoys to or from Murmansk for them to attack. Krancke then reported that he had just received a signal from the Operations Division concerning JW-51B, and asking him to inform the Führer that C-in-C Navy approved in principle the operational use of a cruiser, a pocket battleship, and destroyers. Hitler expressed interest and approval, so late that evening the heavy cruiser *Hipper*, the pocket battleship *Lützow*, and six destroyers put to sea. But Hitler's concern about the possibility of losing large surface ships caused a signal to be sent to the officer-in-charge, Admiral Kummetz, less than an hour after sailing, cautioning against the taking of "great risks," and Hitler told Krancke that he wished to have all reports at once, because he "could not sleep a wink when ships were operating."[15] The inhibiting effect of these cautionary orders contributed to the total failure of the operations; no ships of the convoy were sunk, one German destroyer was lost, the *Hipper*

12. Anthony Martienssen, *Hitler and His Admirals* (London: Secker and Warburg, 1948), p. 3.

13. Dudley Pope, "Battle of the Barents Sea," in *History of the Second World War*, ed. Barrie Pitt (London: Purnell, 1967), Vol. III, pp. 1261–1268.

14. Ibid., p. 1263.

15. Edward P. von der Porten, *The German Navy in World War Two* (London: Pan Books, 1972), pp. 229–232.

was damaged, and the German units turned tail before an inferior but much more confidently handled British escort force.

There would seem to be no doubt that Hitler was hoping to bring in the New Year with the announcement of a naval victory which would to some extent counteract the depressing events on the Eastern Front and in Africa, and he was infuriated by the Navy's failure to deliver one. The outcome was to be a drastic decision on 1 January, and an argument that eventually resulted in Raeder's resignation.

JANUARY 1943

During January 1943, the crisis at Stalingrad moved inexorably to its close. A Soviet offer of surrender terms, made on the 8th, was rejected on the 9th, whereupon the Red Army attacked on the 10th. Within four days, it had captured half of 6th Army's position, deprived it of its main supply airfield, and split it in two. On the 19th, a further Soviet attack across the Don completed the rout of Germany's allies by smashing the Hungarian 2nd Army. The southern "cauldron" at Stalingrad was wiped out on 31 January, and all fighting in the city had ceased by 2 February. However, the German resistance tied up major Soviet forces that could otherwise have been used against Army Group A, thus facilitating its withdrawal to the Taman Peninsula and Rostov, so that by 22 January it was clearly out of danger for the time being.

In Africa, central Tunisia was held, but Rommel's forces continued to retreat toward the old French defense line at Mareth in eastern Tunisia. Raeder resigned over Hitler's decision to scrap the large surface warships, and was succeeded by the U-boat admiral, Dönitz.

Some problems are encountered in attempting to pinpoint decisions taken in early 1943. Responsibility for the war diary had been taken over from 1 January by Professor Dr. P. E. Schramm, but he did not arrive at FHQ until the beginning of March, so the diary for the first two months was reconstructed from the Wfst file and notes which Greiner had continued to keep. Hitler's practice of deciding Eastern Front matters privately with Zeitzler means that probably some decisions, especially short-term ones, went unrecorded, as the OKH diary did not survive the war.

At the midday conference on 1 January, Hitler ordered that wherever possible Army Group A should take with it the civilian population of areas being evacuated. He ordered some units belonging to 10th Panzer Division to be resubordinated, but refused a proposal by Zeitzler to move the 97th Light Division to a flanking position, because he still thought, incorrectly, that the greatest danger facing Army Groups A and Don was a Russian advance southward to Rostov. On this day also, in his disappointment at the results of the naval battle off Bear Island, Hitler decided to scrap the large surface ships, redistribute their crews, and use their guns and armor in building up the defenses of "Fortress Europe."[16] Concern for the southeast and Romania caused him to order strengthening of anti-aircraft on Rhodes, the Salonica-Athens railroad, and in the Romanian oil district, and to place air defense of the Romanian oil district under German control.

On the 2nd, Stalingrad was quiet, Army Group A's withdrawal was proceeding as planned, and arrangements were being made to supply it via the Kerch Straits. Apart from an order affecting a mountain cyclist detachment in Norway, there was neither cause nor opportunity for decisions affecting the Eastern Front. However, differences emerged between Rommel and the Italian General Bastico about future operations in North Africa, on which Mussolini had been asked to rule. Kesselring reported that Mussolini shared Rommel's view, and Hitler decided, in a rare instance of delegation, to accept Mussolini's decision. The major operation pending in Croatia necessitated some adjustment of boundaries between the Italians and Germans there. And to discourage excessive hopes of autonomy in the collaborationist Croatian government, the Foreign Office was told to notify it that the command in areas of Croatia evacuated by the Italians would be taken over by the Germans, not the Croats.

The 3rd saw a number of detailed decisions concerning the transfer of worn-out divisions from the East to the West to recuperate, and the dispatch of the special-duties "Brandenburg" regiment from Russia to Tunisia. Various command proposals for Africa were discussed. It was decided that Kesselring should retain the headship of Air Fleet II in addition to the post of Commander-in-Chief South, and that an Italian Army Command should be formed in Tunisia, unity of leadership being achieved by its de facto subor-

16. Pope, "Battle of the Barents Sea," p. 1269.

dination to the German 5th Panzer Army. Preoccupation with Tunisia was sufficient to cause the rejection of an OKH proposal to send assault gun batteries of 10th Panzer Division and the anti-tank detachment of the Herman Göring Division to the East.

January 4th saw continued inactivity in the East and a scatter of decisions affecting other theatres: Noting the success of Anglo-American air attacks on trains in Western Europe, Hitler ordered German aircraft to be similarly equipped. In view of the difficult food situation in the French Antilles, he agreed to free passage for certain designated ships between there and the United States. He ordered that U-boat bunkers should be built in Marseilles, and that anti-aircraft equipment sent to Romania should be taken over by the Romanians as soon as possible.

January 5 saw a reversion to discussion of the Eastern Front, Scandinavia, and France, but a paucity of decisions. Commander-in-Chief West was ordered to set the French a deadline for surrendering their hidden arms stocks. Some detailed alterations were made in the German command structure in the Central Mediterranean, without reference to the Italians. Bulgarian units were ordered out of an area in Yugoslavia for political and economic reasons, and harsh reprisals were ordered against another Yugoslav town. A request made by Himmler almost four weeks earlier for 10,000 men to replace police losses in Army and partisan area operations was fulfilled by drafting policemen in Germany under the age of thirty-four, replacing them with older men and young conscripts.

January 6 and 7 saw the Eastern Front continuing reasonably quiet, Army Group A continuing to withdraw in good order, and the Stalingrad front quiescent, though 6th Army reported deterioration in the supply situation and condition of the troops, and critical shortages of fuel and ammunition. Zeitzler proposed to withdraw some Army coast defense artillery batteries from the north coast of the Black Sea to the Crimea, but Hitler refused on the grounds that these batteries were the only ones at the disposal of the Armed Forces Command of the Ukraine. A proposal by the 20th (Mountain) Army to take over part of the Finnish coast was rejected on the grounds that it would exclude the navy from coastal defense. Differences of opinion remained over the handling of the situation in Tunisia, but no decisions were taken. The Bulgarian War Minister arrived at FHQ, and the possibilities of an "Anglo-Saxon" attack through Turkey and a defense against it were discussed; but no decisions were made, except to institute arrangements similar to those with the Italians, which placed the German Commander-in-Chief Southeast at the head of the joint command. Discussions in OKW resulted in a resolve to equip the Bulgarian Army as soon as possible for defense against a "modern" opponent by building up one cavalry and ten infantry divisions to full offensive strength and increasing the Bulgarian tank force from a brigade to a division. It was noted that German units would also be required if Thrace was attacked. The Commander-in-Chief Navy, Grand Admiral Raeder, arrived for discussion, in the course of which he submitted his resignation, and the Commander-in-Chief U-boats, Admiral Dönitz, was appointed in his place.[17]

A proposal drawn up by Wfst on the previous day was considered on 7 January; it entailed the transfer of six divisions from the West to Army Groups Center or North in the East, so that experienced eastern divisions could be transferred to the south of the Eastern Front for the pending mobile battle envisaged by Manstein. On the 7th, Commander-in-Chief West was ordered to withdraw three infantry divisions as soon as possible from coastal defense, and to prepare them to begin transport to the east on 10 February; three Air Force Field Divisions would take their place. Commander-in-Chief West and Commander-in-Chief Navy were ordered to report the prospects and requirements for entry into northern Spain and occupation of the northern Spanish ports under operation "Gisela," in accordance with Directive No. 42.[18] Commander-in-Chief South asked for at least two new formations, preferably motorized, for Tunisia, but was told he could expect only the punishment brigade 999 and special force units plus some personnel and material for the German-Italian Panzer Army (DIPA). Kesselring felt strongly that what was being provided was inadequate, and asked for his opinion to be given orally at the conference; Hitler, however, made it clear that he had no intention of sending any formations beyond those already promised. For the first time, serious anxiety began to be felt about the Hungarian 2nd Army on the Don, but no decisions in respect to it were reported.

The partial lull on the Eastern Front, caused mainly by bad weather, continued. On 8 January, the Soviets offered apparently

17. Raeder had apparently been on the point of dismissing Dönitz. See Speer, *Inside the Third Reich*, pp. 373–374.

18. Hugh R. Trevor-Roper, ed., *Hitler's War Directives* (London: Sidgwick and Jackson, 1964), pp. 121–123.

reasonable surrender terms to 6th Army. A number of detailed decisions affecting units of divisional size or below were made. Two artillery schools (at Rügenwalde and Thorn) were ordered to the West. Special care was to be taken to keep SS Totenkopf in the West as long as possible to build it up; its transfer to the East was postponed so that its first units would not reach their intended unloading area till the beginning of March. The 327th Infantry Division of the Army was ordered in its place, to be ready for transfer by the 20th. French prisoners-of-war taken in North Africa were ordered to be released, and the event suitably exploited for propaganda purposes. Commander-in-Chief Southeast was ordered to deploy the 11th Air Force Field Division in the Peloponnese. And, in an expansion of the order of 19 December 1942, 200,000 persons previously found unfit for combat service were ordered to be called up.

Paulus's request for freedom of action having been curtly rejected by Hitler, the Soviet surrender terms were formally refused on the 9th. Aside from this, the daily conference was remarkable for a plethora of reporting on the Eastern Front, much of it again concerned with petty detail such as the problems of releasing the SS Police Division for service in the West.

Until 14 January, most of the Eastern Front remained quiet: the weather was bad, the Red Army was preparing to liquidate the Stalingrad pocket, and its opponents were in no position to initiate action themselves. The remainder of January 1943 was notable for the sparsity of decisions relevant to Stalingrad, and the plethora of decisions on related, trivial, or non-urgent matters. Specifically, the only Stalingrad-related decisions in the whole month were as follows:

On 9 January. The Soviet surrender terms were formally refused. This was followed on 10 January by an attack by seven Soviet Armies, which captured half of 6th Army's positions by the evening of the 13th and its main airfield at Pitomnik on the 14th.

On 15 January. Field Marshal Milch of the Air Force was appointed to take charge of the airlift to 6th Army. As its main airfield had just been lost, the appointment of this very able officer seems belated; and it may have been made purely to express Hitler's displeasure at Göring's failure to fulfill his airlift promises. This is speculation, but it is significant that Göring was not consulted about the appointment of Milch, who was, after all, his Deputy.

On 22 January. Italian and Hungarian forces in Russia were placed under German command, their own Headquarters being euphemistically withdrawn to "reorganize."

It became clear on this day that Army Group A was no longer in danger of encirclement, and would succeed in withdrawing almost intact from its exposed position in the Caucasus. This made it unnecessary to continue to tie down Soviet troops at Stalingrad, so Paulus, with Manstein's strong support, asked for permission to begin surrender negotiations. Hitler refused.

On 23 January. Hitler was notified that 6th Army had almost no ammunition left. Zeitzler supported Paulus's request for authority to negotiate a surrender. Hitler again refused. He argued that it must "fight to the last in order to gain time" (for what is not clear), and informed Paulus of this personally by radio.

On 24 January. The Russians again offered surrender terms. Paulus asked for permission either to break out or to fly out some important officers. Hitler again refused.

The northern "pocket" in Stalingrad was wiped out on 30 January, but the only reference to the Eastern Front in that day's FHQ Conference was to the possible future capture of Leningrad. Final communication with the southern pocket was on 31 January, on which day Hitler made his last Stalingrad-related decision: to promote 118 senior officers in the trapped Army. Paulus was made a Field Marshal, probably as an invitation to commit suicide rather than become the first German Field Marshal to be captured.

Thus, only seven Stalingrad-related decisions were taken during January. This in part reflects the hopelessness of the situation after the failure of the relief attempt, but it also continues the tendency, already noted in respect to December, for Hitler to postpone or refuse decisions involving positive action. Specifically, Stalingrad-related decisions were taken on only six days; and of the seven decisions taken, only two involved positive action, in both cases belated (to put Milch in charge of the airlift the day after the main reception airfield had been lost, and to place Italian and Hungarian forces under German command after those forces had virtually disintegrated).

Of the remaining five decisions, four involved refusals: of Soviet surrender terms on 9 January; of Paulus's requests for permission to negotiate a surrender on the 22nd and on the 23rd; and of permission to attempt to break out or to fly out senior officers on 24 January. The remaining decision—to promote 118 senior Stalingrad officers on 31 January—was purely symbolic, as many of them had already surrendered, and the rest were to do so over the next two days. The conclusion from this must be that Hitler's decision-making capacity continued to deteriorate under the stress of a situation in which the initiative had been lost and two efforts to retrieve it—the airlift and the relief attempt—had failed. Although there was to be no admission that nothing further could be done, until that implicit in the refusals of Paulus's requests of 22–24 January, Hitler had probably realized it by 23 December, the day on which the relief operation was abandoned. This realization is implicit in the unrealism of Operations Order No. 2 of 28 December, which spoke of the formation of a new relief force by mid-February, at a time when it was already clear that the besieged force could not hold out until then.

During the rest of the crisis period, decisions in respect to other areas of Hitler's responsibility continued to be made, indicating that he suffered no general "paralysis of will." Many of these decisions were trivial, and they are included here in abbreviated form for the sake of completeness (bearing in mind the qualifications already stated about the gaps in sources for this period), and to enable tabular conclusions to be drawn.

On 9 January, the day the Soviet terms for surrender were refused, Hitler asked for exact details "for future operations" of an action in which two German agents had penetrated the Belgian escape organization by posing as shot-down British fliers. He also agreed to Kesselring's request to set up a "fortress" command in Bizerte, but vetoed the dispatch of "Göring" Division units to Tunisia until the whole division was ready.

On the 10th, the Romanian Marshal Antonescu arrived. Also, Admiral Raeder's memorandum on the importance of retaining the large surface warships was rejected,[19] as was a proposal to equip a seized Danish refrigerator ship as a blockade runner.

On the 11th, as a result of a conference held in the Ostministerium (East Ministry) on 13 December concerning the political handling of indigenous professionals (doctors, veterinary surgeons, agronomists, etc.) in the East, Hitler ordered their education and improvement to be promoted, a compromise with the doctrinal position that education of Easterners should be kept to a mini-

---

19. Porten, *The German Navy*, pp. 232–233.

mum. Commander-in-Chief Southeast, who had asked for personnel to staff coastal defenses in Greece, was told that he could have none. OKH, the Navy, and the Air Force were asked for studies of how a Turkish-Anglo-American operation in the Balkans would be conducted. Discussions with Antonescu on 11 and 12 January led to a decision to reconstruct the Romanian Army to provide at least eight divisions equipped up to the German standard, and to step up German training of Romanian officers and NCOs.

Kesselring reported in person on the 12th on the situation in Africa. Most of his report dealt with problems of sea transport between Italy and North Africa, for which he requested more but smaller ships, more anti-aircraft for Tunis, Palermo, and Naples, and more U-boats. Hitler agreed to provide more ships, and ordered the Army to release long-barreled 5cm guns for them. Kesselring asked for the proposed removal of the 164th Infantry Division from Rommel to Tunisia to be rescinded. Hitler approved this and also the dispatch of the "Göring" Division to Tunis. There was a very detailed discussion about movements of divisions and weapons. Expanding on previous orders to establish AA batteries, Hitler ordered that officers up to and including the rank of major should be posted into them even if they had no AA training and could not be used in functions corresponding to their ranks, a curious procedure in an army suffering from manpower shortages. He also declared that arms deliveries to Spain were urgent and that he intended to set up schools for Spanish volunteers in the south of France.

While all these peripheral and detailed decisions were being taken, the situation at Stalingrad was deteriorating further. At 8:05 A.M. on 10 January, the Soviets launched operation "Ring" with a 55-minute air and artillery bombardment, followed by an east-west attack aimed at splitting 6th Army in two[20] and capturing its main airfield, objectives that were achieved by the 14th. During these days, OKW conferences were discussing such minor matters as passwords for the North and Baltic coasts, minor security breaches, and whether to send twenty-four light field howitzers to Norway or to the far north of the Eastern Front.

More relevant to the need to strengthen the Eastern Front were

20. Alexander M. Samsonov, "Stalingrad: The Relief," in *History of the Second World War*, ed. Barrie Pitt (London: Purnell, 1967), Vol. III, p. 1303.

Hitler's orders on 14 January to convert some divisions to a "high value" attack profile by above-scale equipment with modern weapons, to issue new equipment in future only as the battlefield situation required, and to direct all new equipment delivered up to 15 March to the East. However, the orders could not materially affect the situation at Stalingrad. The new "high value" divisions would take time to develop; new heavy equipment could not be delivered to forces whose only supply line was an inadequate airlift; and the rule of priority for the East in the next two months' output had so many exceptions that it became meaningless: the exceptions included not merely a number of German formations in the West and Africa, but arms deliveries to three allies (Italy, Bulgaria, and Romania) and one neutral (Turkey). Arms deliveries to Spain were also to begin soon.

On 15 January, Milch took charge of the airlift, but the rest of that day's conference was taken up with minor decisions concerning Norway and Denmark, the disposal of the stocks in the Toulon arsenal, the downgrading of fortifications on the French south coast, and, in a contradiction of an earlier order concerning the "Göring" Division,[21] an order for some of its units to be dispatched from Italy to Tunisia.

Supply issues again dominated the conference on 16 January. Motor vehicles in the Ukraine and the Baltic states were to be requisitioned; caution in the surveillance of ships waiting to leave Goteborg for England was ordered, for fear of retaliatory Swedish obstruction of transit of supplies from northwest Norway and north Finland (the Swedish reaction to the Allied victories was causing concern); and anti-aircraft protection for Danish shipyards, now required to build shipping for Germany, was to be increased. Commander-in-Chief West was asked what provision he could make in southern France for training Spanish volunteers; Arnim, the commander in Tunisia, was refused further supplies for the time being; and a draft order to provide another 500,000 men to the forces was issued. Hitler had already signed the latter on 13 January, and a three-man committee of Keitel, Bormann (Chief of the Party Chancellory), and Lammers (Head of the Reich Chancellory) was set up to administer it.

---

21. The contradiction involved dispatching the division to Africa before its training was completed.

Resource issues again predominated on the 17th, as Army Commander Norway had indicated on the 11th that the dispatch of experienced officers to the East had made it impossible to staff OKH training schools in Norway. OKW agreed to send officers with Eastern Front experience there, but indicated that the courses should be shortened. A number of detailed decisions concerned small movements of troops between security regiments in Denmark and forces of Army Group Center. Following the Allied sinking in the Gulf of Naples on the 15th of a ship carrying ten tanks, Hitler ordered that tanks should be sent from Italy to Africa in the future only on landing ships.

On the 18th, Commander-in-Chief West recommended the complete dissolution of the French labor service because of its anti-German attitude. This, however, was felt to be politically inadvisable, so it was decided to retain it under tighter controls and use it primarily to build fortifications. Losses of blockade runners prompted Hitler to decree that if further operations proved impossible, the Navy should build transport submarines, provided it could do so without detriment to the construction of combat U-boats.

January 19 saw another decisive Soviet breakthrough against the Hungarian 2nd Army, and a request by Zeitzler for withdrawals to prevent encirclement. Hitler refused, and a heated argument ensued, in which Zeitzler maintained that Hitler did not recognize the seriousness of the situation, and Hitler in reply delivered his by now standard diatribe against Army officers. Leave for all forces in the East was stopped on 17 January, resulting in widespread disorganization because no trains were available to take troops back from Germany to their units. Hitler provided Göring with a list of German cities whose anti-aircraft defenses must be strengthened, and he approved Göring's proposal for an increase in the number of night fighters.

On the 20th, the decision taken on 8 January to retain SS Totenkopf in the West until March was canceled because of the deteriorating situation in the East; its departure for Russia was advanced to the first week of February. Hitler expressed fear of an Anglo-American landing in Sardinia. The Commander-in-Chief of Army Group B (Weichs) reported on the 21st that the Soviet advance could not be stopped. A number of detailed measures were taken to try to reinforce the Hungarian 2nd Army, and Commander-in-

Chief West was ordered to provide 5,000 requisitioned French vehicles to the Eastern Army by mid-February. The collapse of the
satellite forces in the East was acknowledged on 22 January by a
decision to "free" the command of the Italian 8th and the Hungarian 2nd Armies from operational duties so that they could reorganize their forces and subordinate troops still in action to German
command. Hitler's inability to abstain from detailed intervention
was shown by his order that every military train on the Taman Peninsula should be fitted with quadruple anti-aircraft machine guns.
An attempt was made to solve chain-of-command problems between Rommel, who wanted to withdraw to the Mareth position,
and Mussolini, who was reluctant to abandon Tripolitania, by creating German Army Group Africa, but Hitler rejected this on political grounds, in favor of continuing to exercise command through
the Comando Supremo. He resolved a dispute between the Army
and the Air Force over the allocation of 2cm anti-aircraft ammunition by ordering the Air Force to surrender one million rounds a
month to the Army for four months, beginning in February.

By 22 January, Army Group A was out of danger, so Paulus, with
Manstein's strong support, sought permission to begin surrender
negotiations.[22] Hitler, however, refused. On the next day, he was
informed that ammunition had almost run out, and Zeitzler added
his support for surrender. Hitler again refused, arguing that 6th
Army must fight to the last "in order to win time," though he did
not say for what. The Russians again offered surrender terms on
the 24th, and Paulus asked for permission either to try a breakout
or, at the very least, to fly out some important personnel, but he
received yet again a flat refusal. In the next few days, Hitler appears to have avoided taking decisions on the Eastern Front: on the
25th, he discussed the reorganization of the Romanian forces; and
on the 27th, the reorganization of the Italian forces. Decisions relating to Africa in these days were left to Mussolini, who ordered
Rommel to win as much time as possible during his retreat to Mareth, and to hold that position at any price.

A British raid on the Norwegian coast on the night of 23–24
January reactivated Hitler's apprehensions about Norway; given
the importance of the sea route from Narvik for the winter transport of Swedish iron ore, these were never far from the surface. He

22. Manstein, *Lost Victories*, p. 360.

instructed that the incident be publicized to emphasize the consequences of insufficient sentries, and he ordered searchlights and quick-firing guns to be installed at the most important fjord entrances. Goebbels had long urged "total war," and appears at last to have obtained Hitler's acquiescence,[23] though the German war effort was always qualified ·by the Führer's fear of the effects of the consequent hardships upon a skeptical public, and never reached the British or Soviet level. Hitler ordered strong air protection for Army Group A's Kerch Straits supply route, and he insisted that the French, whose railways were under increasing Allied air attacks, should take a more active role in their protection.

At the afternoon conference on the 30th, Hitler expressed high expectations of the SS Panzer Corps, about to enter the fray on the Eastern Front. January 30 was the day on which the northern cauldron in Stalingrad was wiped out, but this went unmentioned, his only other reference to the East that day being to the need to hold Demyansk as a jumping-off point for the future capture of Leningrad. Orders were issued for the defense of the Balkans without consulting the Italians. Raeder's resignation as head of the Navy took effect, and Dönitz reported to FHQ on succeeding him; he was granted an additional steel allocation for the Navy[24] and, in due course, a reprieve for some of the large surface warships. Hitler formally buried his feud with Keitel and Jodl by shaking hands with them again.

The last radio messages from the southern cauldron in Stalingrad arrived on the 31st, the day on which Hitler promoted 118 Stalingrad officers. Paulus became a Field Marshal, less in recognition of services than as an invitation to commit suicide, no German Field Marshal ever having been captured. On February 2, all fighting in Stalingrad ended, except for a very small pocket of 11th Army Corps north of the city. Engel recorded that FHQ was dominated by the recognition that the end had come, and that Hitler was deeply distressed, "looking for faults and failures," and criticizing Paulus heavily for surrendering rather than killing himself.[25] The 11th Army Corps reported the end of resistance at 8:14 A.M. on 2 February. The Stalingrad battle concluded, and with it the crisis period.

23. See, for example, Lochner, ed., *The Goebbels Diaries*, pp. 178 and 216; and an article by Goebbels in *Das Reich*, 17 January 1943.
24. Speer, *Inside the Third Reich*, p. 375.
25. Kotze, ed., *Heeresadjutant bei Hitler*, p. 143.

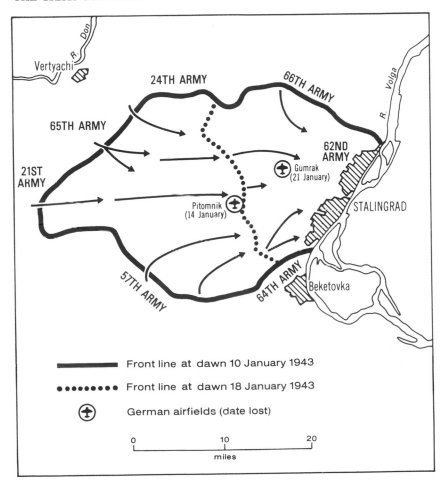

MAP 5.
THE FINALE AT STALINGRAD,
10 JANUARY–2 FEBRUARY 1943

CRISIS COMPONENTS

Environmental Change

The crisis period had as its source the launching of a major Soviet counteroffensive north and south of Stalingrad on 19–20 November 1942. The German High Command had vague forewarnings that it was pending, but no inkling of its imminence, scale, or intensity. The transition from pre-crisis to crisis was therefore very abrupt.

Threat to Basic Values

During the pre-crisis period, the perception of threat was merely one of failure to achieve objectives. The intensity of threat perception increased rapidly as the besiegers at Stalingrad became the besieged, with twenty German and two Romanian divisions threatened with complete annihilation. It was further enhanced by the heavy casualties incurred in divisions that were not encircled, and by the danger that the whole of Army Group A would be cut off from behind by a Soviet drive down the Don to Rostov.

Probability of an Adverse Shift in the Military Balance

With one German army and part of another encircled at Stalingrad, two more German armies threatened in the Caucasus, and one Hungarian, one Italian, and two Romanian armies subject to heavy attrition by the Soviet counteroffensive, the probability of an adverse shift in the military balance was clearly apparent, the more so as the German manpower situation was already strained, and losses could no longer be fully replaced. The consequence was a series of attempts by Generals Paulus, Manstein, Jodl, and Zeitzler to secure permission to withdraw from Stalingrad. A total of at least eleven requests for permission to attempt a breakout are known to have been made between 22 November 1942 and 30 January 1943, as well as at least three requests for authority to negotiate a surrender. All were rejected by Hitler.

Time Pressure

Both the field commanders and the High Command generals, except for the sycophantic Keitel, were acutely aware of time constraints, both on extracting forces at Stalingrad from the trap which the Red Army had sprung on them, and on the withdrawal of Army Group A from its exposed position in the Caucasus. Hitler, however, ignored them in respect to the Stalingrad grouping; in the belief that the besieged force could be adequately supplied from the air, he forbade withdrawal. And with regard to Army Group A, he did not sanction its withdrawal until the end of December. This in turn imposed a requirement on 6th Army to tie down Soviet forces until Army Group A was safe.

COPING MECHANISMS
Information Processing

Information flows, as far as the Germans' own operations went, were adequate throughout. Landline communication with 6th and 4th Panzer Armies was cut by 22 November, but adequate radio links were retained until the end. Information on Soviet operations was inadequate throughout. The Soviet move was foreseen only in the sense of an imprecise warning by Foreign Armies East, a few days before it was launched, of a possible attack on a scale much smaller than that actually undertaken. On the other contributions to the crisis—the British offensive in Egypt and the Anglo-American landing in French North Africa—there was no more than a few hours of forewarning. Difficulties in the processing of information were self-created by Hitler's retreat to the Berghof after his visit to Munich on 8 November, from which he did not return to FHQ until late on 23 November. Though this caused problems in the handling of information, there is no evidence that these problems had any serious effect on the decision-making process. Hitler made no recorded complaint about lack of information.

Consultations: Persons and Groups

With the increase in stress, there was some temporary widening of the circle of persons consulted. Hitler decided on 16 November to relinquish command of Army Group A to Manstein; but four days later, when the magnitude of the Soviet counterstroke was beginning to be realized, he appointed Manstein to command a new Army Group Don instead, his place at Army Group A being taken by Kleist. From then on, Manstein insisted on putting forward his views about the need for a relief operation, and eventually won his point.

Göring was added to the group on 24 November, because of Hitler's decision that the forces in Stalingrad should stand fast and be supplied by air. Göring's assurance that it could be done was given over the protests of the Air Force Chief of Staff, Jeschonnek. Göring was not consulted further after his assurance had been accepted. Attempts to persuade Hitler that the airlift could not work included the bringing of a junior officer, Major Christian, to FHQ on 26 or 27 November for a discussion with Hitler, but his views were rejected out of hand. Rommel also visited FHQ, on 28 November, to try to persuade Hitler that withdrawal from Africa was the only feasible course, but his views also were rejected. Early in 1943, increased contact with the Naval leaders resulted from Hitler's decision to scrap the larger surface warships after their poor performance in the Battle of Bear Island. Raeder resigned as Commander-in-Chief, and was replaced by Dönitz, who succeeded in persuading Hitler to rescind the decree in part, after which contact subsided to its former low level.

The increases in the group were temporary and ad hoc; no permanent addition to the group, even for the duration of the crisis period, was made. Because of the regular pattern of daily meetings which already existed, and because of the custom developed by Zeitzler of discussing Eastern Front matters privately with Hitler (which would be recorded, if at all, in the OKH Diary, destroyed in the last days of the war, not in that of OKW), it is not possible to decide whether there was any significant increase in the number of consultative meetings held by Hitler in the crisis period. He had already in the pre-crisis period reduced the amount of his contact with others after his arguments with Jodl and Halder in September. The onset of the crisis does not seem to have drawn him out of isolation; rather, on the contrary, he "retreated" to the Berghof in November, and spoke of doing so again in December, though Zeitzler succeeded in dissuading him.

Decisional Forums

The decisional unit remained Hitler personally, and the institutional daily meetings continued to be the machinery by which he evolved decisions. Hitler's concept of decision-making was not based on consultation so much as on maintenance of divided jurisdictions, which prevented or hindered the making of decisions by others. It is by no means clear that he regarded the OKW/OKH apparatus as essential to decision-making, because in December he spoke of (but was dissuaded from) "retreating" to the Berghof for a longish period to "clear his head" for new decisions. This carries an implied wish to shed some decision-making load, but the question was never pursued, as all of Zeitzler's effort went into persuading him to stay at FHQ.

Alternatives: Search and Evaluation

The Soviet preparations for launching an offensive were well concealed; and in the last fortnight before it was launched, when complete concealment was no longer possible, Hitler's attention was largely engaged with other matters (Africa and his invasion of unoccupied France, in particular). So no consideration was given to, or plans prepared for, countering the possibility of a Soviet attack. Apart from ordering Manstein to replace Weichs in command of Army Group Don (created from forces of Army Group B in the Stalingrad area and vicinity) and ordering some units as reinforcement, no action was taken between 19 November, when the offensive opened north of the city, and the 22nd, when the encirclement was closed. Once that had happened, the range of alternatives became very circumscribed. They were:

1. To withdraw westward, abandoning the line of the Volga. This was first put forward by Jodl on 21 November—that is, when a route westward was still open. Hitler rejected it; his reasons were not recorded. Paulus asked for freedom to do it on the evening of the 23rd—that is, a few hours after the two claws of the Soviet pincer movement had met, but before Soviet forces had had time to consolidate. This request was also rejected.

2. To withdraw eastward—that is, hold on to the Volga line. This was possible only if supply could be arranged. Hitler first referred to the possibility of supply by air on 22 November. On the 24th, Göring stated that the Air Force could carry out the task; neither Zeitzler nor Göring's own Chief of Staff, Jeschonnek, believed it could be done, but both were overruled by Hitler.

3. To withdraw the encircled forces southwestward toward existing German positions, while Army Group Don safeguarded their rear. This was proposed by Manstein on 25 November, and also turned down by Hitler.

4. To be relieved by a land attack. A firm decision to attempt this was taken by Hitler on 2 December. However, there was a basic unclarity: Hitler's apparent intention was that the relief operation should enable the forces at Stalingrad to hold on to their positions, while Manstein, who was to command the relief, intended to extract them southwestward. Since the relief attempt failed, this unclarity was never resolved.

A fifth alternative—to end the war with Russia—was not considered by the German decision-making group, but was advocated by Mussolini, as a means of making forces available to meet the expected Anglo-American invasion of western and southern Europe. Mussolini put this view to Göring in Rome on 1 December, and his Foreign Minister, Ciano, advocated it to Hitler on the 18th. It was not seriously entertained by Hitler, whose campaign in Russia had been undertaken in order to gain "living space" for German expansion, and who believed that compromise with the Anglo-Americans was more feasible than with the Soviet regime.

It cannot be said that any serious search for alternatives in respect to the forces marooned at Stalingrad took place. At the level below Hitler, withdrawal was unsuccessfully urged by Jodl, Manstein, Zeitzler, and numerous others, until failure of the relief operation made it impossible.

In respect to Army Group A, the alternatives were to remain where they were (advance had ceased to be feasible before 19 November), and thus risk being cut off by a Soviet advance down the Don to the coast in their rear, or to withdraw partly into the easily defended Taman Peninsula and partly behind the Don. This latter course was first considered on 13 December, but no conclusion was reached.

A breakpoint in decision-making occurs in the period 26–28 December. An order drafted on the 26th shows Hitler still determined on a standfast both at Stalingrad and in the Caucasus; relief of 6th Army was the main objective for the immediate future, and Army Groups A, B, and Don were all told to hold their existing positions. But on 28 December, Hitler issued another order, which spoke only of "creating the preconditions" for relief of 6th Army, authorized both Army Groups A and Don to make limited withdrawals, except at Stalingrad, and gave Manstein control of both Army Groups. Three days later, on 31 December, Hitler decided to transfer six divisions from the West and one from Army Group Center, with a view to a renewed relief operation in mid-February. This was not realistic in terms of its stated objective: the forces surrounded at Stalingrad were already acutely short of food, fuel, and ammunition before the end of December; the airlift had proved totally incapable of supplying even half of the minimum daily requirement of 700 tons; and Soviet attrition of it was increasing as the Red Army widened the corridor which the Germans had to overfly, and installed increasing numbers of anti-aircraft guns in it, while Red Air Force fighters grew daily more active against the airlift. The operation was, however, realistic in terms of the possibility of at least a temporary stabilization of the front with a severe local defeat upon the Red Army, and recovery of a substantial amount of lost territory, in an operation conducted during the post-crisis period.

Two other fundamental alternatives were posed during the crisis period. One, put by Rommel, was to abandon North Africa altogether. The other, put by Mussolini and Ciano, was to end the war with the Soviet Union. If Rommel's proposal had been accepted, the effects during November-December would have been intangible, as the only forces that would have been "freed" for deployment elsewhere would have been the four German divisions of the German-Italian Panzer Army—provided, of course, that they could have been evacuated intact, which they almost certainly could not have been. A more important effect would have been the retention in Europe of the more substantial army and air forces that were dispatched to Tunisia. A substantial part of these could have been employed in December on the Eastern Front, where, if added to the relief force, they would have improved its prospects, though not necessarily to the extent of turning failure into success.

The second alternative would at best have meant a negotiated peace with the Soviet Union, at worst a rapid withdrawal to the Soviet-Polish border of 1941. The first would presumably have saved the 6th Army and the other formations destroyed or mangled in the Stalingrad operation, while the second clearly would not. In both cases, Germany would have had more forces available to face Allied invasions of Western Europe—in the first case, at least three times as many as there actually were when the invasions eventuated. In the second case, the reinforcement available for the West would have been much less, but defense of the eastern frontiers of the Reich would have been better prepared and with stronger forces than were available to Germany when these frontiers were actually reached almost two years later. But Hitler rejected both radical alternatives out of hand.

CHAPTER SIX

The Post-crisis Period

THE POST-CRISIS PERIOD lasted from 3 February through 24 March. Soviet forces continued to advance on most sectors until 19 February, but achieved no further major encirclements. The German retreats during February were for the most part planned withdrawals to more easily defended positions, designed to free forces for a counteroffensive. Soviet overoptimism led the Red Army to pursue its offensive too far; Manstein's counteroffensive, launched on 20 February, drove the Soviets out of the recently captured major centers of Kharkov and Belgorod back to the Northern Donets river. By 24 March, the front had stabilized; the spring thaw then immobilized both sides for several weeks, thereby ending the Stalingrad crisis.

The post-crisis period saw a decline in German perception of threat and of unfavorable change in the military balance; the danger to Army Group A had already been averted, and after the surrender at Stalingrad, the Soviet offensive gradually lost its impetus and was even turned back. Before the end of February, Manstein had already proposed to follow his local counteroffensive with a new offensive to be launched as soon as the spring thaw was over— that is, during April. Although Hitler rejected this plan, preferring to wait until new types of tanks (Tiger and Panther) and assault guns (Ferdinand/Elephant and Hornet) were available in adequate numbers, the planning for a large-scale summer offensive went ahead. The post-crisis period therefore saw the German leadership recovering from the Stalingrad trauma, and planning to regain the initiative. Although abortive attempts were made by some generals to enlarge the decisional forum and persuade Hitler to relinquish field command by appointing a Commander-in-Chief East, and to diminish the influence of Keitel by securing the appointment of a Chief of General Staff of OKW, Hitler refused to sanction either appointment. His decision-making authority survived the challenge, and the only new appointment made was that of Colonel-General Guderian as Inspector-General of Armored Troops, a post with no operational authority and incomplete jurisdiction, since self-propelled guns, an increasingly important element of Panzer divisions, were not covered by it.

For a short period after the surrender in Stalingrad, Hitler appears to have conceded greater freedom of decision-making to senior field commanders, in that very few decisions by him are recorded up to 13 February, and still fewer involve interference in field operations. However, beginning with 13 February, the frequency and breadth of Hitler's decisions returned to pre-crisis dimensions. This aspect of the post-crisis period is discussed in greater detail at the end of this chapter.

Under the impact of the disaster, Germany was plunged into deep mourning, as was Hitler himself, according to Engel.[1] More than 100,000 restaurants, amusement centers, and shops were closed, to secure additional manpower for the "total war" now being advocated by Goebbels.[2] Hitler's attention shifted to Africa, where he appears to have convinced himself that something could be saved. On 2 February, he ordered the strongest possible combat groups to be prepared for shipment to Tunisia, and gave attention to command organization in North Africa, to the defense of Sicily and Sardinia, and to convoy and shipping questions.

His search for scapegoats for Stalingrad extended to the Romanians: on 2 February, the German General at Romanian headquarters was asked to hand to Antonescu a letter from Hitler which asked him to take countermeasures against "signs of disintegration" alleged to have appeared in Romanian formations transferred to the German 17th Army after the virtual annihilation of their parent formations, the 3rd and 4th Romanian Armies.

On the 5th, Wfst issued an appreciation of the defenses in Scandinavia and Western Europe; it indicated that enemy landings could be expected in Spain or Portugal at any time, Scandinavia in March

---

1. Hildegard von Kotze, ed., *Heeresadjutant bei Hitler, 1938–1943: Aufzeichnungen des Major Engel* (Stuttgart: Deutsche Verlags-Anstalt, 1974), p. 143.
2. Louis P. Lochner, ed., *The Goebbels Diaries* (London: Hamish Hamilton, 1948), p. 193.

or April, and Western Europe at any time from May onward.[3] Hitler's only recorded reaction was his agreement on 5 February to a proposal by Commander-in-Chief West to cancel a relatively minor movement of an SS division in France, the first mention for several days of a current decision by him. On 5–6 February, Manstein was summoned to FHQ, after pleading with Hitler either to visit the front himself or at least to send a senior officer such as Jodl.[4] Hitler refused to do so, and indicated the depth of his preoccupation, notwithstanding his persistent search for scapegoats, by telling Manstein, "I alone bear the responsibility for Stalingrad."[5] Manstein attempted to persuade him to appoint a Commander-in-Chief East, but failed. He was slightly more successful in securing Hitler's agreement to a limited withdrawal to a more defensible line along the Mius River, but was unable to secure approval to abandon the whole of the eastern part of the Donets Basin.[6]

The German preoccupation with the possibility of Allied invasions at all points of the compass continued to appear throughout February, as the weakness of their situation became increasingly evident to both OKH and OKW. On the Eastern Front, the disorganization of the Italian and Hungarian forces caused them to be withdrawn entirely from the front for reorganization. Anxiety about Norway led to increases in the defenses of the most important fjords, using captured Russian artillery, anti-aircraft guns, searchlights, and sound locators. On the same day, 7 February, Kesselring's request for further forces for Africa was considered, as was strengthening security in the relatively small Croatian oil field at Gojlo with a security battalion formed from German soldiers born in 1900 or earlier, oil company workers, ethnic Germans, and Ukrainians recruited by Himmler's office.

With the mounting problems on the central sector of the Eastern Front, Army Group Center was under pressure not merely from the Red Army but also from severe partisan activity in its

---

3. This is an interestingly complete misreading of Allied intentions. As early as January 1942, Churchill pressed for the publicized dispatch of American troops to the U.K. as a means of fixing German attention on the West, while even then his intention was to invade French North Africa. See Winston S. Churchill, *The Second World War* (London: Cassell, 1948–1954), Vol. III, pp. 606–607, 624.

4. Erich von Manstein, *Lost Victories* (London: Methuen, 1958), p. 365.

5. Ibid.

6. Ibid., pp. 408–413.

rear. OKH proposed on 9 February to place most of Latvia, Lithuania, and Belorussia under the control of Army Group Center in order to facilitate centralized decision-making for military operations there. Wfst and the Commander-in-Chief Ostland regarded this as psychologically inadvisable and militarily unnecessary, so Hitler refused to sanction it. As he now considered an Allied landing in the Iberian Peninsula probable, he authorized a number of steps to be taken against the possibility of an enemy landing in Portugal. After a conference with Dönitz on 8 February, he signed a draft order on the 9th, exempting men required for building U-boats, and for surface warships and armaments directly associated with the U-boat war, from military service.[7]

On 10 February, a long report from Kesselring on the situation in Africa was considered. Kesselring made a number of proposals, and Hitler agreed to all of them without introducing any modifications of his own. This episode, in conjunction with the limited freedom of action reluctantly given to Manstein, suggests that, in the aftermath of Stalingrad, Hitler was at least temporarily permitting greater initiative to his senior commanders. However, on the 11th, Kesselring complained that his autonomy had been reduced by the introduction, under an order of 30 January, of a Chief of Command Staff to C-in-C South, and was not convinced by assurances that it had not. And a request from the Commander-in-Chief Southeast for some Mark III tanks had to be declined by OKW, on the grounds that Hitler had ordered them to be converted to assault guns.[8]

The preoccupation with other invasion areas was manifested again on the 12th, when an OKW study on the possibility of a joint Anglo-American-Turkish invasion of the Balkans was issued, and on the 13th, when the Chief of General Staff in the west (Blumentritt) indicated that he considered an enemy attack on the French coast to be possible in the near future. However, Hitler's only recorded decision on these days is an order, made sometime between 10 and 13 February, that railway locomotives in the west should be given

7. Karl Dönitz, *Memoirs: Ten Years and Twenty Days* (London: Weidenfeld and Nicolson, 1959), p. 348.

8. Hitler believed that hollow-charge ammunition would considerably increase the power of artillery against tanks, and had on 23 January 1942 ordered an increase in the production of self-propelled guns at the expense of tanks. Production of the Mark III tank was discontinued in December 1942. See Heinz Guderian, *Panzer Leader* (London: Futura, 1974), pp. 277–281.

active anti-aircraft defenses against enemy fliers, and that locomotive cabs should be armored.

On the 13th, against the advice of Manstein, Hitler ordered that Kharkov was to be held at all costs, thereby encroaching on the freedom of action that Manstein believed he had secured, and that had led to an OKH Directive being issued on the same day for two new armies to be formed in the east. This directive was a response to Manstein's own proposals of four days before, but in fact neither army was ever formed.

From 14 February onward, Hitler's decision-making resumed the frequency and breadth that had characterized the pre-crisis period. On that day, his decisions included orders for "correct" treatment of the remnants of the Italian, Romanian, and Hungarian armies in the east; for an Air Force Field Division and personnel designated for another to be dispatched to the west; for the army in Western Europe to provide three combat-strength divisions for the east as soon as possible; for the "Göring" Division to be moved to the 1st Army area and combined with the "Göring" Panzer regiment; for the 2nd Parachute Division to be set up in France, and an SS assault brigade to be deployed in the west as an intervention reserve; and for U-boat bases to be secured against major air attacks. He also approved a proposal by C-in-C West for a strengthened mobile brigade, decreed guidelines for pending operations against the partisans in Yugoslavia, ordered the Reichsführer-SS to form three SS divisions (one each of Croats, Lithuanians, and Latvians) by the beginning of June, and refused a request by the Navy that its allocation of 2cm anti-aircraft shells not be reduced further.

On the 15th, Hitler sent a letter to Antonescu, thanking him for steps he was taking to deal with signs of disintegration in the Romanian forces, and held a conference concerning Scandinavia, at which the matters discussed ranged from the building of an operational reserve in Norway to the use of captured tanks for airfield protection. The refusal of the Swedish government to allow transit by German guns, intended for heavy batteries in Norway, was mentioned, and he made it clear that no pressure was to be put on Sweden.

There was an argument at the daily conference on 16 February concerning troop dispositions in Finland; and on the proposal of Jodl, Hitler ordered that Mannerheim (Finnish President and Commander-in-Chief) should be "met halfway."

Manstein's plan for a counteroffensive had been drawn up during the first two weeks of February, while Hitler's readiness to intervene in field operations was temporarily at a low ebb. It entailed voluntary withdrawals from the Eastern Donbass and Kharkov to entice the Russians to overextension, and Hitler had accepted this, though without enthusiasm, when Manstein had discussed the matter with him at FHQ on 6 February. But on the 13th, Hitler ordered Kharkov to be held. It fell on 15–16 February, and on 17 February he descended upon Manstein's headquarters at Zaporozh'ye, urging him to recapture Kharkov at once and mount a frontal offensive.

Manstein argued for his plan, which involved permitting the Soviets to advance to the upper Dnieper, and then releasing Panzer forces from Krasnograd in the north and Krasnoarmeyskoye in the south to snip off their overextended columns. By careful timing, this could be done just before the spring thaw made the ground too soft for swift movement of tanks, so an immediate Soviet riposte would be impossible. The Russians would have no choice but to abandon Kharkov and fall back across the Northern Donets. The thaw would then immobilize both sides for several weeks, giving the Germans and their allies a respite to prepare for renewed operations in the spring.

At first, Hitler refused to consider the sequence of operations which Manstein had proposed; and according to Engel, the tone of the discussions was very unpleasant.[9] Manstein at one stage said, "things can't go on like this, my Führer," and displayed anxiety to get Hitler away as soon as possible, so that he could continue to work independently. Soviet tanks were roaming the steppes not far from Manstein's headquarters, and he also had to oversee last-minute preparations for the attack, which was to commence on the night of 19/20 February. On the 18th, Hitler reluctantly agreed to give him the SS Division "Das Reich" as a reinforcement for 4th Panzer Army; and on the 19th, the Führer left Zaporozh'ye to return to FHQ.

At this stage, another abortive attempt was made to rectify the deficiencies which many senior field commanders saw in the High Command structure, and to broaden the decision-making group. The perceived deficiencies were that, first, there were "profes-

9. Kotze, ed., *Heeresadjutant bei Hitler*, p. 144.

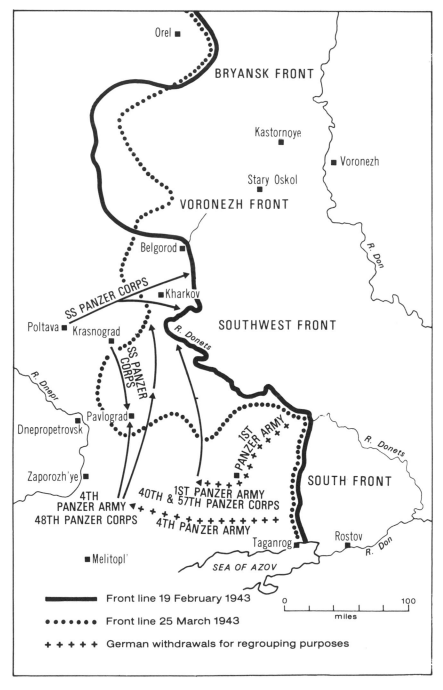

MAP 6.
THE POST-CRISIS PERIOD: THE GERMAN COUNTER-
OFFENSIVE, 19 FEBRUARY–25 MARCH 1943

sional" Commanders-in-Chief for three European areas (West, South, and Southeast), but none for the Eastern Front, where Hitler exercised the role himself; and second, that while OKW was responsible for all theatres except the East, it had no Chief of General Staff analogous to Zeitzler.

By mid-February, the crisis of confidence between Hitler and the Army Commanders had reached such a point that Engel decided, on his own initiative, to pay a visit to Rundstedt, in an attempt to persuade him to use his influence to induce Hitler to appoint a senior officer as Commander-in-Chief East, with functions analogous to those of C-in-C West, South, and Southeast.[10]

On the 19th, Hitler, before returning to FHQ, ordered Army Group A to transfer whatever forces it could possibly spare to Manstein's Southern Army Group. This meant the tacit abandonment of the plan to use the sole remaining foothold in the Caucasus, the Kuban bridgehead, as a base for its reconquest. Before returning to FHQ, Hitler issued an exhortatory proclamation to Army Group South and Air Fleet IV.[11] On his return, he approved proposals by OKH for arms deliveries to Spain.

February 20 saw an acceptance of proposals made by the Army Commander in Norway postponing railway construction in the Arctic area north of Narvik, and a major formal decision to reappoint Colonel-General Heinz Guderian to an active post as Inspector General of Armored Troops.[12] Guderian, the main architect of the Blitzkrieg doctrine that had proved so successful in the first two years of the war, had been inactive since his dismissal from command in December 1941, and his recall to office was a direct response to the changing balance of power in armored warfare, especially Soviet successes against the German armored divisions. It may also have been intended as a partial response to the pressures from the Army for an appointment of a Commander-in-Chief in the east, though as such it was more of a diversionary tactic, since Guderian was given no operational command responsibilities, and opposition from the artillery generals confined his jurisdiction to tanks, a crippling restriction, since Hitler had already decided to

10. Ibid.
11. This was a very rare occurrence by this stage of the war, Hitler's appearances in public and communications with his subjects having become very infrequent. The probable reason for this departure from practice was that the victory gained by these forces to some extent effaced the Stalingrad debacle.
12. Guderian, *Panzer Leader*, pp. 287–295.

increase the production of assault guns at the expense of tanks, on the ground that they were cheaper.[13]

Resolution of the problems of Germany's allies dominated conferences on the 21st and 22nd. A decree of 21 February combined the remnants of the Italian 8th Army into two divisions, and ordered all units not needed for this reorganization to be withdrawn to Italy. On 22 February, proposals for the reconstruction of the French armed forces were considered; their object was to provide some limited capacity to fight the expected Allied invasion, but none for fighting the German and Italian forces. Reconstruction of the Croatian army was also discussed in detail. Growing suspicion of Italy was shown in instructions that German troops would hold areas cleared by them in pending anti-partisan operations, unless specifically ordered to hand over control to Italian troops, and that the bauxite district around Mostar was to be kept under German occupation. Hitler agreed to exempt two police regiments from requisition of police vehicles for the eastern front. In Paris, Engel secured a four-hour audience with Rundstedt, who declined to ask Hitler to appoint a Commander-in-Chief for the east and a Chief of General Staff for OKW, suggesting that Manstein and Kluge should do it instead.[14]

The 23rd saw Hitler ordering the first company of Tiger tanks for Africa to leave by the 27th, and there was a discussion of a report by the Chief of Armed Forces Hygiene on enemy preparations for biological warfare. (Hitler had prohibited preparation for offensive biological warfare on 23 May 1942.[15]) The report indicated that Russia, England, and America appeared to be preparing for biological attack, as France had been, while German preparations were adequate only for defense. Wfst proposed to prepare for reprisals by producing and deploying biological warfare agents. Hitler sharply rejected this, and it was decided that only research already ordered and approved should continue. On this day also, Hitler reluctantly agreed to Dönitz's proposal to retain some of the large surface warships, whose decommissioning had been ordered. Dönitz had concluded that their mere existence helped the U-boat arm by forcing the British to retain large numbers of heavy warships of their own,

13. Ibid., p. 298.
14. Kotze, ed., *Heeresadjutant bei Hitler*, p. 144.
15. OKH/Gen. St. d. H./Gen. d. Nb. Tr. (Ib), Nr. 297/42.

whose crews and escort vessels could otherwise be diverted to anti-submarine warfare. He therefore proposed to decommission only five ships and to retain six, deploying two (the battleship *Tirpitz* and the battlecruiser *Scharnhorst*) to defend Norway and, where possible, to attack the Murmansk convoys.[16]

On the 24th, Hitler issued an order to the Army Groups in the east and the Commander-in-Chief of the Air Force concerning breakdowns of discipline during withdrawal. Undisciplined behavior, especially in big towns and on main routes, was to be suppressed with all due severity. The disobedient were to be shot on the spot, those who did not exert their authority punished, and energetic leaders protected against the legal consequences of their actions.[17] Hitler's only other recorded decision on that day concerns a matter of detail, the deployment of a regiment of SS "Reich."

The 25th saw detailed interventions by Hitler in a series of orders concerning new lines of demarcation between Army Groups South and Center, the authorization for gradual withdrawals by Army Group Center, the closing of gaps between the two Army Groups, and the assembly by Army Group South of strong mobile formations behind its north wing. Wfst attempted to exploit the limited permission for withdrawals by having defensive positions built behind the eastern front, using Polish forced labor. It was also decided to assess whether men could be withdrawn from Ukrainian agriculture and be replaced by women, so as to increase the amount of male forced labor available. The Chief of Foreign Intelligence Operations reported the belief that a substantial enemy landing, probably on one of the larger Mediterranean islands, was likely to take place in March. Kluge, presumably as a consequence of peer pressures, telephoned Engel to ask if he could arrange a private meeting with the Führer;[18] he was particularly anxious that Keitel, Jodl, Zeitzler, and Schmundt should not be present. Engel secured Hitler's agreement on the 27th to see Kluge on the following day.

On the 26th, Hitler issued guidelines for Tunisia: Rommel was to be Commander-in-Chief of Army Group Africa, and von Arnim (whom Kesselring had proposed as Commander-in-Chief) was to

16. Edward P. von der Porten, *The German Navy in World War Two* (London: Pan Books, 1972), p. 235.

17. This order was issued by the Army General Staff as Führer Order No. 7, of 24 February 1943.

18. Kotze, ed., *Heeresadjutant bei Hitler*, p. 144.

head 5th Panzer Army and was to command the Army Group temporarily during Rommel's illness. Dönitz conferred again with Hitler, securing his formal endorsement of the limited reduction of the German large surface warships. The Commander-in-Chief West reported that the 39th Division, which was due to begin moving to the east on 3 March, was not yet fit for use there.

Hitler responded to this on the 27th by ordering that the division should be regarded as "available" for deployment in the east on 4 March, but that its capability for use must first be ascertained. He also ordered that Army Coast Artillery should be strengthened with 2cm anti-aircraft guns at the end of June and with searchlights by the end of October.

A blockade runner bringing rubber from Malaya was sunk in the Bay of Biscay on 26 February. Therefore, on the 27th, Hitler ordered improvements in air reconnaissance and surveillance over the Bay of Biscay, in order to improve the protection of these vital cargoes on the final stage of their journey.

By the 28th, the evidence of Hitler's resumption of direct control is complete. A supplement to operation order No. 4, which concerned Army Groups South and Center and was issued on 25 February, contained orders on matters of detail within the Army Group Commanders' competence.[19] Kluge arrived for his meeting with Hitler fully determined to resign if he was not successful in securing the appointment of a Commander-in-Chief East and the replacement of Keitel by an acceptable Chief of General Staff for OKW. However, he emerged from the meeting depressed and pensive, having failed at both points.[20]

Thus, February, which began with the surrender at Stalingrad and with Hitler apparently reluctant to exercise authority over senior field commanders, ended with that authority completely restored, the attempt to challenge or circumscribe it repulsed, and a successful counteroffensive launched against the Russians.

MARCH 1943

Military uneasiness at the lack of a professional Commander-in-Chief of the Eastern Front was paralleled by political disquiet at

---

19. The supplement not merely laid down new boundaries and front lines, it also prescribed how they were to be achieved. *KTB/OKW*, Vol. III, Part I, p. 160.

20. Kotze, ed., *Heeresadjutant bei Hitler*, p. 144.

the lack of any positive measures to attract the non-Russian minorities of the Soviet Union to the Nazi cause. Goebbels and Göring met on 2 March, agreed, against the opposition of the party ideologist, Rosenberg, to urge Hitler to issue a proclamation for the east, and decided to seek an early meeting with him.[21]

Göring reported on 3 March that air cover over the Bay of Biscay had been strengthened as ordered. The rest of the conference concerned Southeastern Europe. Hitler ordered Commander-in-Chief Southeast (Colonel-General Löhr), who was present, to stop enemy landings at the beaches, and to stockpile six months' requirements in Crete. A lengthy discussion of political consolidation in Croatia took place, and it was agreed to keep it under strict German administration. The order covering the requisition of vehicles for the Eastern Front was extended to cover Germany and the occupied West and to include uncompleted vehicles. A jurisdictional dispute between the Reich labor front and the Army was left unresolved. The order of 20 January, which had accorded first defense priority to the Greek islands and the Peloponnese, was amended by the addition of Sicily, Sardinia, and Corsica.

The only decision recorded on 4 March was one of detail: Hitler ordered 8.8cm anti-aircraft guns destined for Africa to be shipped only from the Sicilian port of Trapani, and, wherever possible, only on small ships. However, Hitler conceded that the port of Marsala could also be used, provided it could be protected to the same degree as Trapani.

On 5 March, the decisions concerned Hungarian troops in Russia and the German position in North Africa. The Hungarian Chief of General Staff had already asked for the Hungarian 2nd Army to be withdrawn west of the Dnieper, so Hitler ordered the Army to be reorganized into two full divisions and twelve construction battalions, with the remaining troops speedily returned to Hungary. Growing equipment shortages were reflected in the decision that the two divisions and twelve battalions would have to be equipped entirely from 2nd Army's existing stocks.[22]

The reports from North Africa complained bitterly of lack of supplies and of the unsatisfactory equipment and morale of Italian

21. Lochner, ed., *The Goebbels Diaries*, p. 200.

22. The point here concerns not the quantity of the available equipment (Hungarian 2nd Army comprised ten divisions on 22 December 1942) but the quality, most of the Hungarian equipment being outdated. See Table, "Die Gliederung des deutschen Heeres" (22 December 1942), in *KTB/OKW*, Vol. II, Part II, p. 1394.

units. Hitler merely noted for transmission to Kesselring that both he and Rommel had greatly changed their opinions (that is, become less optimistic) since the end of 1942. Hitler argued that withdrawal into a narrow bridgehead would be disastrous, and that immediate increases in shipping capacity, enabling transits to be doubled and later trebled, were possible and essential. (This line of argument ensured that large quantities of men and equipment were transported to Africa, in time for a surrender in May of proportions little short of that at Stalingrad.)

March 6 saw attention returned to Yugoslavia; operations against the Communists were to continue, but no more arms were to be issued to Chetniks, who were to be disarmed where appropriate, by force if necessary. The Chetnik center in Montenegro was to be attacked later; and to ensure Italian cooperation (the Chetniks and Italians had collaborated extensively against Tito's partisans), the Italian commander, General Ambrosio, and Mussolini should be shown intercepted messages from Mihailovich to his units. The high hopes for the U-boat campaign (actually, though not yet obviously, on the verge of collapse) led to an increase in the Navy's allocation of 45,000 tons of steel per month.[23]

To eliminate organizational confusion in directing the effort in Africa, Wfst prepared a new directive for Commander-in-Chief South. This, however, rejected a number of changes proposed by Kesselring and essentially merely reaffirmed Directive 38 of 2 December 1941[24] and the Führer order of 27 January 1943[25] on duties and subordinations. Hitler signed it on 8 March. But any idea that organizational measures could save the situation in Africa was dashed by a report on the Mark VI (Tiger) tank, which showed that only three were available for use.

A special conference on 9 March considered Guderian's propo-

23. March 1943 was in fact the most successful month of the whole war for the U-boats, which sank ninety-five ships of 627,000 tons, at a loss of fifteen submarines. However, Allied countermeasures, already introduced by March but not fully effective, improved the situation dramatically. In May, Allied tonnage lost had fallen to 264,000 tons, and forty-one German submarines were sunk. On 24 May, Dönitz conceded defeat and withdrew his submarines from the North Atlantic. See Patrick Beesly, *Very Special Intelligence*, revised edition (London; Sphere Books, 1978), pp. 234–245.

24. Hugh R. Trevor-Roper, ed., *Hitler's War Directives* (London: Sidgwick and Jackson, 1964), pp. 105–106.

25. This was issued on 28 January 1943 as Führer Order on the subordination of 5th Panzer Army and the duties of the Commander-in-Chief South. OKW/Wfst, Op. Nr. 66214/43.

sals designed to give him control over armored forces developments. Only Speer (who bore the main responsibility for production) supported his request for inclusion of assault artillery,[26] and Hitler deferred to majority opinion, with demonstrably bad later effects upon armored forces. On the same day, the Führer gave Goebbels several directives aimed at increasing manpower by 800,000, improving civilian air raid protection, confirming Goebbels's position as sole commander of Berlin, and removing all Jews from the city. Hitler sanctioned the award of the casualty ribbon for air raid injuries and, on hearing that Nuremberg had been bombed, summoned the Air Force liaison officer, General Bodenschatz, from bed to express his anger at Göring's inefficiency. However, he refused Goebbels's suggestion of 2 March for a proclamation on the east.[27]

Surrounded as it was by German-dominated territory, Sweden had pursued official neutrality, but public opinion there was predominantly pro-Ally, and anti-German sentiments were being more openly expressed following the Allied successes. Wfst had therefore prepared contingent orders for the military commander in Norway, while Hitler ordered the commanders in both Norway and Finland to prepare a short study of requirements for invading Sweden. In view of the sensitivity of the issue, Hitler decreed that this order should be communicated orally, not in writing.

The other problem dealt with on 10 March concerned the call-up of older men. Wfst noted that manpower needs could not be met merely by inducting the 1897–1900 classes, and proposed to mobilize part of the 1894–1896 classes as well. Hitler vetoed this for the time being, but ordered that in mobilizing the 1897–1900 classes, the needs of the war economy must be kept in mind and that 120,000 of them should go to the Air Force, to replace younger men who would be transferred to the Army. On 10–11 March, he paid a further visit to Manstein's HQ, chiefly to congratulate Manstein on the recapture of Kharkov.[28] On his return, he ordered that the measures for equipping formations in the east which had been ordered on 14 January must be completed by 14 April.

Göring had gone to Rome for discussions with the Comando Su-

26. Guderian, *Panzer Leader*, p. 298.
27. Lochner, ed., *the Goebbels Diaries*, pp. 215–216.
28. Manstein, *Lost Victories*, p. 426; and Lochner, ed., *The Goebbels Diaries*, p. 225.

premo, and Hitler's anger at the Air Force's inability to stop night bombing of German cities found further expression on the 12th, when he came to FHQ to report on his discussions with the Italians. In the presence of Rommel, whose health had again broken down, it was decided that Tunisia must be held. at all costs, for the sake of Italian morale. After the talks, Hitler impulsively awarded Rommel a high decoration, and it was decided that he should go on leave at once, his place being taken by Arnim, and the matter kept secret. Hitler endorsed Rommel's proposals for defense of the Mareth and Schott positions, and a conference on supply by sea was arranged for 14 March.

Invasion questions dominated the proceedings on the 13th. The military commander in Norway had reported on the 9th that he needed reinforcements against an expected invasion in the spring, but Wfst had stated that more could not be provided by the Army or Air Force. Hitler reiterated that Norway must be strengthened, but he made no specific decisions. Naval headquarters reported an increasing expectation of a major Western action in France and the western Mediterranean any time after mid-March. Hitler ordered that units of the new assault guns and tanks (Hornet, Ferdinand, Panther, and Tiger) were to be deployed in the west as far as technically possible, remaining under the control of the Inspector General of Armored Forces unless and until they were needed for battle. He also ordered the 11th Air Force Field Division to be fully motorized and to be ready for deployment as a mobile reserve in Greece. Men born between 1919 and 1922 who had not yet been called up were to be mobilized from August onwards.

The conference on supply on 14 March took place in the presence of Dönitz, Keitel, Jodl, Kesselring, and Jeschonnek (Chief of Staff of the Air Force). Hitler insisted that Tunis was a first-class strategic position, and proceeded to attack the Italians for their lack of enthusiasm for its defense. Comando Supremo had suggested that the supply requirement was 80,000 tons a month, but Hitler defined it as 150,000–200,000. He believed that Italy must be faced with the alternatives of either doing everything possible to achieve the supply or facing the possibility that Italy itself would be lost.

The accusation of Italian foot-dragging over the defense of Tunisia was curious, given that it took place immediately after the receipt of a letter from Mussolini which reiterated the need to hold

Tunisia at all costs. Hitler referred to several other issues, but no comments or decisions by him were recorded. No decisions were recorded on the 15th either, other than Hitler's decision to give a high decoration to SS General Dietrich, and a conversation with Goebbels in which Hitler agreed that Goebbels should not pause till not a single Jew was left anywhere in Germany.[29] The paucity of decisions on 15 and 16 March may be partly accounted for by the fact that on those days discussions took place with the Spanish envoy, General Campos, on the question of arms deliveries to Spain, a delicate matter given the shortages under which Germany itself was laboring.

On the 16th, the Abwehr reported that Marshal Pétain was planning to flee to North Africa, so Hitler ordered all airfields in the vicinity of Vichy to be rendered unusable. In recognition of Manstein's successful counteroffensive at Kharkov, Hitler awarded him a high decoration. And in an attempt to bring some order into the chaos of conflicting authorities over the manpower program, he gave Sauckel complete authority over departments of the Ministry of Labor already within his jurisdiction, despite the vehement objection of Goebbels.[30]

The record of 17 March shows Hitler in full decision-making stride. His military conference decisions covered all areas. He ordered Air Fleet I to be strengthened because he expected a Soviet attack in the Leningrad area, having convinced himself that attacks against 2nd Panzer Army in the center of the front had ended and that enemy forces were being moved away either to the south for defense against an expected German attack or to the north for a Soviet offensive. Operations order No. 5, issued on 5 March, was supplemented on the 17th with a list of detailed preparations to be undertaken in view of the fact that the spring thaw had come early. Some rearrangement of forces was decreed, with the Eastern Front receiving three divisions and some "Brandenburg" forces (special-purpose units analogous to Commandos, Rangers, or SAS), and surrendering one division to OKW Reserve, two divisions to Commander-in-Chief Southeast (with some of their units going to Norway), and one division to Commander-in-Chief South.

In view of the situation in the east, the planned equipping of the

29. Lochner, ed., *The Goebbels Diaries*, p. 230.
30. Ibid., pp. 230–231.

"Göring" Division, one of the three new SS divisions, two Air Force Field Divisions, and the Croatian Light Infantry Brigade was postponed until after the middle of April. Concern about the possibly imminent invasion of Italy was shown by the issuing of an order (apparently decreed on 15 March) for a party of Italian artillery and pioneer officers to visit the "Atlantic Wall" before the end of the month. Commander-in-Chief West reported on proposals to occupy the Balearic Islands, stating that the forces available could not defend the islands without Spanish cooperation, and that the planned operation was unfeasible. Hitler expressed his agreement.

In respect to Africa, Hitler canceled the planned regrouping on the Mareth-Schott position which had been ordered on 12 March, in view of the issuance of a directive by the Comando Supremo to Army Group Africa on 17 March, which expressed the sense of Hitler's conversation with Kesselring on the 14th.

Hitler also considered a proposal by Goebbels, who was anxious to gain control of propaganda to the east,[31] and gave a compromise decision, allowing Goebbels the same rights as he had over all other propaganda, namely to post representatives at embassies abroad. Hitler also issued a decree warning government and party leaders to conduct themselves "in accordance with the needs of wartime." Goebbels considered these measures inadequate; he had been especially incensed by the luxurious living of many senior party officials, and the bad effects of this on popular attitudes toward the war.[32]

On 18 March, Hitler endorsed a proposal from C-in-C West to transfer the French Garde Mobile to the police force, and to allow the French Government a "government troop" of 2,739 officers and men, provided Italy had no objection. The 715th Division had requested permission to use eight hundred colored French prisoners-of-war as drivers, grooms, and manual laborers, and Hitler approved this. He also ordered an assault brigade to be sent to Sardinia at once.

Hitler's lack of success in Vienna as a youth had left him very hostile to that city. After hearing of an art exhibition that had taken place there, he expressed violent disapproval, and ordered Vien-

31. Ibid., p. 232.
32. Ibid., p. 234.

nese cultural affairs to be placed under Goebbels's supervision, with all subsidies to be cut off if the Viennese objected.[33]

Dönitz informed Hitler of the arrangements made by the Kriegsmarine with the Italian Navy, which gave the Germans a large degree of control over it. The Admiral emphasized the need for air cover on Mediterranean convoy routes to reduce the very high shipping losses, and Hitler concurred. Neither Dönitz nor Hitler knew, and the British did not disclose for over thirty years, that these heavy losses were primarily due to the reading of German and Italian naval ciphers, not to airborne reconnaissance, which was usually dispatched in advance of attacks simply to conceal the true sources of information.

On the 19th, the emphasis shifted back to the Balkans, with a number of minor troop movements ordered, and an assault brigade earmarked for Rhodes. It was reported also that a promised delivery of thirty-six heavy coastal guns to Bulgaria could not be made, but Hitler made no recorded comment. On that day, he attended a demonstration at Rügenwalde of a modified Panzer IV tank, the new "Ferdinand" assault gun, and a rail-mounted heavy gun known as "Gustav." At the demonstration, Guderian found grave fault with the "Ferdinand," which, lacking a machine gun, was very vulnerable to infantry at close range, and was produced only because of Hitler's belief in its designer, Dr. Porsche. Guderian's argument with Hitler, who claimed "Gustav" could fight tanks, crossed into absurdity: the gun, of 800mm (31.5 inches) caliber, could operate only from a double-track railway, and fire one round every forty-five minutes.

On the 20th, Goebbels recorded Hitler's agreement that future bombing raids on England should be directed against "residential sections of the plutocracy," not slums, harbors, or industrial cities, and that air warfare should be psychological rather than military in intent. The point was of little relevance; by 1943, the Air Force could barely attack England, as most of its bomber force was in Russia, while construction was increasingly being diverted from bombers to fighters to meet the twin threats posed by improvements in the Soviet tactical air forces and the ever-increasing weight of Anglo-American bombing. An indication of Hitler's detachment

33. Ibid., p. 238.

from German civil society was that while he interfered in matters of detail concerning both arms production and combat operations, he left the conduct of the "total war" propaganda campaign almost exclusively to Goebbels.[34]

No decisions by Hitler are recorded for 21 or 22 March, but on the 23rd he agreed that the remnants of the Hungarian 2nd Army could remove their headquarters westward to Kiev. Because of unrest in Holland, he ordered 100,000 former Dutch army personnel to be put to forced labor in Germany.

The Commander-in-Chief of Army Group Africa had complained that Kesselring had forbidden him to send tactical reports directly to FHQ. Hitler therefore issued an order on 23 March that no higher agency was to prevent the sending of reports to him, but that such reports should go simultaneously to the next highest superior, so that he could express his opinion.[35]

On 24 March, proposals by the Croatian Prime Minister for reorganizing his administration were vetoed; Hitler's concern was to increase German control over Croatia, at the expense of Italian, rather than enhance Croatian autonomy. Increased partisan activity against the Ukrainian railways led to approval of a series of anti-partisan measures.

Noteworthy after 19 February is the paucity of orders relating to Manstein's offensive. In part, this is due to the exclusion of OKW from conferences at which OKH matters were decided, but it seems from Manstein's own account that he achieved at least temporary freedom from interference. The Russians were forced back across the Northern Donets; but on 24 March, the OKW diary noted that the offensive had come to an end, and most units had taken up defensive positions. The spring thaw then enforced inactivity on both sides for several weeks; 24 March therefore serves to mark the end of the post-crisis period and consequently of the Stalingrad crisis as a whole.

The post-crisis period will now be discussed in terms of the four crisis components and variables of the typologies.

---

34. Ibid., pp. 241–242.

35. The grounds for this order appear to have been an attempt by the Commander-in-Chief South (Field Marshal Kesselring) to prevent direct reporting to OKW by the Commander-in-Chief of Army Group Africa (Colonel-General von Arnim). See *KTB/OKW*, Vol. III, Part I, p. 239.

CRISIS COMPONENTS

Environmental Change

The post-crisis period was initiated by the surrender of the trapped forces at Stalingrad between 30 January and 2 February 1943. At that point, the worst was known; a major defeat had been suffered, but an entire collapse in the south had been averted by the extrication from the Caucasus of Army Group A, an undertaking to which continued German resistance at Stalingrad had contributed. Although the Soviet offensive continued until 19 February, it achieved no further encirclements of large Axis forces, while the Red Army became seriously overextended in following up what was in fact a planned German withdrawal, designed to lure them into a trap. German perception of unfavorable environmental change therefore decreased during the post-crisis period. There may have been a brief period (15–16 February) when Hitler perceived an increased threat from Manstein's yielding of Kharkov after he had been categorically ordered to hold it. But it is equally likely that his visit to Manstein's headquarters on 17–19 February was prompted merely by a desire for reassurance, because although he attempted to urge an immediate frontal assault to recapture the city, he eventually accepted Manstein's reasoning and appears from the incomplete surviving records not to have interfered further with Manstein's conduct of the operation. Soviet forces suffered substantial losses during Manstein's counteroffensive (20 February–24 March); they were forced to surrender Kharkov and retreat to the east bank of the Northern Donets river.

Threat to Values

Belief in an important value—the professional superiority of German war-making ability—had been shaken by the Red Army. The skill shown in extricating Army Group A and in Manstein's counteroffensive went some way toward rehabilitating belief in that value. Although the importance of the defeat at Stalingrad could not be minimized, the partial recovery of the initiative during the post-crisis period prevented the defeat from being seen as definitive; and even before the end of the crisis, planning had already begun for a major new offensive to take place in late spring or early summer. It would be left to that offensive, against the Kursk salient in

July 1943, not Stalingrad, to provide the definitive German defeat in Russia.

It should be noted, however, that Hitler, in the post-crisis period, perceived a number of potential threats to values arising from the defeats in the East and in North Africa, namely of invasion at various points from Norway to Greece, and of possible intervention by Sweden and Turkey on the Allied side.

Change in the Military Balance

Overall, the military balance was, of course, more adverse to Germany at the end of the total crisis than at the beginning, but it was less adverse at the end of the post-crisis period than at the beginning of it. Although a great deal of territory had to be surrendered, no further disasters befell the German Army in Russia during February, and Manstein's successful counteroffensive demonstrated that the Red Army could still be beaten in the field. Austerity measures initiated by Goebbels in the days immediately following the Stalingrad surrender were only perfunctorily backed up by Hitler, who before the end of the post-crisis period had already turned his attention to a renewed offensive in Russia.

Time Pressure

Hitler was sensitive to time pressure relating to other theatres of war, especially in respect to the dispatch of forces to North Africa and to peripheral areas of Europe (Norway and the Balkans) which he wrongly regarded as likely to be invaded in the near future. But in regard to the Eastern Front, he displayed a sense of time pressure only in urging the immediate recapture of Kharkov during his visit to Manstein's headquarters on 17–19 February.

Manstein was subject to time pressure, not in the sense of a need to take decisions quickly, but in the sense of having to phase his counteroffensive so as to exploit the weather and Soviet difficulties of supply, and force the Red Army back across the Northern Donets—that is, across a river line which the Germans could more easily defend later, before the spring thaw enforced inactivity on both sides. The assembly of forces for his counterstroke was carried out under severe time constraints, but these were overcome.

The lessening of time pressure on FHQ was shown in the reduction in the number of recorded decisions relating to the southern sector of the Eastern Front. During the full crisis period of seventy-seven days, from 20 November to 2 February, sixty-six such decisions were recorded; in the fifty days of the post-crisis period, from 3 February to 24 March, only thirteen.

COPING MECHANISMS

Information Processing

The established FHQ procedures for processing and acting on information at the daily conference continued in force throughout the post-crisis period, with no change in the information flow. However, Manstein perceived his difficulties in securing Hitler's acquiescence to withdrawals as based on inadequate understanding at FHQ of his intentions and possibilities. Having pleaded with Hitler to come to the front himself, or to send a trusted representative such as Jodl, he was summoned to FHQ by Hitler on 5 February, and was further visited by Hitler at his own headquarters on 17–19 February. There is no evidence to suggest that Hitler was imperfectly informed of Manstein's plans; it is likely that such misperceptions as existed arose from the generalized mistrust of withdrawals which characterized Hitler's decisions throughout the crisis rather than from lack of information about Manstein's intentions. As the Soviet offensive manifestly lost its impetus in the first half of February, and the initiative passed back into German hands, information about Soviet intentions became of less importance than during the pre-crisis and crisis periods.

Consultation: Persons and Groups

For much of February, Manstein acquired an importance not hitherto accorded to a senior field commander; but in general, Hitler's and FHQ's pattern of minimal consultation was sustained. Goebbels's attempt to secure Hitler's involvement in home-front matters by public propagation of the "total war" concept was unsuccessful. Although much of Hitler's and OKW's time was occupied in consideration of matters unconnected with the Eastern Front, here too the activity consisted of considering reports prepared entirely within FHQ or adjudicating on reports and requests passed upwards from the commanders in the areas concerned, rather than in consultation with them.

Decisional Forums

From the beginning of the post-crisis period to 13 February, Hitler took very few decisions; preparations for Manstein's counterstroke were made by Manstein's HQ in conjunction with Zeitzler and OKH. However, Manstein had to visit FHQ on 6 February to secure Hitler's permission for preliminary withdrawals, believed he had secured it, but found on 13 February that this permission was qualified, when Hitler called for Kharkov to be held, against Manstein's wishes. The sequel, Hitler's visit to Manstein on 17–19 February, gave Manstein the freedom of action he had sought, his HQ thereby in effect becoming the decisional forum for the southern sector of the Eastern Front until the conclusion of his offensive on 24–25 March. During the period 1–24 March, Hitler is recorded in the OKW diary as having made fifty-one decisions; of these, only four related to the Eastern Front, and only one of those to the southern sector. The record is biased by OKW's exclusion from private meetings between Hitler and Zeitzler, but this was already in force during the crisis period, in which the OKW diary nevertheless recorded Hitler as taking sixty-six decisions in respect to Army Groups A, B, and Don, versus fifteen relating to other Eastern Front sectors and one hundred and forty-two relating to other theatres of military operations.

During the post-crisis period, an attempt was made to enlarge the decisional forum by securing the appointment of a Commander-in-Chief East. This was initiated by Hitler's Army adjutant, Major Engel, who tried to persuade the Commander-in-Chief West to approach Hitler about it. When Rundstedt declined, Manstein discussed it with Hitler on 6 February, and Kluge made a further attempt on 28 February, but both failed. Hitler did, however, appoint Colonel-General Guderian to the post of Inspector-General of Armored Troops on 28 February; but Guderian's duties included no operational control of forces, and were further circumscribed by the exclusion from his competence of assault guns, which were to become an increasingly important component of Panzer divisions.

Hitler's decision-making authority survived the Stalingrad debacle sufficiently intact to repel the senior field commanders' attempt to circumscribe it. Even Kluge, who had sworn to resign if Hitler refused to appoint a Commander-in-Chief East, did not do so. The reluctance of the senior officers to carry their opposition further can be explained in terms of loyalty to a Head of State to whom all had taken a personal oath of obedience in 1934. But a contributory factor was undoubtedly the success of Manstein's offensive and the renewed optimism about the prospects of a German summer offensive which this induced.

Alternatives: Search and Evaluation

The only debate about operational alternatives in the post-crisis period was between Manstein's concept of yielding territory in order to regroup his own forces and to tempt the Soviets to overextend themselves, and Hitler's by now routine insistence on holding on to positions. This led to two meetings (at FHQ on 6 February, and at Manstein's HQ on 17–19 February), at the second of which Manstein succeeded in securing Hitler's acquiescence to his more flexible concept.

More fundamentally, an abortive attempt was made to find an alternative to Hitler as the overall commander in the East; but at meetings with Manstein on 6 February and Kluge on 28 February, the Führer refused to appoint a Commander-in-Chief East, and the attempt was abandoned.

CHAPTER SEVEN

Overall Conclusions

THE STALINGRAD CRISIS will now be examined in terms of the nine research questions set out in the Introduction. The relevant research findings will be discussed, qualitative comparisons will be drawn between the three subdivisions of the crisis, and some quantitative comparisons of the decision-making patterns in the three subdivisions will also be attempted, to the extent that the limitations of the data permit.

Some difficulties are encountered in interpreting the research questions, conceived in the 1970s, in terms of a situation of more than thirty years earlier, and in applying questions concerned with the initiation of war to an intra-war crisis. The peculiarly personalized character of German decision-making during the Second World War, and Hitler's characteristic and, on the whole, only too successful tactics of dividing responsibilities between agencies and of creating competing agencies to cover the same section of the war effort, mean that the full reasoning behind some of the decisions is not known and never will be, because it was neither communicated to anyone nor committed to paper. Nevertheless, enough information has survived about the decision-making processes in Nazi Germany to enable at least some generalizations to be made in terms of the research questions. German meticulousness in keeping records and statistics assists powerfully in this connection.

Within the period July 1942 to February 1943, the pressures of Threat and Time, initially not perceived at all by Hitler and those who surrounded him, grew inexorably as it was realized, first, that the summer offensive in Russia could not achieve its objectives before the onset of winter; secondly, that a substantial proportion of the forces involved in it were faced with the prospect of destruction; and thirdly, that a comparable catastrophe was impending in North Africa. The German decision-making apparatus was therefore confronted with a growing level of stress. But before attempting to consider how it reacted to that stress, it is advisable to look at the pre-crisis German perception of the enemy in fairly general terms.

THE PSYCHOLOGICAL ENVIRONMENT

German perceptions of Russia, and especially of Russian military capacity, had been conditioned by many centuries of interaction in which Russia had sometimes been politically dominant, but German cultural ascendancy had almost always been assured. Germans had played important roles in Russia as rulers, administrators, soldiers, scholars, and businessmen, while Russians had played no comparable role in Germany. The Russian Academy of Sciences had been established by Peter the Great in 1725 on German advice and, to begin with, had consisted almost entirely of German scholars. The Empress Catherine the Great, herself German, had, among other things, imported German peasants to improve Russian agriculture. Reorganization of the Russian Army in the 1860s had leaned heavily on the Prussian model in respect both to its conscription system and to the institution of a General Staff. In intellectual circles, the two sides of the Slavophile-Westernizer debate had derived most of their ideas from German historians and philosophers—Herder, Hegel, Fichte, and Schelling being particularly influential. And the post-1917 state philosophy originated in the writings of two exiled Germans, Marx and Engels. A patronizing Social-Darwinist attitude toward all Slavs, and especially Russians, was long-established in Germany. At the outset of the nineteenth century, Herder had characterized the Slavs as peaceful agriculturists, incapable of permanent military organization and "unfortunate" to have found themselves located between the more dynamic Germans on one side and Tartars on the other.[1] Hegel had described them as coming "only late into the series of historical states."[2] Max Weber claimed that Poles had only "become human

1. Cited in Janko Lavrin, *Russia, Slavdom and the Western World* (London: Bles, 1969), p. 24.

2. Georg W. F. Hegel, *Lectures on the Philosophy of History*, trans. J. Sibree (London: George Bell, 1905), p. 107.

beings" by courtesy of Germany.[3] And Hitler himself argued that "the Russian State was not organized by the constructive political talent of the Slav element in Russia, but was much more a marvellous exemplification of the capacity for state-building possessed by the Germanic element in a race of inferior worth."[4] And because that element had been replaced in the Russian Revolution by a Jewish one (by definition an agent of corruption), "this colossal Empire in the East is ripe for dissolution."[5]

An attitude likely to result in a tendency to underestimate Soviet capacity was therefore well-established before the Nazi ideology of race was devised; it underlay the decision to invade the Soviet Union with forces which it was known would be outnumbered by the defenders (and which were even more outnumbered than expected, because Soviet mobilization capacity was itself underestimated).[6]

The first major German land defeat of the war was suffered in the Battle of Moscow, but the tendency to "blame it on the weather" rather than on the Soviet opponent was widespread (though not universal) among senior officers,[7] troops, and civilian populations[8] alike. Even after Stalingrad, fear of defeat in the East was associated with the Russian winter, and the German perception of Soviet military capability remained low. In fact, the defense of Moscow was skillfully conducted, and with resources that were more meager than the Germans realized. And while the weather was bad for the Russians, too, they exploited it by destroying before withdrawal as much fuel and shelter as possible, so that much German effort was expended on simple survival, to the detriment of military operations. It can also be argued that to invade Russia without adequate cold-weather clothing, antifreeze, and lubricants was foolhardy.[9] The point is not to denigrate German performance but

3. Robert G. L. Waite, *The Psychopathic God: Adolf Hitler* (New York: Basic Books, 1977), p. 288.

4. Adolf Hitler, *Mein Kampf* (London: Hutchinson, no date [late 1930s]), p. 557.

5. Ibid.

6. Basil H. Liddell Hart, *The Other Side of the Hill* (London: Panther, 1956), p. 189, quotes Halder as follows: "We underestimated Russia: we reckoned with 200 divisions, but now [August 1941] we have already identified 360." See also Warlimont's comments on the same page.

7. See statements by Kleist and Rundstedt in Liddell Hart, *Other Side of the Hill*, pp. 206–209 and 212–213.

8. Examples are given in the Appendix.

9. Geoffrey Jukes, *The Defense of Moscow* (New York: Ballantine, 1969).

to indicate that the tendency to underestimate the Russians had already proved deep-seated enough to survive one major defeat, and that the existence of this tendency played a not insignificant part in the development of the Stalingrad crisis, specifically in conditioning German perceptions as to whether the Russians could mount a threat at all and, when it turned out that they could, in German responses to it.

The first question concerns the effects of increasing and decreasing levels of crisis-induced stress on cognitive performance, and two associated hypotheses:

1. The greater the stress, the greater the conceptual rigidity of an individual, and the more closed to new information the individual becomes.

2. The greater the crisis, the greater the propensity for decision-makers to supplement information about the objective state of affairs with information drawn from their own past experience.[10]

Both hypotheses are concerned solely with changes in attitude under the effects of passage of time and changing levels of stress; neither involves any assumptions about the attitudinal base with respect to which changes are assessed. Where Hitler is concerned, this creates problems, especially in regard to the first hypothesis, because his conceptual rigidity was already high, and his receptivity to information low, before the pre-crisis period. In passages in Chapter 14 of *Mein Kampf*, he had discussed information in terms not of contribution to knowledge but rather as a process intended to "impress definite political ideas" on left-wingers whose former teaching had been "partly counterbalanced by the residue of sound and natural instincts which remained," or, "much more difficult," on "representatives of our so-called intellectual circles," who "have sacrificed the last residue of their national instincts to the worship of some abstract and entirely objective theory."[11] In short, it is "instinct," which precedes knowledge, that is the important factor.

Similarly, Hitler's attitude to information was instrumental. "It

10. From Michael Brecher with Benjamin Geist, *Decisions in Crisis* (Berkeley, Los Angeles, and London: University of California Press, 1980), p. 343, where the consensus findings of the literature are also summarized.

11. Hitler, *Mein Kampf*, p. 546.

was the total failure of the whole German system of information [in World War I] . . . that urged me to consider the problem of propaganda in a comprehensive way."[12] The discussions of propaganda in *Mein Kampf* concentrate on the functions and transmission of information as a means of persuasion, and say next to nothing about the nature of information.[13] In summary, therefore, the question of effects of stress on cognitive performance, and of the two associated hypotheses, can be conducted only on the basis that Hitler was conceptually rigid and resistant to new information even in no-stress or low-stress situations. He had fixed views about the inferiority of Russians, formed before 1924, the year in which these views were incorporated into *Mein Kampf*. His conceptual rigidity and low receptivity to new information demonstrated themselves in a reluctance to admit to himself or others that his perception of Russians could be wrong.

In the pre-crisis period, he attributed the successful Soviet withdrawal to the Don bend in July 1942 not to Russian military skill but to Bock's preoccupation with Voronezh, which, though an important factor, was not the sole or even the determinant one. Nevertheless, Bock was dismissed.

Similarly, in August, when List failed to achieve his objectives in the Caucasus, Hitler attributed this not to the physical difficulties of the undertaking, or the strength of Soviet resistance, but to List's disobedience of orders, and dismissed him. When Jodl attempted to defend List by claiming that he had obeyed his orders to the letter, Hitler quarreled with Jodl and contemplated dismissing him also. And Halder's reservations about the possibilities of success led to Halder's removal in September. All these events occurred in the pre-crisis period, when the level of adversary-imposed stress was not high, Soviet forces being for most of the period in full withdrawal.

When the full crisis erupted in November, Hitler's response to it was curiously slow: he was absent from FHQ from 7 November, the day before the Allied landings in North Africa, to 23 November, two days after closure of the encirclement at Stalingrad. Though parts of the FHQ staff traveled with him, their physical dispersal at the Berghof, Strub, and Salzburg, their remoteness from FHQ,

12. Ibid., p. 161.
13. Ibid., pp. 161–168 and 297–298.

and the lack of any high-level OKH representative among the party that accompanied Hitler made it difficult to respond quickly to pressures of time and threat. Yet, when Hitler did arrive back at FHQ, he attempted to postpone the discussion of matters that Zeitzler regarded as urgent. He again showed conceptual rigidity in refusing to sanction withdrawals and in accepting, over the misgivings of senior Air Force and Army professionals, Göring's assurance that the beleaguered forces could be supplied by air. This, of course, enabled him to sustain his opposition to withdrawals and thereby maintain his conceptual rigidity, reject the "new information" that the Soviets were far more formidable than he conceived them to be, and continue in the belief, derived from his experience of the previous winter, that refusal to withdraw was the correct response to Soviet attacks.

Contrary to the first hypothesis, Hitler's conceptual rigidity declined somewhat under the stress of the crisis period. After the failure of the relief attempt, he sanctioned withdrawal of Army Group A from the Caucasus; and in the post-crisis period, he gave Manstein freedom to make withdrawals in order to regroup for his counteroffensive. And when, in mid-February, his doubts about withdrawals surfaced again, leading him to order the holding of Kharkov (and, when it was lost, urging its immediate recapture), Manstein was able to persuade him to change his mind.

The relaxation of conceptual rigidity was not, however, complete. Hitler angrily rejected Rommel's advice to abandon North Africa, and neither Manstein nor Zeitzler found it easy to obtain his sanction for withdrawals. Nevertheless, this sanction was obtained in both the crisis and post-crisis periods, suggesting that under stress Hitler's conceptual rigidity relaxed somewhat. The first hypothesis is therefore not supported by Hitler's behavior.

The second hypothesis, concerning a decision-maker's propensity to draw on his own past experience, derives rather more support from Hitler's actions. Where this hypothesis is concerned, Hitler's wide interpretation of history was rooted in the Social Darwinism of the late nineteenth century and in his experience of the dissolution of the Austro-Hungarian empire in 1918. His historical views are set out in *Mein Kampf*, in the conference of 5 November 1937 noted in the Hossbach Memorandum, and in many speeches, as well as in interpretative articles by Goebbels in *Das Reich* and elsewhere. This historical perspective has been discussed in a number of works on Nazism,[14] and can be summarized as based on nationalism, fear of revolution from the left, obsession with racial and biological questions, and a cataclysmic perception of history. The concept of struggle dominated his thinking ("Mankind has grown great in eternal struggle, and only in eternal peace does it perish"), led to his exaltation of obedience over intelligence, and generated his idea of German misfortunes as the consequences of the loss of racial purity.[15] Historical greatness and geographical magnitude were linked, and the restoration of the racial integrity of the Germans was to be accompanied by the acquisition of living space in the east, where a German master race, restored to pure Aryanism by selective breeding, would dominate a residual population of Slav helots. "If land was desired in Europe, it could be obtained by and large only at the expense of Russia, and this meant that the new Reich must again set itself on the march along the road of the Teutonic knights of old."[16] The invasion of Russia was therefore itself a product of Hitler's reading of the historical legacy.

In narrower terms, his interpretation of Stalin's options was historically based, in that he developed a fear, *before* the Soviet counteroffensive began, that Stalin would repeat his offensive of 1920—that is, would attempt a drive down the Don to Rostov, similar to that with which he had defeated the White forces in the Russian civil war.[17] In fact, this was only a partial misperception. The Soviet offensive was originally planned along these lines, with the intention of cutting off both Army Group B in the space between the Don and the Volga, and Army Group A in the Caucasus. Nevertheless, the primary emphasis of the Soviet offensive plan was on the destruction of the troops in the Stalingrad area, and when the numbers encircled proved to be much larger than expected, no hesitation was shown in diverting forces from the drive toward Rostov in order to reinforce the encirclement at Stalingrad. But even after Army Group A had withdrawn out of danger, a movement essentially completed by 24 January 1943, and despite the ample evi-

---

14. For example, Joachim C. Fest, *Hitler* (New York: Harcourt Brace Jovanovich, 1974), pp. 54–57.

15. Hitler, *Mein Kampf*, pp. 313–316, 324, 360, 436 and 444–446.

16. Ibid., p. 154.

17. This "Stalin offensive" was in fact a piece of Stalinist mythmaking. The drive to Rostov was in pursuit of the already defeated White armies of General Denikin, and was neither conceived nor directed by Stalin.

dence that the Soviet advance along the southern reaches of the Don was not being pursued in massive strength, Hitler refused to permit a surrender at Stalingrad. In this case, Hitler proved to be more dominated by Stalin's historical experience than was Stalin himself.

As disagreements with his military subordinates became more frequent and acrimonious, Hitler often resorted to pseudohistorical reflections upon the German officer class in general and the General Staff in particular. For example, on 4 September 1942, he contrasted his own experience as a combat soldier in World War I with Halder's "sitting on a swivel chair"; and on 30 September, he harangued Engel and Schmundt about the General Staff's alleged "loss of vision" after 1914. These references are in marked contrast to his eulogy of the German Army in *Mein Kampf*,[18] but they do not reflect a recourse to past experience or to history under the influence of stress. They are polemical devices, not a guide to action, and they become more frequent because disagreements with the military become more frequent.

It is likely, however, that the impetuous decision to decommission and scrap the larger surface warships does reflect recourse to past experience under stress. The immediate cause of it was the disappointing outcome of the Battle of Bear Island on 31 December 1942, at a time when Hitler was hoping for a victory with which to usher in the New Year and counterbalance the depressing picture on the Eastern Front. His remarks to Krancke before the battle ("Our own Navy is only a copy of the British—and a poor one at that") and his ready acceptance of Raeder's resignation on 6 January 1943 are consonant with passages in *Mein Kampf* which criticize the pre-1914 Naval leadership for halfheartedness, lack of foresight, a tendency to build inferior copies of British ships, irresolution, and contamination by "parliamentarian considerations."[19]

The partially incorrect recourse to historical analogy in respect to the anticipated Soviet drive down the Don to Rostov contributed to the loss at Stalingrad, but also to the salvaging of Army Group A by timely withdrawal. It expressed adherence to a perception reached during the pre-crisis period, which was in fact a correct reading of Soviet intentions at the time, but was adhered to

18. Hitler, *Mein Kampf*, pp. 241–242.
19. Ibid., pp. 236–237.

after it had been invalidated by a change in the Soviet plan. It cannot be viewed as the product of increasing stress, but must rather be seen as justified by circumstance, albeit fortuitously: the Soviet change of plan resulted from encirclement at Stalingrad of about four times as many forces as expected, which forced them to retain in the area troops who would otherwise have been employed in the intended drive to Rostov, and it was this that made Army Group A's timely withdrawal a possibility. Where conceptual rigidity and recourse to past experience under stress did play a part was in Hitler's initial reluctance to permit Army Group A to withdraw, and in his enduring refusal to allow Stalingrad to be abandoned. Here he was influenced by the experience of the winter of 1941–42, in which generals who had advocated withdrawals subsequently admitted that they might have resulted in a rout.

In summary, therefore, the evidence presents some support for both hypotheses. However, while it points strongly to increased conceptual rigidity under the stress of the full crisis period, it does not support to the same extent an *increased* recourse to past experience. The most crucial instance of the latter, the reluctance to permit withdrawals, was the *repeated* application of a solution derived from the previous winter. In respect to one of the threatened forces, Army Group A, it was overcome by persuasion in the full crisis period; and when in the post-crisis period it reemerged in respect to Kharkov, it was again overcome by the same means.

There is no evidence to suggest that Hitler's cognitive performance was impaired by fatigue; his habit of sleeping till late in the morning and working into the night was followed by most of the officers closely associated with him, so that he was seldom prematurely disturbed from sleep.[20] The decline in the number of Stalingrad-related decisions between the failure of the relief attempt and the final surrender is probably no more than a tacit recognition that no more could be done, and is balanced by increases in decision-making activity in relation to other theatres such as North Africa, where he did not share Rommel's view that the situation was beyond redemption.

There is, however, a suggestion not necessarily of impaired cognitive performance but of impaired readiness to take decisions dur-

20. Walter Warlimont, *Inside Hitler's Headquarters, 1939–45*, trans. R. H. Barry (London: Weidenfeld and Nicolson, 1964), p. 225.

ing the immediate aftermath of the surrender in Stalingrad. From 2
to 12 February 1943, the number of decisions attributed to Hitler
in respect to both OKH and OKW theatres falls to a very low level:
during these eleven days, he is mentioned in connection with only
eight Army-related decisions, most of which were reactions to proposals made by others rather than positive initiatives of his own.

COPING: PROCESSES AND MECHANISMS

Information

The second and third research questions concern the impact of
changing crisis-induced stress on: (2) the perceived need and consequent probe for information; and (3) the receptivity and size of
the information-processing group.

The basic problem here is that the flow of information coming to
Hitler was copious, but the full extent to which it was "tainted,"
especially through British deception operations, including the ma-
nipulation of German spies and the exploitation of knowledge derived from the penetration of the German ciphers, was not disclosed at all until comparatively recently, and has not yet been fully
disclosed.[21] However, if we distinguish between information itself
and Hitler's perceived need for it, a judgment is easier to reach.
When the summer offensive of 1942 in the Soviet Union was going
well, Hitler expressed no dissatisfaction with either the volume of
information reaching him or its accuracy. When it began to become
clear during August that the summer offensive was not attaining its
objectives, a change occurred, not in the direction of a search for
more information but toward a reduction of it, by excluding information that did not fit in with Hitler's preconceptions. This was
shown, for example, on 21 August 1942, when Halder stated that
German strength was insufficient for two wearing offensives such as
those being carried on simultaneously by Army Groups A and B,
and an angry argument took place. In the course of it, Halder
pointed out that the Soviets were producing 1,200 tanks a month
(in fact, an underestimate), whereupon Hitler forbade him to utter
"such idiotic nonsense." The dispute with Jodl in September, as
well as the dismissal of Halder, resulted from a visit by Jodl to

---

21. Francis H. Hinsley et al., *British Intelligence in the Second World War* (London;
Her Majesty's Stationery Office, 1979), Vol. I, pp. vii–x.

Army Group A and his subsequent defense of the Army Group's leadership. Hitler asserted that their failures were due to disobedience of orders, and Jodl pointed out that, on the contrary, they had made an attempt to carry out, to the letter, orders that were themselves misconceived. After this, Hitler confined himself to his quarters, and for some time forbade Jodl to appear before him at the conferences. Jodl himself later told Warlimont that he (Jodl) had been wrong to dispute with Hitler, because the source of a dictator's strength was his self-confidence, which should not be shaken. By this remark, he indicated awareness of, and agreement with, the restriction of the flow of information reaching Hitler.

When it became necessary to institute an airlift to supply the troops in Stalingrad, Hitler chose to believe Göring's assurances about the quantities that could be conveyed, over the strongly and frequently expressed misgivings not only of the Army leadership but of the senior officers of the Air Force. A serving officer, Major Christian, was brought to headquarters in an attempt to persuade Hitler that the airlift could not work. When the Major said that an average of 100–150 tons a day was all that could be expected against the 500–700 tons needed and promised, Hitler flatly contradicted him. Two days later, when Rommel told Hitler that Africa was lost and that the only possible course was to extract the Afrika Korps so that it could fight in Italy, Hitler "shouted at him,"[22] and Africa was reinforced.

Information from the Romanians, which indicated during November that large Soviet forces were being assembled on their front, was noted but not acted upon, beyond a totally inadequate "corsetting" of Axis ally formations with small numbers of German units. While Hitler believed that some sort of offensive was pending, neither he nor the intelligence branch, Foreign Armies East, sought any clear idea of its scope and timing. There is no evidence, for example, that a serious effort was made to investigate the Romanian reports by intensified air reconnaissance either of Soviet bridgeheads south of the Don or likely assembly areas north of it. The issuing of orders[23] for the completion of the capture of Stalingrad a mere two days before the launching of the Soviet counterof-

22. Alan Bullock, *Hitler: A Study in Tyranny* (Harmondsworth: Penguin Books, 1962), p. 688.

23. Bundesarchiv/Militärarchiv, Freiburg, AOK6 1b Nr. 4640/42, of 17 November 1942.

fensive was a clear indication of an ignorance that in large part was willful and voluntaristic.

Hitler also rejected arguments for coming to terms with Russia, put forward by Mussolini in November 1942 and again by the Italian Foreign Minister, Count Ciano, in December.[24] The limiting factor on the information flow throughout was not what was available but what Hitler was willing to hear, and that was a diminishing quantity as the crisis progressed. It must be noted, however, that Hitler's receptivity to new information was already low in the pre-crisis period, and that subordinates such as Halder and his successor Zeitzler both made repeated attempts to bring new information to his attention.

The third research question concerns the impact of changing levels of stress on the receptivity and size of the information-processing group.

It has already been noted that Hitler rejected unpalatable information at all stages of the crisis. If a distinction is made between Hitler as decision-maker and Hitler plus Keitel, Jodl, and Halder/Zeitzler as information processors, Keitel is never recorded as dissenting from Hitler, whereas Jodl had a major difference of opinion with him over Army Group A during the pre-crisis period, but subsequently made a conscious effort to avoid dissent, on the grounds that a dictator's self-confidence should not be assailed.

The relationship between Hitler and Halder can be followed in more detail through the pages of Halder's diary, supplemented by that of Major Engel and references in the OKW Diary itself. The first sign of Halder's dissatisfaction emerges in a comment on the "lack of fundamental discussion" at the Führer conference on 4 July, the seventh day of the German offensive. During July, dissent between Hitler and Halder was noted on eight days, in August on twelve, and in September on seven. The intensity of the disputes between them also increased: whereas, in July, Halder talks mostly of "lively debate" or "lively exchanges," his comments in August refer to "impossible demands"; on 21 August, there was the incident previously mentioned in which Halder's estimates of Soviet tank production were dismissed as "nonsense"; and on the following day, Warlimont noted that the tension between Hitler and Halder "could be felt in the room." In September, major clashes

24. Bullock, *Hitler*, p. 689.

occurred on the 4th and 8th (the larger one involving Jodl as well); on the 9th, Hitler replaced List by himself, and declared his intention to dismiss all his closer military subordinates (Keitel, Halder, Jodl, and Warlimont, though in fact only Halder was removed).

All these disputes revolved around the fact that Jodl and Halder were more receptive than Hitler to new information. That this problem of receptivity was recognized by the field commanders, though they did not perceive its precise nature, is apparent from Engel's diary entry of 29 August, in which, having visited the commanders of Army Group B and 6th Army (Weichs and Paulus), he describes both as convinced that the discrepancy between the tasks set and the forces provided resulted from Halder's failure to give Hitler a true picture of the problems. The increase in the frequency and intensity of the arguments between Hitler and Halder shows that Hitler, under the stress induced by the growing realization that the offensive was failing, was becoming less receptive to information that confirmed this, and sought to avoid acknowledgment of its validity by dismissing executants rather than scaling down tasks.

This tendency, most marked in the pre-crisis period, is also observable in the earlier part of the crisis period, not merely in Hitler's refusal to order 6th Army to withdraw but, having instituted the airlift, in his lack of receptivity to evidence that it was abjectly incapable of delivering the required 700 tons a day. When an Air Force combat officer, Major Christian, was brought to FHQ on 28 December 1942 in an effort to persuade Hitler of this, he dismissed Christian's observations by suggesting that more efficient loading of the aircraft was all that was needed.

There were a few instances in the pre-crisis period when Hitler sought more information: by visiting Bock on 3 July; by sending his Adjutant, Major Engel, to Army Group B at the end of August; and by sending Jodl to Army Group A a few days later. In each case, the visits resulted from failure to achieve objectives; in two cases, they led to dismissal of the Army Group Commander, but in no case did they lead to a scaling down of objectives.

Decreasing receptivity is further indicated in Hitler's behavior after the dismissals of 9 September. From that date on, he led an even more isolated existence than before: the Führer conferences were held in his quarters rather than in a Wfst conference room, he took his meals there by himself instead of in the FHQ mess, and he left there for fresh air and exercise only after dark. For several weeks, he refused to have Jodl appear at the daily conferences; and after Zeitzler's appointment, he took to discussing Eastern Front matters with him privately, OKW officers being excluded. This change in his life-style supports the conclusion invited by the evidence of the daily conferences that during the pre-crisis and crisis periods intra-group tension increased because, on balance, Hitler's receptivity declined while that of Jodl and Halder did not. Hitler's proposed remedy was to change not the tasks but the composition of the group, and to reduce his contact with it.

In the post-crisis period, Hitler accorded more freedom to Manstein than to previous field commanders, but stress induced by doubt as to the possible outcome led him to visit Manstein's headquarters for the unusually long period of three days on 17–19 February. However, the outcome of this visit was that Manstein was not dismissed, and was allowed to retain the degree of freedom which he had achieved. This indicates an association between Hitler's decreasing stress and increasing receptivity as an information processor. It does not point to increased size of the "group," which comprised only Hitler, Manstein, and Zeitzler, but suggests a temporary transference of the leading tactical decision-making role to Manstein, and decreased intra-group tension associated with decreasing stress.

Consultation: Persons and Groups

Two research questions are concerned with the effects of changing stress on: (4) the type and size of consultative units; and (5) group participation in the consultative process.

The type and size of consultative units and the nature of group participation in the consultative process were both affected by two circumstances. First, there was the fact that the nation had already been at war for almost three years before the Stalingrad crisis began, and therefore already had a fully developed organization capable of and accustomed to directing military operations on a large scale, including, where necessary, reacting to enemy moves. There was therefore no perceived need for improvization.

The second circumstance was the nature of the Nazi state itself, with its basis in the Führerprinzip (leadership principle). The relationship between Hitler and his subordinates was based essentially on a division of powers, competing jurisdictions, and a centralization of actual power in Hitler himself, by virtue of his multiple offices as Head of State, Government, Armed Forces in general (Wehrmacht), Army (Heer), and Party.

All the major nations involved in the war in Europe were characterized by centralized decision-making, in that all were headed by an individual (Roosevelt, Churchill, Stalin, Hitler, Mussolini) endowed with supreme decision-making powers by virtue of his office. However, there were varying degrees of decentralization of decision-making with regard to details: Churchill, Stalin, and Hitler took a great interest in details, and quite frequently interfered in the execution of their decisions, while Roosevelt and Mussolini intervened to a much lesser extent.

In Stalin's case, detailed intervention, which was very marked in the early stages of the war, arose from suspicion not merely of the competence but of the integrity of the senior military, which noticeably decreased as the war went on, so that dismissals became rare and total dismissals, as opposed to demotion and/or reassignment, rarer still. At the same time, Stalin's direction of military operations became increasingly a matter of choosing between alternatives put forward by the General Staff, with considerable decision-making powers entrusted to his Deputy Supreme Commander, Marshal Zhukov, and the Chief of General Staff, Colonel-General (later Marshal) Vasilevsky.

In Churchill's case, a committee system of directing warfare, notably by the War Cabinet and the Chiefs of Staff Committee, ensured that detailed interventions by the Prime Minister were subjected to prolonged discussion, while overall direction of the war effort was, in the end, accountable to the Parliament. The force of Churchill's personality and the fertility of his imagination sometimes led him into ill-considered interventions in detail,[25] but the various checks upon him, and the very high quality of information available to him and his advisers, especially from the broken German ciphers, in most cases ensured a consensus on a reasonable course of action.

In Hitler's case, no such restraints operated, and his exercise of decision-making power was littered with dismissals of subordinates. Before the war, he succeeded in dismissing the conservative military leaders Blomberg and Fritsch; and after the failure of the

25. Arthur Bryant, *Triumph in the West, 1943–1946* (London: Collins, 1959), p. 389.

offensive before Moscow at the end of 1941, he dismissed or procured the resignations of the Commander-in-Chief of the Army, Brauchitsch, all three Army Group Commanders (Leeb, Bock, and Rundstedt), and a number of subordinate commanders. During the period from mid-1942 to mid-1943, he exercised his power of dismissal over the Commanders of Army Group South (Bock), A (List), and B (Weichs), the Chief of the General Staff (Halder), the Deputy Chief of the Wehrmacht Commander Staff (Warlimont, though this was rescinded in a few days), and a number of corps and divisional commanders, while an orderly officer who failed to wake him early with some information about which he could have done nothing was threatened with execution, dismissed from his post, and reduced to the rank of private. In the aftermath of Jodl's defense of the command of Army group A, Hitler announced his intention of dismissing both Jodl and Keitel. Though he did not in fact carry out his threat, his relations with both remained cool for a long time thereafter, and Jodl never again enjoyed his full confidence.

The selection of officers for the immediate entourage indicated that, unlike the other supreme commanders with an interest in detailed execution of their orders, Churchill and Stalin, Hitler did not wish to be surrounded with strong personalities. Keitel had had a relatively undistinguished career up to his appointment as Chief of Staff of OKW, and the general contempt in which he was held by the other field marshals is indicated by the contemptuous names of "*Lakeitel*" (a pun on the word for "lackey") and "*Nickesel*" ("nodding donkey") which were attached to him. He was once described by Blomberg as "nothing but the man who runs my office," to which Hitler replied: "That's exactly the man I am looking for!"[26] While Keitel was hampered in the execution of his duties by the fact that he had no actual control of anything, there is no reason to believe that according him powers beyond those of a mere executant of Hitler's decisions would in fact have made any difference. It is, for example, a fact that he lent no support to the numbers of senior officers who attempted to persuade Hitler to sanction the withdrawal of the encircled troops in Stalingrad from this exposed position. It is also true that even his own brother, the Chief of the Army Personnel Office, transmitted to Halder the feelings of the senior military that their interests were not adequately repre-

26. Warlimont, *Inside Hitler's Headquarters*, p. 13.

sented by Keitel, because of his failure to stand up to Hitler, and that the efforts by officers such as Manstein and Kluge to secure the appointment of an Army officer as Commander-in-Chief East were motivated not merely by a desire to detach Hitler from the detailed conduct of operations, but also by an aspiration to remove Keitel from office. After his outburst in September, Jodl never again opposed Hitler on any major matter, justifying his failure to take a stand by the need to sustain Hitler's self-confidence, which Jodl saw as a dictator's basic source of strength.

The frequency of dismissals within the German High Command clearly related to Hitler's search for scapegoats. The promotion of Paulus to Field Marshal, immediately before the surrender of Stalingrad, was not a recognition of services rendered (Hitler was bitterly critical of Paulus),[27] but an invitation to commit suicide, as no German Field Marshal had ever fallen alive into enemy hands. The limited freedom of action accorded to Manstein in the later stages of the operations during the winter of 1942–43 was significantly hedged about with restrictions, which Manstein ignored to the best of his ability. Rommel solved the problem of the relationship with Hitler in less subtle ways—for example, by carrying out a forbidden withdrawal and mentioning it only in his situation report afterward.

The dismissal in September of the Chief of General Staff of the Army, Halder, was a direct consequence of Halder's opposition to Hitler's military decision-making, especially to the decision to attempt to capture Stalingrad and the Caucasus simultaneously rather than consecutively, as had been envisaged in the original operational plan.

In the naval sphere, Hitler's subordinates enjoyed greater autonomy because of his admitted lack of expertise in naval warfare. Nevertheless, the restriction that he placed upon risk-taking by the major surface units, prompted mainly by political considerations (specifically his fear of the loss of prestige entailed in the sinking of large warships), led to excessive caution among his admirals, especially after the loss of the *Bismark* in 1941, and resulted in indecision in the handling of the German surface forces in the Battle of Bear Island on New Year's Eve 1942.[28] Consequently, a force of

27. Hildegard von Kotze, ed., *Heeresadjutant bei Hitler, 1938–1943: Aufzeichnungen des Major Engel* (Stuttgart: Deutsche Verlags-Anstalt, 1974), p. 143.
28. Dudley Pope, "Battle of the Barents Sea," in *History of the Second World War*, ed. Barrie Pitt (London: Purnell, 1967), Vol. III, pp. 1261–1269.

German heavy ships was outmaneuvred and outfought by inferior British forces, and a major victory at sea, which Hitler was hoping would inaugurate 1943 and to some extent counterbalance the impending catastrophe at Stalingrad, was not achieved. He therefore decreed the total deactivation of the major surface ships. This led to the resignation of the Commander-in-Chief of the Navy, Admiral Raeder, and his replacement by the U-boat Admiral Dönitz, who, with some difficulty, was able to achieve a partial cancellation of the decision.

It can also be argued that Hitler's relative lack of knowledge of and interest in naval warfare, while giving his Admirals somewhat greater autonomy of action than his Generals enjoyed, were responsible for his failure to accord priority to submarine building, which could have had a decisive effect on the Battle of the Atlantic. Only after Dönitz had become Commander-in-Chief of the Navy in January 1943 and established a close working relationship with Speer, who was in charge of production, was a major increase in submarine production made possible; and by then, though it was not yet apparent to either Dönitz or his adversaries, the acute phase of the battle of the Atlantic was almost over. Despite major successes in the early months of 1943, a number of factors, chief among them the recovery by the British of the ability to read the U-boat ciphers, which they had temporarily lost in February 1942, brought about a dramatic change, so that by May 1943 Dönitz had been forced to withdraw his U-boats from the North Atlantic.[29]

Hitler laid claim to no particular expertise in the field of air power either, but because the German Air Force was geared primarily to tactical support of the Army, his decisions had a more direct impact upon it than they had upon the Navy. The German Air Force, which had held the initiative in the early stages of the war, was increasingly losing it during 1942–43, and was being significantly outproduced by all its adversaries. Technologically erroneous attempts to ensure that all bombers were capable of dive-bombing held back the development of large bombers such as were already being produced in quantity by the Americans and British, and made it impossible to attack Soviet arms factories in the Urals and Siberia; while the necessity to concentrate more and more air production effort into fighters for defense of the homeland starved

---

29. Karl Dönitz, *Memoirs: Ten Years and Twenty Days* (London: Weidenfeld and Nicolson, 1959), p. 341.

the Air Force of offensive possibilities. The result was the suicide of two successive Chiefs of Staff of the Air Force, Udet and Jeschonnek, and a deteriorating relationship between Hitler and Göring. Nevertheless, Hitler chose to accept Göring's assurance that the besieged forces at Stalingrad could be supplied by air, because this made it possible for him to resist Army pressures to withdraw the encircled troops.

In contradistinction to his admitted lack of expertise in naval and air warfare, Hitler claimed to be an expert in war production. While he displayed a knowledge of the details of individual weapons which was frequently embarrassing to his generals and admirals, German organization of war production was in fact chaotic. Göring, in addition to being Commander-in-Chief of the Air Force, was head of the economic Four Year Plan, while the Minister for Armaments and Production, Dr. Todt, was also responsible for the construction industry, especially the building of fortifications along the west coast of Europe, U-boat shelters, and road construction in all occupied territories. The lines of demarcation between Todt and Göring were not clearly defined, and Speer has described the system that he introduced after Todt's death as "organized improvization." Although it improved matters greatly, it did not bring German armament production to the levels reached by Germany and Austro-Hungary in the First World War,[30] even though the industrial resources of Italy and occupied Europe were available and exploited. While much of this shortfall resulted from sabotage and Allied bombing, the decisive factor was the disorganized nature of the production process, a direct result of Hitler's reluctance to diminish his own decision-making role by granting overriding powers in any one field to a single individual.

It should also be noted that Hitler preferred consultation to be on a one-to-one basis rather than in a group, especially with persons who might disagree with him. He never convened the Cabinet, for example, between 1938 and his death in 1945, and accounts of meetings with him by Speer, Goebbels, and others from outside FHQ seldom refer to the presence of third parties other than subordinates. His closest military advisers, Keitel and Jodl, seldom opposed his wishes, and it was with them only that he nor-

---

30. Albert Speer, *Inside the Third Reich* (London: Weidenfeld and Nicolson, 1970), p. 299.

mally took his meals—until, after the dispute with Jodl in September 1942, he eschewed even their company. His reluctance to meet possible opponents in groups appears to have been accepted by the senior field commanders, for no attempt was made to appear in a body to advocate the appointment of a Commander-in-Chief East. When Rundstedt declined to make the proposal, he suggested that Manstein and Kluge should do it, and both made the attempt; but there is no evidence to suggest that they sought either to appear together before him or to organize support for a collective approach among the other Commanders of Army Groups and Armies.

The implications of the above for the fourth and fifth research questions are:

(4) The type and size of consultative units varied only to a very minor extent during the crisis overall, because a well-developed and formalized consultative system, normally involving a minimum of two conferences a day, already existed. Although Hitler made some changes in the personnel closest to him, he never suggested that he perceived any need to increase or decrease their numbers. The temporary exclusion of Jodl after the September dispute resulted from annoyance at Jodl's defense of the Commander-in-Chief and staff of Army Group A, but Jodl's place was not filled by anyone else, and he was eventually restored to favor.

(5) Group participation in the consultative process also showed only minor variations during the crisis. The main variation was to reduce it by excluding OKW staff from discussion of OKH matters after Zeitzler replaced Halder. This in turn is linked not to the periodization of the crisis but to the growth in stress within the pre-crisis period which led to Halder's dismissal. With a new Chief of Staff of OKH, it was possible to introduce a new procedure which perpetuated OKW/OKH rivalries—during the dispute—on 8 September. OKW/OKH, in the persons of Halder and Jodl, had collaborated in opposing Hitler, prompting him to dismiss one and banish the other; and the strict separation of conference discussions which was introduced with (though not necessarily *by*) Zeitzler rendered such future OKW/OKH collaboration less likely. Diffusion of the powers of others was an essential prerequisite to their centralization in Hitler; so that it is barely possible even to speak of group participation in the consultative process at any stage of the crisis. Decisions that ran counter to previous ones (for example, those

which authorized withdrawals) are associated with the persuasive powers of Manstein and, to a lesser extent, Zeitzler, rather than with any group activity.

Decisional Forums

Two research questions concern the effects of changing crisis-induced stress on: (6) the size and structure of decisional forums; and (7) authority patterns within decisional units.

The possibility of variation in the size of the decisional forum is limited by the fact that the basic decisional unit was Hitler himself, and therefore was irreducible. Nevertheless, Hitler could not take every decision, so some elements of decision-making were "sub-contracted" to senior officers of OKH and OKW, or to commanders in the field. But as the crisis progressed, Hitler tended to interfere at lower and lower levels of decision-making, including even deployment of divisions or smaller units. The crisis in September 1942, after Jodl's defense of Army Group A, led Hitler to take command of it, exclude OKW from Eastern operations, and, at least temporarily, ban Wfst staff from the situation conferences.[31]

The replacement of Halder by Zeitzler also tended to increase Hitler's direct influence on decision-making at all levels, because he had chosen Zeitzler, a relatively junior officer, in the expectation that he would be more pliable than Halder. In fact, Zeitzler proved less pliant than expected, and resisted a number of Hitler's decisions that he regarded as mistaken. From October 1942 onwards, Hitler took to arranging Eastern Front matters in private sessions with Zeitzler, thereby further diminishing the group aspect of the decisional forum. After the dispute with Jodl, Hitler rarely left his own quarters, and saw less and less of his entourage outside the formal conferences.

The senior field commanders in particular attempted to alter the structure of the decisional forum and reduce Hitler's role in Eastern Front decision-making by advocating the appointment of a Commander-in-Chief East with functions analogous to those of the existing Commanders-in-Chief Southeast (Balkans), South (Mediterranean), and West (Northwestern Europe), but all their attempts failed.

In nonmilitary decision-making, the "committee of three" (Bor-

31. Warlimont, *Inside Hitler's Headquarters*, p. 257.

mann, Keitel, and Lammers) attempted to increase their own influence within the decision-making process by having all orders for signature by Hitler cleared through themselves. In practice, this system did not work well, as the Air Force and Naval leaderships would not accept Keitel's authority, while Lammers, responsible for ministerial powers, constitutional affairs, and administrative matters, remained in Berlin and had little access to Hitler. This increased the influence of Hitler's secretary at FHQ, and there seems to be general agreement among ex-functionaries of the regime[32] that it was Bormann's powers, rather than those of the committee as a whole, that were enhanced. Although Hitler retained the power of final decisions, Bormann obtained close control over the kind of material that was submitted for decisions, and Speer has testified that Bormann would often draft lengthy directives on the basis of brief or vague comments by Hitler.[33] Bormann thwarted Goebbels's efforts to win support for a policy of "total war" for fear that an increase in Goebbels's power would mean a diminution in his own. In April 1943, Bormann succeeded in having himself officially appointed as the Führer's Secretary; and although this appeared merely to ratify the existing state of affairs, the official designation gave him increased influence over the nature of materials submitted to Hitler, thereby further reducing the size of the decisional unit.

In general, therefore, it can be said that the decisional unit became smaller as the crisis proceeded, both because Hitler decided that it should be so and because maneuvres among his entourage increased the influence of Bormann, to the virtual exclusion of a number of other ministers who had previously contradicted Hitler. Mutual mistrust between leading members of the regime hampered such attempts as were made to increase the size of the decisional unit (for example, the efforts of Goebbels and Speer to enlist Göring's support for "total war" measures) to the extent of rendering them largely nugatory.

Similar considerations affected the structure of the decision-making group. Because of Hitler's highly personalized habits in decision-making, it is difficult to speak of a structured decision-

32. For example, Speer, *Inside the Third Reich*, p. 363, records efforts by Göring, Goebbels, and himself to curb Bormann's powers.
33. Ibid., p. 350.

making group. Throughout his career, he exhibited a preference for associates who did not query or criticize his decisions, and a readiness to dismiss those who did. The formal decision-making structure in the military field consisted of the OKW and OKH headquarters, and Hitler was careful, especially after his dispute with Jodl in September 1942, to exclude OKW from Eastern Front matters. Formally, the highest decision-making body in the country was the Cabinet, but it never met throughout the war. Hitler's deliberate preference for divided and overlapping jurisdiction facilitated his own control over decision-making, though frequently to the detriment of the overall effort.

Given, however, that a decision-making group need not and usually does not consist wholly of equals, some points may be made about the structure of the German military decision-making group in this period. The formal structure of the group—which may be taken to include Keitel, Jodl, and Halder (until 24 September 1942, and thereafter Zeitzler), plus, for certain matters, the Commanders-in-Chief of the Air Force and the Navy and the senior Field Commanders of the Army—did not change. However, there was a very heavy turnover among its membership because of the successive dismissals of Bock, List, Halder, and Admiral Raeder, and the envisaged dismissal of Keitel and Jodl. In all cases, the dismissals resulted from Hitler's conviction that his orders were being resisted, disobeyed, or obeyed only with reservations. Military efforts to change the structure of the military decision-making group by procuring the appointment of a Commander-in-Chief East were vetoed.

During the crisis, an apparent structural change took place with the formation of a "Committee of Three" (Keitel, Lammers, and Bormann), which was meant to act as a "clearinghouse" for all orders, other than operational military ones, for signature by Hitler, but in practice the formal change of structure made little difference. The Naval and Air Force Commanders-in-Chief simply declined to acknowledge Keitel's authority, while Lammers had little access to Hitler, so responsibility devolved increasingly upon Bormann, enhancing his influence within the decision-making group, but without altering its structure.

Apart from an examination of the effects of changing stress levels upon the size and structure of decisional forums, the sixth research question involves a consideration of consensual findings that not merely do decision groups tend to become smaller in high-stress situations but that their group cohesion increases, often leading to more harmony and emotional support, that face-to-face interaction may increase in frequency and intensity, and that pressure for conformity under the impact of threat brings about "group think," a tendency to group concurrence and subordination of dissent.[34]

While the evidence supports a finding that the decisional forum tended to become smaller under the impact of the crisis, growth of group cohesion occurred between the field commanders and Zeitzler in respect to the surrounded troops. Here there was a growth in consensus among the senior military officers in favor of the opinion, held by Paulus, Zeitzler, and Weichs from the beginning, that 6th Army and associated formations should be withdrawn from the Stalingrad area. This view eventually came to be shared by Manstein, who had initially left open the question of whether a corridor through to 6th Army should be used to reinforce it or withdraw it. However, Hitler did not share the view, and neither did Keitel, while Jodl appears to have been uncommitted, unconsulted, or both. Manstein was given permission to break through, without any ruling being given as to what 6th Army should do once the corridor had been established; and the question was never put to the test, because the relieving force not merely failed in its objective but was driven back well beyond its original starting line. The growth of consensus among the military therefore made no difference to the outcome of the battle of Stalingrad.

In respect to Army Group A in the Caucasus, a consensus was reached, after the failure of the Stalingrad relief attempt in late December, that it must be withdrawn, and the withdrawal was carried out successfully.

The situation in North Africa was more complex, because the decision to commit substantial German forces to holding it was taken only after Allied control of sea and air space over the Mediterranean had made the commitment unlikely to succeed. Rommel advocated abandonment of North Africa rather than reinforcement, primarily because of the correct perception, which Mussolini also urged upon Hitler, that the loss of North Africa would inevitably

34. Ole R. Holsti and Alexander L. George, "The Effects of Stress on Performance of Foreign-Policy Makers," *Political Science Annual*, 6 (1975), 286–290; see also Brecher with Geist, *Decisions in Crisis*, p. 354.

and quickly be followed by an invasion of Italy, and that forces that would be needed to defend Italy should not be frittered away by dispatching them across an Allied-controlled sea to an area from which they could not be recovered if, as seemed all too probable, they were defeated. There was, however, no FHQ consensus in support of Rommel, and the C-in-C South (Kesselring) was far more optimistic about the prospects of success in Africa. No *realistic* consensus was therefore reached in respect to that theatre, and it seems that here the influence of "group think" was strongest because Kesselring's unrealistic optimism reinforced Hitler's; whereas where Stalingrad was concerned, the consensus pessimism of Zeitzler and the field commanders was contrary to Hitler's view.

In the later stages of the crisis period, there is what may be termed a tacit consensus on the impossibility of saving the Stalingrad force. Very few Stalingrad-related decisions are recorded, and there is a lack of reference to the possibilities of relief. But the consensus, if such it may be termed, involved no more than a silent acceptance of an overwhelmingly apparent reality and a turning of attention to other areas where genuine choices could be made between alternatives, and where group decisions could still appear to have a genuine likelihood of determining outcomes.

The seventh research question specifically concerns the relationship between changing levels of stress and authority patterns within decisional units. Because of the several authority-conferring posts held by Hitler, this question has to be considered in relation to each.

At the outset of the crisis, Hitler's authority as Head of State, Government, Party, Armed Forces, and Army was unquestioned except by very small civilian and military resistance groups. Nothing that happened during the crisis created any threat to his authority as Head of State. At no time and from no quarter within the leadership did any suggestion arise that his place as Leader of the German Nation should be taken over by someone else, nor was there any suggestion that he should become merely a symbolic figure by yielding his post of Head of Government. However, Goebbels, as Minister of Propaganda, expressed disappointment at Hitler's reluctance to give full support to his "total war" campaign, launched during the post-crisis period. By virtue of his office, Goebbels was particularly sensitive to public opinion, and to the reports on it provided twice weekly by the Security Service (SD). During February and March, these reports recorded rumors among the general population that Hitler had been removed to a sanatorium in Dresden or Obersalzberg, or, in another version, that he had suffered a nervous breakdown at FHQ, and famous doctors had been summoned to treat him.[35] In March also, the SD reported widespread concern among the public at Hitler's failure to appear in public, and lack of photographs of him, and rumors that his hair had turned white.[36] But by his birthday (20 April), the reports stated that "despite numerous expressions of doubt after Stalingrad, and many rumors, the general belief in the Führer among the broad mass of the people is unshaken." The report also recorded that in some areas fewer flags or pictures of Hitler than in previous years had been exhibited, but perhaps rather disingenuously attributed this to the lack of any special request to display them.[37]

It is clear from the reports that some degree of disillusionment with Hitler as an authority figure resulted among the general public, but that criticism concerned most of all his failure to appear in public; that is, it expressed a need for reassurance about his continued ability to provide leadership rather than a desire for his removal from it. Goebbels echoed this attitude within the higher leadership during the crisis and post-crisis periods, both in his unsuccessful attempts to secure Hitler's active support for the "total war" campaign, and in his abortive efforts to bring more coordination into war production. There is no evidence that Hitler ever read the SD reports, but Goebbels clearly did, and served as the link between Hitler and public opinion. In summary, his efforts were directed to persuading Hitler toward more public display of his authority, not toward abrogation of any important part of it.

The same can be said of Hitler's role as Party leader. Goebbels attempted to have Hitler exert his authority against conspicuous consumption and high living by senior Party officials such as Gauleiters, but neither he nor any other Party leader suggested Hitler's replacement. Power politics among the higher Party leadership centered on attempts to exploit Hitler's authority (for example, in

35. Bundesarchiv, Koblenz, R58/181/87 and 87 r.s.
36. Ibid., R58/182/113 r.s.
37. Ibid., R58/182/126.

Goebbels's seeking confirmation of his control over Berlin, or Bormann's control of access to Hitler), not to usurp it.

In the military field, the position was somewhat different. There was no attempt to persuade Hitler to yield either of his posts as Commander-in-Chief of OKW and of OKH, but there were several efforts to confine him to control of overall strategy by creating a new post of Commander-in-Chief East. Had this post been created, an experienced professional officer would have had overall detailed control of the Eastern Front similar to that possessed by the other "area" Commanders-in-Chief (South, Southeast and West). The proposition arose among the senior field commanders, not the staffs of OKW and OKH, and was designed to subvert not Hitler's position as an authority figure at the highest level, but that of the "Headquarters Generals," specifically Keitel, Jodl, and Halder/Zeitzler, who, the field generals believed, did not adequately inform Hitler of the true state of affairs at the front. That this supposition was wholly correct only in respect to Keitel, true only with qualifications of Jodl and Zeitzler, and wholly incorrect where Halder was concerned merely reinforces the point that the field commanders' belief in Hitler suffered only minor erosion by the crisis. Their waning of confidence was directed instead at their FHQ colleagues, and this is shown especially in the behavior of Kluge, C-in-C of Army Group Center: when, after Manstein's earlier failure, he agreed to a further attempt to persuade Hitler, he asked Engel on 25 February 1943 to arrange an appointment for him, and specifically asked that Keitel, Jodl, Zeitzler, and Schmundt should not be present. Before seeing Hitler on 28 February, he informed Engel of his intention to resign if Hitler refused to appoint a C-in-C East and to dismiss Keitel. But Hitler did neither, and Kluge did not resign. Nor, among the welter of Army dismissals that punctuate the crisis, is there a single voluntary resignation.

It may be argued that the lack of resignations reflects not the preservation of Hitler's authority but the ethics of the German officer corps. While it is generally true that resignation or request for reassignment were not lightly regarded in the German Army, there were ample precedents. These included, between 1807 and 1812, not merely resignation but taking service with an enemy (Russia), after Prussia had been conquered and forced into alliance with France. The officers concerned were later described by Prince Frederick Charles of Prussia as including "men of the noblest name

and character."[38] Among them was the later author of *On War*, Karl
von Clausewitz. Also in that war, the commander of the Prussian
forces with the French Army in Russia, General Count Yorck von
Wartenburg, had, with the encouragement of his officers, committed a formal act of treason by changing sides, conceiving (correctly) that this, rather than obedience or mere resignation, was
what Prussia's true interests required him to do. There had been
similar instances in 1848, which need not be detailed. The point to
be made is that the German officer corps had a concept of honor
which could on occasion transcend mere obedience to encompass
not merely resignation but formal treason.

That this code was not a dead letter is shown (1) by Halder's involvement in an abortive plot to remove Hitler in 1938; (2) by the
continued existence of a group of younger officers, mostly at HQ
Army Group Center, who made several unsuccessful attempts to
assassinate Hitler between 1941 and 1944; (3) by the fact that though
most of the senior officers whom they approached declined to join
them, many citing their personal oath of loyalty to Hitler as a bar,
none reported them; in other words, they were prepared to accept
the consequences of oath-breaking by others, and did not feel that
their own adherence to the oath required them to protect Hitler
against the ill-intended actions of other officers; and (4) while the
activities of the "officer opposition" were not known at the time,
there had been a recent and public example of a senior officer re-
signing his post. This had taken place on 3 December 1941, when
Rundstedt, the senior officer who was probably the most universally respected by his colleagues, had responded to Hitler's coun-
termanding of one of his orders by on-the-spot resignation from the
command of Army Group South. This action had neither incurred
the odium of his colleagues nor diminished his stature in Hitler's
eyes. Only three months later, on 1 March 1942, Hitler had appointed him as Commander-in-Chief West, despite the fact that at
sixty-six years of age he could legitimately have been left on the
retired list. So resignation, though not common, was not unprecedented, and the fact that no Army Group Commander or Army
Commander resorted to it during the crisis indicates that the perceived need for more effective exertion of decision-making au-

---

38. Essay of 1860, in Karl Demeter, *The German Officer Corps in Society and State,
1650–1945*, trans. Angus Malcolm (London: Weidenfeld and Nicolson, 1965), p. 258.

thority did not extend to perception of a need to replace Hitler's authority with that of someone else.

The only resignation during the crisis was that of Admiral Raeder. It is perhaps significant that he resigned because of an arbitrary act (the decision to scrap the major surface warships) in a field of warfare in which Hitler claimed no special expertise. That no Field Marshal or General resigned over Hitler's far more numerous arbitrary decisions on the land battle provides additional evidence that they continued, to and beyond the end of the crisis, to accept his authority and expertise in the realm of land warfare.

It may be argued against this that two military attempts to assassinate Hitler late in the post-crisis period demonstrate rather forcibly the erosion of his status as an authority figure. The first of these, in March 1943, involved the placing of two bombs on his aircraft by staff officers of Headquarters of Army Group Center, which he was visiting. These failed to explode. A week later, it was planned to blow him up during a visit to the Berlin Arsenal, but at the last moment he cut the visit short, and the time fuse could not be set to explode before his departure.[39] These and subsequent attempts were organized by Staff Colonels and Majors belonging to mixed civilian-military opposition groups that had existed since before the war. Many of them were reservists rather than career officers, so they did not represent a distinctively military viewpoint. Few senior officers supported them, they had no large bodies of troops at their disposal, and the predominance of army officers in the assassination attempts denotes no more than the fact that only the military had relative ease of access both to explosives and to Hitler.

Alternatives: Search and Evaluation

The last two research questions derived from the ICB model concern the effects of changing stress on: (8) the search for and evaluation of alternatives; and (9) the perceived range of available alternatives.

In the pre-crisis period, there were three points at which major alternative courses of action arose for consideration. These were:

39. Eberhard Zeller, *The Flame of Freedom*, trans. R. P. Heller and D. R. Masters (London: Oswald Wolff, 1967), pp. 160–164.

   a. In early July, whether or not to take Voronezh.

   b. In late July, whether to retain the original concept of consecutive drives to the Volga and the Caucasus, or whether to make them simultaneous.

   c. In and from mid-August, whether to attempt to take the city of Stalingrad rather than adhere to the original concept of a lodgment on the Volga north of it.

At the relevant times, such stress as existed was internally generated within FHQ rather than imposed by enemy action. In hindsight, it can be seen that the decisions in cases (b) and (c) above, to depart from the original plan, were probably wrong (which does not imply that the original plan would have succeeded, but merely that it would at least have failed at a lower cost), and that the same is probably true of decision (a), when Bock's diversion of his mobile forces to a task for which they were not suited made it possible for the Red Army, pursued mainly only by infantry on foot, to withdraw along the Don without major losses. The outcome of the choice made in decision (a) therefore affected the outcome of the choices made at (b) and (c), by preserving more Soviet strength than if Bock had sent his motorized forces eastward as quickly as possible. In case (a), pressure of time was not considered; but Hitler's perception that it should have been, because Bock's dilatoriness made the Soviet escape possible, caused him to dismiss Bock.

In case (b), it was Hitler's (in this case incorrect) perception of a time constraint (the possibility of catching large Soviet forces north and west of the Don) that prompted him to send 4th Panzer Army southward where it was not needed, Soviet forces having already made their escape. But, having returned it to its original location, he then decided to conduct simultaneously operations by Army Groups B and A which had been planned as consecutive. Without attempting to pronounce on the feasibility of the original plan, one can at least say that the splitting of forces entailed by this change substantially increased the possibility that neither Army Group would attain its objectives.

Decision (c) was ultimately to prove the most fateful, because it tied down major forces in a position where they were later to be encircled and destroyed. But it is the case that in the pre-crisis period the three major "probably wrong" choices between alternatives were not made under pressure of time or a high level of stress other than the self-imposed stress already mentioned. This stress was created by differences within FHQ, notably those between Hitler and Halder, not by the external environment.

In the crisis period, the climate in which alternatives had to be considered was much different, and the stress levels much higher, because the threat had grown from one of mere failure to achieve objectives to one involving the physical annihilation of forces and the massive loss of territory in the areas of Army Group B (around Stalingrad) and Army Group A (the Caucasus) in Russia, and in North Africa. Both threats became acutely apparent during the first three weeks of November 1942, beginning with the British advance from El Alamein on 2 November, continuing with the Allied invasion of French North Africa on the night of 7/8 November, and climaxing with the Soviet counteroffensive at Stalingrad, which was launched on the 19th and achieved encirclement of a major part of Army Group B on the 21st.

In the case of Army Group B, four alternatives existed:

a. To withdraw eastward into Stalingrad and attempt to make it a "fortress" supplied by air.

b. To withdraw westward, abandoning Stalingrad.

c. To relieve the troops in Stalingrad by an advance from outside the Soviet encirclement.

d. To open a passage from both sides of the encirclement, through which 6th Army could either withdraw or be relieved.

All these alternatives were considered, with the Army commander, Paulus, and the Army Group commander, Weichs, being in favor of withdrawal westward. Manstein, who was appointed to command the new Army Group Don, at first favored the westward withdrawal, but then came to believe it preferable for 6th Army to remain in place and a corridor to be broken through to it, leaving open the question of whether the corridor should be used to reinforce it or to withdraw it. Hitler, in accordance with his usual practice, forbade abandonment of the position and ordered encircled troops to withdraw eastward into the city area rather than westward toward the bulk of the German forces.

The question of air supply was decided in an arbitrary and haphazard fashion. Göring, who was smarting under criticism of his leadership of the Air Force, especially of its inability to prevent Allied bombing of German cities, saw an airlift as a way to retrieve his reputation, and guaranteed its success over the profound misgivings of his deputy, Milch, and the Chief of Staff of the Air Force, Jeschonnek. Hitler thereafter remained deaf to attempts to obtain sanction for a westward withdrawal by the Chief of Staff of OKH, Zeitzler, and senior field commanders such as Manstein, and to appeals for freedom of action from the commander in Stalingrad, Paulus. Hitler's unwillingness to sanction a withdrawal, though bolstered by reasoning about the importance of holding Soviet forces at Stalingrad, seemed to have been prompted by no more than his reluctance, after the experience of the winter of 1941, to authorize retreats, and, in his arguments with Zeitzler, he used the support of Keitel and Jodl as an indication of military support for his thinking.[40]

There were only two alternatives for Army Group A: to withdraw from the Caucasus or not to withdraw. In this case, the decision to withdraw seems to have been more easily arrived at, prompted by the vulnerable location of this group and by Hitler's belief that Stalin would attempt to repeat the success he had achieved in 1920 by a strike down the Don from Stalingrad (then Tsaritsyn) to Rostov in order to cut it off. The Soviet plan did in fact contain such a provision,[41] but was modified in the course of the operation when the Stavka realized that it had far more German and Axis troops encircled at Stalingrad than it had expected. Hitler did not know this, and the decision to withdraw Army Group A, which was undoubtedly correct, was made in time for the withdrawal to be undertaken successfully. However, the need for Army Group B to "tie up" Soviet forces in the Stalingrad area which might otherwise be used to drive down the Don and cut off Army Group A was exploited by Hitler as an additional reason for refusing permission to withdraw from Stalingrad.

Soviet analyses of the Stalingrad battle and associated operations concede that the resistance by the encircled forces did indeed contribute to the successful withdrawal of Army Group A, but point out that this withdrawal was complete in all essentials by 24 January 1943, so that resistance after that date served no useful purpose.[42] However, once it became apparent that the airlift of sup-

40. Fest, *Hitler*, p. 664.

41. Georgy K. Zhukov, *Vospominaniia i razmyshleniia* (Moscow: Novosti Press Agency Publishing House, 1969), pp. 412–413.

42. Most of 1st Panzer Army reached Taganrog, about fifty miles west of Rostov, by 31 January. Rear-guard formations evacuated Rostov on 6 February. See Paul Carell, *Scorched Earth* (London: George G. Harrap, 1970), pp. 140–143.

plies was incapable of keeping the encircled forces in being, and after the failure of the relief expedition in December, the only alternatives open to Hitler in respect to Army Group B were to authorize a surrender or to order continued resistance. The option of surrender was unpalatable to Hitler in any circumstances. On the eve of the final collapse, Paulus was promoted to Field Marshal in a clear indication that he was expected to commit suicide. It is difficult to avoid the conclusion that Hitler remained throughout impervious to the attempt of Field Commanders or members of his headquarters to urge upon him any alternative that involved withdrawal from the banks of the Volga.

In the case of Africa, Hitler's belief in the necessity to prop up his weaker Axis partner, Italy, coupled with his ignorance of the theatre, led to a decision to reinforce it after an objective consideration of Allied ground, air, and naval strength in the Mediterranean would probably have pointed to abandonment of North Africa as the most realistic course, as Rommel indeed suggested.[43] In this case, while prompt military action prevented a swift Allied takeover, and probably postponed the Allied invasion of Italy, and the Italian change of sides, by several months, no evidence has been found to suggest that either Hitler or OKW had envisaged the situation sufficiently far in advance for a detailed and timely consideration of the alternatives open to them. Basically, the African theatre remained undersupplied and underestimated until it was too late. There is also no reason to believe that the postponement of the collapse of Italy until the summer and autumn of 1943 either resulted from a considered German review of policy alternatives or had any significant effect upon the course and outcome of the intramural crisis of alliance between Germany and Italy. The German reinforcement of the African theatre was essentially an improvisation in response to a situation in which Hitler no longer held the initiative, and in which the Allies' control of the sea and air space of the Mediterranean made the progress of their land forces from its southern to its northern littoral a function of their own planning and logistical processes, upon which Axis forces could have little or no influence.

As the crisis at Stalingrad deepened, the range of alternatives open to German decision-makers inevitably diminished. More and

43. Bullock, *Hitler*, p. 689.

more efforts were made to extract 6th Army from its predicament, but the growing strength of the Soviet encirclement rendered even the attempt to undertake them impracticable. It is probable that 6th Army could have been relieved or extracted in late November or early December 1942, when the Soviet High Command had not yet realized that it had encircled over 300,000 Axis troops rather than the 80,000 or so it had expected. But once the Soviet leadership realized the true situation, operational plans were readjusted, resources intended for a drive down the Don to cut off Army Group A were applied instead to strengthening the encirclement at Stalingrad, and from then on, given the relative strength of the two sides, it is unlikely that any German attempt at relief could have succeeded. The possibility of realistic alternatives had been largely preempted when Hitler decided, on the advice of Göring, that 6th Army could be maintained from the air, and therefore need not withdraw.

The stress that was inevitably generated by the Soviet counter-offensive was increased by the German physical and psychological unpreparedness for it. Because it had not been seriously envisaged, and its magnitude, when it eventuated, was totally unexpected, all decisions connected with the evaluation of alternatives had to be taken under the severe pressure of finite time. The decision to attempt to retain the encircled forces in place and supply them by air was taken in extreme haste, and over the misgivings of those most closely concerned with the attempt to carry it out, Jeschonnek and Milch. At the level of implementation of decision, there is much point in Halder's aphorism that Hitler was interested only in grand strategic decisions and those affecting the lowest levels of the military hierarchy, whereas the most important problems arise at the intermediate level. For example, the airlift and operations associated with it were not placed under a single unified direction until the Soviets had overrun most of the possible airfield sites, including the main supply field at Pitomnik, had placed large numbers of anti-aircraft artillery units in the corridor, and had intensified fighter harassment of the transport to an extent that eroded the already slim prospect that the airlift could succeed.

The decision to reinforce the African theatre was taken in equal haste, and without any evidence of debate other than Hitler's brusque rejection of Rommel's attempt to persuade him to abandon Africa altogether. In the post-crisis period, the only operational alternatives were Manstein's concept of using tactical withdrawals as a means both of regrouping his own forces and tempting the Soviets to advance into a trap, and Hitler's by now stereotyped insistence on holding on to positions. Manstein's concept prevailed, though two meetings with Hitler were necessary. The level of stress in this period was relatively low compared to the crisis period. Such time pressure as existed was imposed on Manstein rather than Hitler, and was the product of weather conditions; the Red Army was still advancing, but clearly running out of supplies and, with them, out of momentum. The time constraint was the imminence of the spring thaw, which would render movement by both sides very difficult to impossible for several weeks from early or mid-March. Manstein aspired to throw the Soviets back across the Northern Donets before that happened, but needed several weeks of the residual winter campaigning weather if he was to succeed. This, the major time constraint, was surmounted; and the minor one—Hitler's presence at his HQ for three days, during which Manstein wished to give his full attention to the final preparations for his offensive—was overcome when Hitler, having accepted Manstein's plan, left on 19 February.

In summary, therefore, an examination connected with the two final research questions suggests that the effects of changing stress on (8) the search for and evaluation of alternatives were somewhat indeterminate. Three major choices taken in the pre-crisis period, without serious time constraints operating on the decision-maker, were probably all as wrong as the decision, taken under a much higher level of stress and under extreme time constraint, to withdraw *into* Stalingrad rather than *from* it; while the choice to withdraw Army Group A, also taken under a high level of crisis-induced stress, was probably a correct one, even though the main reason for it, a perceived Soviet intention to advance down the Don and attack Army Group A in the rear, was erroneous, the Soviets having altered their plans, which had originally included such an advance, before the decision was taken.

In regard to the effects of changing stress on (9) the perceived range of available alternatives, the finding from other crises that under increased stress the range of perceived alternatives is restricted does not find support. The range was restricted by circumstances, not choice.

In the most crucial decision of the whole crisis, the four alternatives open to the beleaguered force were all considered, though, as no verbatim record of the discussion survives, it is impossible to say whether all were adequately considered. However, the fact that all were discussed tends to controvert the finding of Holsti and George that high stress leads to only a restricted search for alternatives.[44] Their finding that it leads to a reduced time perspective, with a higher value placed on immediate goals and less attention paid to the distant future, is confirmed by the fact that in the lower-stress pre-crisis and post-crisis periods a significant role was played by distant goals: the severance of Soviet oil supplies and their seizure by Germany in the pre-crisis period; the recapture of territory, the destruction of Soviet forces, and the gaining of a stable line from which to mount a spring or summer offensive in the post-crisis period. In the crisis period, the time perspective was shorter, and the goal—saving the threatened forces of Army Groups B and A—more immediate. But in such circumstances the finding may be no more than a truism, the real point being that in the pre-crisis and post-crisis periods, when the Germans held the initiative, longer perspectives and distant goals were more appropriate to the objective circumstances than in the crisis period, when the initiative had unexpectedly and massively passed into Soviet hands. In the absence of verbatim records, it cannot be said with any certainty whether or not the pressure for rapid closure led to a less constrictive evaluation of alternatives and their consequences, but the mere fact that the alternative chosen—to supply by air—was adopted solely on Göring's assurance, over the serious misgivings of most of the professionals present, and that the Air Force proved incapable of delivering even one-third of what was needed, tends to confirm the finding from other empirical studies that analysis is reduced and assessment of costs and benefits less rigorous under pressure for rapid decision.

Hitler's acceptance of the necessity to withdraw Army Group A came at a time of high stress, late on 28 December. This was five days after the abandonment of the attempt to relieve Stalingrad, only a few hours after the meeting at which Major Christian told him the airlift had no chance of succeeding, and immediately after an angry discussion with Zeitzler and Jodl. It indicated, first, that high stress in this case reduced rather than increased Hitler's con-

44. Holsti and George, "The Effects of Stress", pp. 280, 291.

ceptual rigidity, and secondly, caused a greater than usual willingness to accept military advice. Why he should have shown these
traits at this time is not known for certain, but the strategic linkage
is a simple one to make: if the troops at Stalingrad could hold out,
the Soviet drive down the Don might not be possible, and there
would be no danger that Army Group A would be taken in the rear.
But as it had proved impossible to relieve them, and as Christian
may have convinced him, on reflection, despite his denials at the
time, that they could not be supplied by air either, their collapse
was inevitable and might be rapid, in which case Army Group A
would be in serious danger. After this, only seven Stalingrad-related
decisions were taken in the thirty-five days remaining before the
final surrender. In brief, 28 December appears to be the day on
which, under high stress, Hitler adapted to the objective reality of
inevitable disaster at Stalingrad, and set about limiting its consequences. His behavior therefore tends on this day not to conform
to the findings which generally associate increased stress with a reduced time perspective and an increase in cognitive rigidity, and
which tend to be confirmed by his behavior at the outset of the
crisis period. In short, a decision-maker may react differently at
different times to similar stimuli, and conclusions can be expressed
only in terms of predominant tendencies to react in given ways to
crisis-induced stress.

In a number of previous crises during his life, Hitler had shown a
propensity to withdraw when under stress,[45] and the crisis of late
1942 was no exception. After his dispute with Jodl in September,
he ceased to take meals in the FHQ mess, and thereafter rarely left
his quarters. He left FHQ on the afternoon of 7 November for
Munich, went on from there to the Berghof at Berchtesgaden, and
did not return to FHQ until late on 23 November. There were no
adequate arrangements for the exercise of command and control
functions: Keitel and Jodl occupied offices in the "Small Chancellory," twenty minutes by road from the Berghof, while the staff
of Wfst was in a special train at Salzburg station, a further forty
minutes' drive away, and no representative of OKH was present at
all. These arrangements might have sufficed for a quiet period of
the war, but Hitler remained there while Anglo-American forces
landed in French North Africa (7–8 November), German forces in-

---

45. See, for example, the discussion in Waite, *The Psychopathic God*; pp. 353–354.

vaded France (11–12 November), and the Soviet counteroffensive achieved its first major successes (19–22 November). And when Hitler finally returned to FHQ, he attempted to put off a meeting with Zeitzler, who had a number of urgent matters to discuss. There is, in fact, evidence here of a tendency not so much to restrict the range of alternatives under increased stress as to withdraw from decision-making altogether. Having returned from the Berghof only on 23 November, Hitler expressed a wish on 9 December to go back there "to clear his head for new decisions," and he did not abandon the idea until a full week had elapsed. Furthermore, in the first ten days of the post-crisis period in February, he took few decisions of any kind.

If, as seems legitimate, reduced rigor of analysis under high stress is considered proven by the taking of irrelevant or counterproductive decisions, the transition period from pre-crisis to crisis was especially rich in them. The invasion of unoccupied France was intended to preempt a nonexistent imminent Allied invasion. The signs of Soviet activity reported by Army Group B were ignored, and instead a series of decisions were taken to preempt nonexistent dangers, including the dispatch of troops to Finland and Norway to deter action by Sweden, which did not contemplate any, and to Crete and the Peloponnese, which the Allies had no plans to invade.

After the failure of the relief attempt at Stalingrad, and the apparent agreement within FHQ that no further alternatives existed there other than the precise timing of a surrender (necessary because of the need to keep the Red Army occupied until Army Group A had withdrawn to the west bank of the Don), many of FHQ's concerns suggest that it not merely transferred its attention to other areas where it could make effective choices, but to some extent took refuge in displacement activities. Between 10 and 14 January 1943, for example, while the Soviets captured half the ground held by 6th Army, as well as its main supply airfield at Pitomnik, the OKW situation conferences discussed trivia such as passwords, the security breaches in a minor report, and whether to send an insignificant number of light field howitzers to Norway or to northern Russia. Only after Pitomnik had been lost was a senior Air Force officer, Field Marshal Milch, given charge of the airlift, with powers to give orders to Army units which had previously been denied.

Numerous witnesses testify to a deterioration in Hitler's physical and mental condition following Stalingrad,[46] but the relative importance of stress and of the controversial drug treatments (some of which contained strychnine) administered by his personal physician, Dr. Morell, are still a matter of controversy which is unlikely ever to be resolved.

Summary of Findings on the Stalingrad Crisis

The findings on the nine research questions as applied to the Stalingrad crisis can be briefly summarized as follows.

1. The effects of increasing and decreasing levels of crisis-induced stress on cognitive performance:

Hitler's conceptual rigidity and reluctance to receive new "disturbing" information were both high before the crisis began, and continued high throughout the pre-crisis and crisis periods, until the failure of the relief attempt. After that, he became somewhat more flexible in the later crisis and post-crisis periods. A tendency to withdrawal under stress manifested itself in his almost complete severance of social relationships with the FHQ staff after his dispute with Jodl in September, in the dilatoriness of his return to FHQ in November after the Allies had seized the initiative in Africa and the Soviets at Stalingrad, and in his almost total retreat from decision-making for about ten days after the surrender at Stalingrad on 2 February.

His tendency to resort to historical experience was marked before the crisis began, and did not increase significantly under crisis-induced stress, except perhaps in the (later partially rescinded) decision to scrap the larger surface warships.

2. The impact of changing stress on the perceived need and consequent probe for information:

On four occasions in the pre-crisis, one in the crisis, and two in the post-crisis period, Hitler sought more information by visiting or sending an emissary to an Army Group headquarters, or summoning an Army Group commander to FHQ. In general, however, he expressed no perceived need for more information; and a limiting factor at all stages of the crisis, especially in the pre-crisis and early crisis periods, was his rejection of information that conflicted with his perceptions.

---

46. For example see Speer, *Inside the Third Reich*, pp. 399–403; Louis P. Lochner, ed., *The Goebbels Diaries* (London: Hamish Hamilton, 1948), p. 200; Roger Manvell and Heinrich Fraenkel, *The July Plot* (London: Bodley Head, 1964), p. 191; and Fest, *Hitler*, pp. 663, 667–677.

3. *The impact of changing crisis-induced stress on the receptivity and size of the information-processing group*:

If the "group" is taken as comprising Hitler, Keitel, Jodl, and Halder/Zeitzler, it can be concluded that the greater receptivity of Jodl and Halder to new information caused increasing tension between them and Hitler, leading to Halder's dismissal and an estrangement between Hitler and Jodl. Keitel's role was a passive one throughout, with no recorded dissent from Hitler. The size of the group did not change, but its composition was altered by Halder's dismissal and Hitler's contemplation of similar action in respect to Jodl.

4. *The effects of changing stress on the type and size of consultative units*:

Because Germany had already been at war for three years before the Stalingrad crisis, a fully developed war-directing organization already existed. There was no perceived need for changes, except of personnel. Hitler dismissed Halder and thought of dismissing Jodl and Keitel, in all cases because of differences of opinion with them.

5. *The effects of changing stress on group participation in the consultative process*:

The only significant variation here was that after Halder's dismissal, group participation was reduced from its already low level by the exclusion of OKW from discussion of Eastern Front matters.

6. *The effects of changing stress on the size and structure of decisional forums*:

Hitler was the basic decisional forum, and in the pre-crisis and crisis periods showed an increasing tendency to extend his decision-making authority downwards. Attempts to enlarge the "forum," in both military (appointment of a Commander-in-Chief East) and nonmilitary fields (the "Committee of Three" and Goebbels's "Total War" measures), were unsuccessful. The structure of the decisional forum did not change, but there was a heavy turnover of membership, reflecting Hitler's readiness and power to dismiss those who incurred his displeasure, or, in short, the essentially one-man nature of the decisional forum of the Nazi state. Group cohesion increased only among "outsiders" (the senior field commanders) and Zeitzler on the desirability of withdrawal from Stalingrad, and had no effect.

7. *The relationship between changing levels of stress and authority patterns within decisional units*:

The crisis did not erode Hitler's authority as Head of State, Government, or Party. Such doubts as were expressed among the leadership and public concerned only a perceived need in the crisis period and (especially) the post-crisis period for reassurance that he could still exert leadership (for example, by making more public appearances). The military did not question his authority in the above capacities or as Commander-in-Chief of OKW and OKH, but some senior field commanders attempted unsuccessfully to persuade him to appoint a Commander-in-Chief East, with a view to reducing not so much his overall authority as that of the "headquarters generals" around him.

8. *The effects of changing stress on the search for and evaluation of alternatives:*

Choice between major alternatives took place on three occasions in the pre-crisis period, in each case involving two alternatives. On each occasion, the choice made was to depart from the original plan, and was probably wrong.

In the crisis period, choice had to be made between four possible courses of action in relation to Stalingrad, and two in respect to Army Group A. The two courses chosen for Stalingrad involved withdrawal eastward for 6th Army and an attempt to drive a corridor through to it. The first was probably the worst choice for 6th Army; but one alternative, to withdraw westward, might have saved it only at the expense of allowing the Red Army to cut off Army Group A instead. The second was correct in principle, but proved impossible in practice. The decision to withdraw Army Group A from the Caucasus was undoubtedly correct, both in that it saved the Army Group and that it enabled the forces at Stalingrad to continue to perform the useful function of tying down Soviet forces, after it had been shown that 6th Army could not be saved.

In the post-crisis period, two alternatives had to be considered: whether to withdraw to regroup for a counteroffensive (Manstein's plan) or to attempt to hold fast (as Hitler wished). The choice of Manstein's proposal was almost certainly the correct one.

Overall, therefore, it would seem that more errors of choice were committed in the pre-crisis period than in either the crisis or post-crisis periods, suggesting that the restriction of choices imposed by circumstance and time pressure contributed to correct decisions. However, the one wrong decision had consequences more directly catastrophic than did the three probably wrong choices of the pre-crisis period which put the German forces into the ultimately catastrophic position.

9. *The effects of changing stress on the perceived range of alternatives*:

The perceived range of alternatives became more restricted in the crisis and post-crisis periods, but this merely reflects the reality of a massive, well-planned, and skillfully conducted surprise Soviet counteroffensive. The range of alternatives was perceived as more restricted because it *was* more restricted.

Some Quantitative Points

Because of gaps in the available material, it is not possible to attempt a quantitative assessment in the same detail as would be feasible when considering a more recent crisis involving a country with a more open form of government than that of Nazi Germany. However, some quantitative reinforcement for qualitative judgments is possible on the basis of surviving documents and post-war memoirs.

Bearing in mind that the reasons for decisions were rarely given and cannot always be reliably inferred from the context, one cannot suggest that quantitative treatment of the issues is more than illustrative. This is especially so in regard to the evaluation of cognitive performance. War is an interactive process in which decisions often have to be taken on the basis of incomplete information, sometimes on no definite information at all. This is especially the case with moves intended to forestall enemy action, as many of them will forestall a move that the enemy has no current intention of making. It has been assumed, therefore, in respect to the first research question, that a high absolute level of mistaken decisions would not in itself reflect on cognitive performance, but that fluctuations in their incidence would be significant. It has also been assumed that to list the numbers of such decisions can be misleading: Hitler's habit of not merely deciding that an operation should be undertaken, but also specifying which forces should undertake it, frequently creates a cluster of sub-decisions that are not necessarily incorrect in themselves simply because the main decision is mistaken. Rather than attempting to discriminate between decisions and the sub-decisions flowing from them, no more has been done than to tabulate the days on which decisions were taken which either confronted nonexistent threats or were shown by subsequent events to have adverse consequences. Nor has any attempt been made here to discriminate between mistaken decisions in terms of their consequences.

In Table 1, all Hitler's recorded decisions, not merely those relative to Stalingrad, have been taken into account.

Summarizing the table, "wrong" decisions were made on the following number and proportion of days:

Pre-crisis period: On 18 days out of 143, or 1 per 7.9 days

Crisis period: On 34 days out of 77, or 1 per 2.3 days

Post-crisis period: On 12 days out of 51, or 1 per 4.3 days

The month of January 1943 (18 days) shows the highest incidence of "wrong" decisions. It is also a month in which relatively few Stalingrad-related decisions were taken. It will now be examined in more detail, to illustrate the criteria employed in evaluating "wrong" decisions.

The main source of such decisions in January 1943 was preoccupation with nonexistent threats. Specifically, decisions were taken to meet these as follows:

Envisaged Threat	Date mentioned (in January 1943)
A Soviet advance down the Don to Rostov	1
Allied invasion of northern Norway/northern Finland	2, 14, 18, 23
Allied invasion of Spain	7, 12, 14
Allied invasion of Bulgaria from Turkey	6, 11
Allied invasion of France	3
Allied invasion of Greek mainland or islands	8, 9, 14, 30
Allied invasion of Sardinia	20

The second source of such decisions was injunctions to the encircled forces at Stalingrad to continue resistance past the point where to do so served any useful purpose. Orders to this effect were issued five times: on 8/9, 22, 23, 24, and 30 January. The first order served the practical purpose of tying down at Stalingrad Soviet forces that would otherwise have been free to drive along the lower Don into the rear of Army Group A. But by 24 January,

Table 1　"Wrong" Decisions

Day	July	Aug.	Sept.	Oct.	Nov.	Dec.	Jan.	Feb.	March
1	Pre-Crisis						x	x	x
2	↓						x	Post-Crisis	
3					x		x	↓	x
4			x						
5	x							x	
6			x				x		
7					x	x	x		
8			x		x		x		
9	x					x	x	x	
10							x		
11							x		
12						x	x		
13	x					x		x	x
14							x	x	
15			x						
16					x				x
17					x	x		x	x
18					Crisis	x	x		x
19					↓ x ↓	x	x		
20			x	x	x		x		
21					x	x	x		
22		x		x	x	x	x		
23	x						x		
24					x		x		x
25									End of Crisis
26									
27									
28						x			
29									
30							x		
31									
TOTAL	4	1	5	3	10	10	18	6	7

Army Group A had withdrawn out of danger. Paulus, almost certainly because he knew this to be so, asked on 22 January for permission to open surrender negotiations (which could be expected to take at least forty-eight hours to conclude), but permission was refused. This refusal, and the three subsequent orders to continue fighting, served no strategic purpose, and it is hard to endow them with any political value.

In the preceding August, by contrast, only one order responding to a nonexistent threat was issued in the entire month. This was on 22 August, when Hitler withdrew the 16th Motorized Infantry Division from 1st Panzer Army to a flank position north of Elista, fearing a Soviet attack from the direction of Astrakhan which was not planned and for which no forces existed.

Even when allowance is made for arbitrariness and use of hindsight in evaluating decisions as "wrong," the quantitative evidence points to an increase of almost 350 percent in the incidence of such decisions as the pre-crisis period gave way to that of crisis, and a drop of nearly 50 percent in their incidence as crisis was succeeded by post-crisis. The quantitative evidence therefore suggests a major decline in Hitler's decision-making performance under the increased stress of the crisis period, and a partial recovery as stress diminished in the post-crisis period. This conflicts somewhat with the qualitative judgment, but only because that takes consequences into account; three probably wrong major decisions in the pre-crisis period largely predetermined the form the crisis would take, and therefore had more direct effects than a plethora of responses to nonexistent threats. These responses entailed the dispersion of forces and effort, but their consequences were indirect, and were not experienced until the Stalingrad crisis itself was over.

No additional quantitative points can be made in respect to research questions 2, 3, 4, or 6. But some light can be shed on questions 5 (on group participation in the consultative process) and 7 (on authority patterns within decisional units) by a tabulation of Hitler's interventions in the details of military operations. The criterion used here is the frequency with which he gave a specific order relating to a unit of divisional size or smaller of Army Groups South, A, B, or Don, including decisions *not* to allocate a particular unit to them. The results are given in Table 2.

The reliability of the figures is affected by the fact that from

Table 2   Interventions by Hitler in Deployments of
Divisions or Smaller Formations

	Southern sector, Eastern Front	Other	Total
28 June–31 July	11	4	15
1–31 August	32	32	64
1–30 September	19	19	38
1–31 October	8	20	28
1–19 November	7	24	31
20–30 November	14	12	26
1–31 December	29	22	51
1 January–2 February	2	49	51
3–28 February	0	14	14
1–25 March	0	14	14

1 January 1943 the conference notes were reconstructed for the
OKW War Diary by Greiner from the files of Wfst, no originals
being in existence, and that Wfst was excluded from the making of
Eastern Front decisions. However, the reconstructed War Diary
entries show that information on the Eastern Front continued to be
made available to Wfst, so that there is unlikely to be a large body
of unrecorded decisions affecting Eastern Front unit movements.
While it has to be noted that to intervene in detailed deployments
to the extent that Hitler did is unusual for a Supreme Commander,
it should also be noted that the peak month for such interventions
was August 1942, at a time when crisis-induced stress was far lower
than during the crisis period proper, and when there was no Allied
invasion of North Africa to occupy Hitler's attention. The figures
for 1 January–2 February illustrate particularly clearly the shift in
his attention, and hence that of FHQ, away from the encircled
forces to other areas where German actions were still perceived as
capable of affecting the outcome.

Totaling the interventions and dividing them by the number of
days in each period of the crisis gives an "index of frequency of intervention" as follows:

Period	Days	Number of interventions	Average frequency	Of which Stalingrad-related
Pre-crisis	143	176	1.23 per day	0.54
Crisis	77	128	1.66 per day	0.58
Post-crisis	51	28	0.55 per day	0

The sharp rise in the frequency of intervention in the crisis period is largely accounted for by decisions in respect to areas other than Stalingrad. The data provide no support for the post-war contentions of some German generals, at least for this period of the war, that Hitler's interventions in matters of detail were baneful in their effects. His interventions were at their most frequent in August, when they averaged just over one a day; and in that period, the offensive was succeeding in terms of territorial gains, though falling below expectations (as in July, when he intervened relatively infrequently) in terms of destruction of Red Army units. What is perhaps more relevant is that at a time when choices between stark alternatives had to be made under severe constraints of time, the lack of a significant rise in Hitler's frequency of intervention hampered action because no other member of FHQ, and no field commander, could assume his decision-making function, or attempted to. The War Diary entry for 21 December 1942 notes, "It is as if the Führer was no longer capable of deciding"; and Warlimont comments on the entry for 12 January 1943 that "Hitler's immobility in regard to Stalingrad handed the initiative to the enemy time after time." In respect to the fifth research question, therefore, the figures suggest that Hitler's tendency to dominate the group, and thereby limit or exclude its participation in the consultative process, was little affected until the post-crisis period, when his interventions in the details of deployments, taken overall, fell off very sharply, from fifty-one in the month before the Stalingrad surrender to fourteen in the month after it.

Where the seventh question is concerned, the figures indicate that Hitler's authority within the decisional unit was essentially unimpaired. He was able to intervene in detailed deployments on fifty-one occasions in the two disastrous months of December and January; that is, more frequently than in any other month of the crisis except August.

Table 3   Hitler's Recorded Decisions

	Stalin-grad-related	Eastern Front	Other	No decision	Total
1–31 July	14	2	2	2	20
1–31 August	28	33	4	2	67
1–30 September	24	13	23	1	61
1–31 October	11	10	26	4	51
1–19 November	9	4	24	4	41
20–30 November	16	1	11	—	28
1–31 December	32	9	48	7	96
1–31 January	17	5	83	2	107
1–2 February	1	—	—	—	1
3–28 February	12	6	24	1	43
1–2 March	1	3	47	—	51
Pre-crisis period [143 days]	86	62	79	13	240
Crisis period [77 days]	66	15	142	9	232
Post-crisis period [51 days]	13	9	71	1	94

This conclusion is further borne out by a tabulation of his full range of recorded decisions, given in Table 3. Including nonmilitary decisions, the table shows that the highest numbers in any one month were in December (96) and January (107), compared to only 67 in the preceding August. Apart from indicating the lack of any preemption of his authority to make decisions, the conclusion has some implications for the eighth and ninth research questions, which concern (8) the search for and evaluation of alternatives, and (9) the perceived range of available alternatives.

Table 3 shows the increasing role played by the need to take decisions in respect to areas other than Stalingrad. The point is more clearly made if Stalingrad-related decisions are converted into percentages of all recorded decisions on a month-by-month basis, as follows:

Pre-crisis	Percent	Crisis	Percent	Post-crisis	Percent
July	22	20–30 November	57	3–28 February	28
August	42			1–24 March	2
September	39	December	33		
October	22	1 January– 2 February	17		
1–19 November	22				

While this study has paid only minimal attention to the events in other areas, the above figures show that the responses to the eighth and ninth research questions have to reflect the existence of "alternatives" in the shape of *other crises*, in this case the one that began in North Africa between 23 October and 8 November, as well as other anticipated crises implied by the "wrong decisions" referred to in the discussion of Table 1. Although the formal end of the crisis period has been taken as the date of the surrender at Stalingrad, the above figures suggest that for Hitler and FHQ the crisis ended *conceptually* between 23 December, when the relief attempt was abandoned, and 28 December, when Hitler agreed to withdraw Army Groups A and Don. To include *other crises* among the perceived range of alternatives would extend this study unmanageably, but it seems that, at least tacitly, Hitler accepted that the Stalingrad crisis was over before the end of the year, and concentrated from then on upon the actual crisis in North Africa and the anticipated crises around the periphery of his conquests.

CHAPTER EIGHT

Hitler and Stalin Compared

THE GERMAN and Soviet dictators had numerous features in common. Both ruled one-party states and enjoyed autocratic powers, which they employed ruthlessly against their opponents. Both had a personal preference for rising late and working till early the next morning (a personal rather than institutional characteristic, as it was shared by Churchill). More germane to this study, both believed themselves gifted in military matters, and took personal charge of their countries' armed forces: Hitler through his roles as Head of State, Government, Party, Armed Forces, and Army; Stalin as Secretary-General of the Party, Chairman of the Council of Ministers, Chairman of the State Defense Committee, and Supreme Commander-in-Chief of the Armed Forces, all of which posts he held by the beginning of 1942. Although a full study of Stalin as a crisis decision-maker cannot be attempted here, there is nevertheless scope to examine some of the similarities and differences between the decision-making "styles" of the two dictators.

In Stalin's case, a detailed study of his day-to-day decisions is not possible, because neither the Stavka (GHQ) nor the General Staff war diaries have been published. However, a number of high-ranking Soviet officers have published either complete or partial memoirs, which throw a good deal of light on their day-to-day relationships with Stalin during the war. Those of Marshal Zhukov (Deputy Supreme Commander-in-Chief), Marshal Vasilevsky (Chief of the General Staff), and Marshals Yeremenko and Rokossovsky (both of whom commanded Army Groups at Stalingrad) have proved especially illuminating, as has the first volume of the two-volume study by Army General S. M. Shtemenko, who served on the General Staff throughout the war and subsequently headed it. These memoirs have been used as the basis for this chapter, along with more episodic recollections contained in the Soviet *Journal of Military History*, many of which have been collected together in Seweryn Bialer's excellent anthology *Stalin and his Generals*.[1]

While the main object here is to compare Stalin's decision-making with Hitler's during the Stalingrad crisis, some reference to the previous context of Stalin's relationship with his military is necessary.

Stalin had not been called up for military service in the First World War, perhaps because of his revolutionary activities, but more likely because he had a withered arm. However, he occupied high supervisory posts as a Political Commissar both during the Civil War (where he was given much of the credit for the successful defense of Tsaritsyn, the city later renamed Stalingrad) and in the war against Poland in 1920 (where a later generation of military historians has held him largely responsible for the Red Army's defeat outside Warsaw). But the most notorious pre-war episode in his relations with the military was the purge of the late 1930s, in which three of the five Marshals and over half the officers of the rank of Divisional Commander or above were executed, and thousands of others imprisoned. Their places were taken by personal cronies of Stalin's such as Kulik (Head of Artillery) and Mekhlis (Head of the Main Political Administration), or by inexperienced officers hastily promoted, and numerous Soviet generals have referred, though mostly in somewhat guarded terms, to the harm this did to the Red Army, while the official rehabilitation of the victims, undertaken soon after Stalin's death, showed clearly how much the military had resented his action.

At the outbreak of war, therefore, Stalin's relationship with his military contained elements of conflict, and his action in having the Commander of West Front (Army Group), General Pavlov, and his Chief of Staff shot for what was in fact no more than incompetence was hardly likely to have sweetened it. Hitler, by contrast, was enjoying something of a honeymoon with the German generals: the dismissals of Blomberg, the Minister of War, and Fritsch, the Chief of General Staff, were several years behind, and were overshadowed by almost two years of unparalleled military success in western, northern, and southern Europe. But Stalin's relationship with his generals improved, while Hitler's deteriorated. The process be-

1. Seweryn Bialer, ed., *Stalin and His Generals* (New York: Pegasus, 1969).

gan with the Battle of Moscow, and continued through and beyond the Stalingrad crisis. While in part this resulted naturally from So viet success and German failure at Moscow, Leningrad, and Rostov in December 1941, it was not solely attributable to these factors, because in 1942 Stalin did not revert to Draconian methods under the spur of renewed setbacks, while Hitler in that year resorted to dismissing senior commanders, not for failing but for achieving less complete success than he demanded of them.

The highest corporate Soviet military institution was the Stavka. This was established on 23 June 1941, the day after the German attack. Its Chairman was the People's Commissar (Minister) for Defense, initially Marshal S. K. Timoshenko, later Stalin himself. The members were: Stalin; the Chief of General Staff (initially Army General, later Marshal G. K. Zhukov; then, from July 1941 to May 1942, Marshal B. M. Shaposhnikov; and for the rest of the war, Colonel-General, later Marshal A. M. Vasilevsky); V. M. Molotov (Foreign Minister); Marshal K. E. Voroshilov (a former Minister of Defense); Marshal S. M. Budenny (a Civil War hero); and Admiral N. G. Kuznetsov (the Navy Minister). There was also attached to the Stavka a body of "Permanent Advisers," which included among its members: three civilian production experts (Mikoyan, Voznesensky, and Zhdanov); Marshal Shaposhnikov (another former Chief of General Staff); General, later Marshal K. A. Meretskov; General Vatutin (a Deputy Chief of General Staff); and Colonel-General, later Chief Marshal of Artillery N. N. Voronov (the Red Army's most noted gunnery expert). Although no formal order was ever issued, the General Staff became the channel through which Stavka decisions were implemented.[2] A week later, on 30 June, a State Defense Committee (GKO) was established, with Stalin as Chairman. This body, composed of political leaders, had the executive powers which Stavka as a body lacked, and on 8 August it conferred on Stalin the title of Supreme Commander-in-Chief.

Unlike Hitler, Stalin did not isolate himself from the rest of the governmental apparatus in a purely military headquarters. Apart from a period in late 1941, when frequent German air raids compelled him to take shelter with the General Staff in the "Kirovskaya" Metro station, he worked either in the General Staff build-

2. Sergey M. Shtemenko, *General'nyi shtab v gody voiny* (Moscow: Ministry of Defense Publishing House, 1981), Vol. I, p. 31.

ing on Kirov Street or, usually, in his office in the Kremlin.[3] Although much of the governmental apparatus was evacuated to Kuibyshev as the Germans approached Moscow, Stalin never left the city, and thus retained closer contact with the nonmilitary aspects of the war effort than did Hitler. Apart from a rather "staged" visit to a mocked-up command post of Western Front in August 1943,[4] Stalin never visited an Army Group headquarters, as Hitler occasionally did, but his system of liaison with Army Group Commanders was considerably more elaborate and formalized than that which prevailed on the German side.

Hitler's contact with Army Groups was normally effected through OKH channels, with first Halder and later Zeitzler as intermediary (a system which late in 1942 was believed by some Army commanders to result in inadequate representation of local commanders' views). Otherwise, the basis of the contact was ad hoc, by means of radio or telephone conversations, occasional visits by the Führer himself (as to Bock in July 1942, or to Manstein in February 1943), but more frequently by a senior officer (as Jodl's visit to List in September 1942) or even a relatively junior one (as that by Hitler's Army Adjutant, Major Engel, to Weichs and Paulus in August 1942). Stalin's emissaries, on the other hand, were sometimes civilian members of the State Defense Committee or Stavka, such as Malenkov or Molotov, but more often very senior officers with high executive authority such as Marshals Zhukov, Vasilevsky, Voroshilov, or Timoshenko, or powerful politico-military figures such as Mekhlis (former Head of the Main Political Administration of the Armed Forces) or Beria (Minister of the Interior and, as such, head of the secret police), though the last two proved unsuitable and soon ceased to be employed to represent Stavka. The only published statement of the responsibilities of these emissaries is a citation by Shtemenko of a telegram sent by Stalin in May 1942 in reply to complaints by Mekhlis about the commander of the Crimean Front, Lieutenant-General D. T. Kozlov.[5] In it Stalin wrote: "You are not a detached observer but a responsible representative of the Stavka, answerable for all successes and failures of the Front and obliged to correct the Command's mistakes on the

---

3. Ibid., Vol. I, p. 37.
4. According to Marshal Nicolai N. Voronov, in Bialer, ed., *Stalin*, pp. 438–439.
5. Shtemenko, *General'nyi shtab*, Vol. I, pp. 63–64.

spot." Both Mekhlis and Kozlov were removed from their posts and reduced in rank, and Mekhlis was never again employed as a Stavka representative.

An interesting sidelight on the "balance of power" between Stavka representatives and Army Group commanders is provided by Rokossovsky.[6] Having been appointed in early July 1942 to command a new Army Group (the Voronezh Front), he was present when Stalin called in an unidentified "general just removed from the command of a Front," most likely Kozlov, who believed he had been wrongly punished because the Stavka representative had interfered with his orders and attempted to override him. Stalin asked why he had not reported this, to which the general replied, "I didn't dare complain about your representative." Stalin's answer was, "Well, that is what we have punished you for: not daring to pick up the receiver and phone up, as a result of which you failed to carry out the operation." Rokossovsky comments: "I walked out of the Supreme Commander's office with the thought that, as a newly-fledged Front Commander, I had just been taught an object lesson."

Stavka representatives traveled regularly between Moscow and the various Army Group headquarters, not merely conducting a one-way traffic of Stavka orders but conveying suggestions and amendments from the local commanders back to Stalin. Army Group commanders were themselves frequently summoned to the Kremlin, and so relatively detached a member of Stavka as the Commander-in-Chief of the Navy, Admiral Kuznetsov, noted that "All major operations, such as those at Stalingrad, Kursk, etc., were already planned with the full participation of Army Group commanders. Several times I was to observe how Army Group commanders summoned to Stalin did not agree with his opinion. Each time he proposed that everything be weighed again in order to reach the proper decision—and he often agreed with the opinion of the commanders."[7]

By early 1942, according to Shtemenko, a clear decision-making pattern had emerged, under which major strategic planning matters were first decided in principle by a small group within Stavka (comprising at that time Stalin, Shaposhnikov, Zhukov, Vasilevsky,

6. Konstantin K. Rokossovsky, A Soldier's Duty (Moscow: Progress Publishers, 1970), pp. 118–119.

7. In Bialer, ed., Stalin, p. 349.

and Admiral Kuznetsov), then reviewed by the State Defense Committee or the Party Central Committee, and then passed to the General Staff to be worked out in detail.[8] It seems clear that the crucial body was the Stavka group, composed entirely of professional military men except for Stalin, rather than the largely civilian State Defense Committee or the unwieldy Central Committee of the Party. Kuznetsov notes of Stalin: "I suspect he even liked people who had their own point of view and were not afraid to stand up for it." But he goes on to say: "In cases where opinions differed, certain of his closest associates exerted a negative influence. Less knowledgeable about military matters than either the field commanders or Stalin, they usually advised the former not to oppose but to agree with Stalin."[9] This is confirmed by Rokossovsky, who says that when, during the Stalingrad counteroffensive, he found it necessary to deviate from his orders, "I made a habit of appealing directly to Stalin. Usually he endorsed the Front Commander's decision, if the commander could offer weighty reasons for his actions and stuck to his guns in proving his point."[10] Rokossovsky also refers to a later occasion, in May 1944, when he was twice sent out of the room to reconsider his disagreement with an element of the Stavka plan, refused to do so, and finally saw his plan accepted by Stalin with the remark: "The Front Commander's insistence proves that the organization of the offensive has been fully thought out. This is a reliable guarantee of success."[11] Rokossovsky does not mention, but another account does, that while reconsidering he was visited by Molotov and Malenkov, who rebuked him severely for daring to disagree with Stalin.[12]

Toadies are seldom lacking from an autocrat's entourage, but there seems to be a qualitative difference between a Rokossovsky, who stood up to Stalin, and a Jodl, who repented his defiance of Hitler on the grounds that a dictator's self-confidence should not be assailed, or a Keitel, who was recruited specifically for his qualities as an "office manager" and was never known to disagree with Hitler about anything of substance. This is not to say that Stalin was not arbitrary or unjust; he was frequently both. But he appears to have

8. Shtemenko, General'nyi shtab, Vol. I, p. 55.
9. In Bialer, ed., Stalin, p. 349.
10. Rokossovsky, A Soldier's Duty, p. 160.
11. Ibid., p. 235.
12. K. Nepomnyashchy (1964), in Bialer, ed., Stalin, p. 461.

valued strong-mindedness among military leaders, however harshly he dealt with it among politicians (or among soldiers once the war was over). The memoirs of Zhukov and of Rokossovsky record sometimes quite stubborn disagreements with Stalin at critical points in the war, but each man frequently got his own way, and both rose to the highest levels of command.

At the organizations most frequently in contact with Stalin, Stavka and the General Staff, there were certainly clashes that led to frequent dismissals, but these occurred below the highest levels, and mostly early in the war. Because the Soviet Union, unlike Germany, was fighting on only one front, and in a war where naval and strategic air operations were secondary to those of the armies, there was no organizational incentive to copy Hitler's bifurcation of his headquarters into OKW and OKH. The Soviet Chief of General Staff's nearest equivalent in terms of duties was therefore Halder or his successor Zeitzler, rather than Keitel. At the outbreak of war, this post was held by Zhukov, but frequent disagreements with Stalin led him to ask to be sent to field command in July 1941, and he was succeeded by Shaposhnikov, who held the office until failing health compelled him to resign it in June 1942. Among Shaposhnikov's last major actions as chief was his joining with Zhukov during March in opposing Stalin's desire to add a number of local offensives to the general strategic defensive which all three agreed in principle was the most feasible course for the Red Army to follow in the summer of 1942.[13] Stalin's point of view prevailed, largely because of the enthusiastic advocacy by Marshal Timoshenko, commanding the Southwestern "Direction" (an assemblage of three Army Groups), of what was to become the disaster of the Barvenkovo Salient, the prelude to the German summer offensive. What is relevant to decision-making "style," however, is that Shaposhnikov and Zhukov were no more penalized for being right at the wrong time than was Timoshenko for excessive persuasiveness. Shaposhnikov retired to command the General Staff Academy, where future senior staff officers were trained, and Zhukov and Timoshenko continued successful careers in high military office throughout and after the war. Shaposhnikov's successor was his principal deputy, Vasilevsky, then Head of the Operations Directorate and already a member of Stavka. He held the office until

13. Georgy K. Zhukov, *Vospominaniia i razmyshleniia* (Moscow: Novosti Press Agency Publishing House, 1969), pp. 394–396.

February 1945, relinquishing it only to replace an Army Group commander who had been killed in action. There was therefore no equivalent on the Soviet side to Hitler's dismissal of Halder or his threats to dismiss Keitel and Jodl.

However, Vasilevsky's Stavka duties required him to spend most of his time away from Moscow,[14] and it proved extremely difficult to find anyone who could both ensure efficient day-to-day functioning of the General Staff and handle its relations with Stavka and Stalin. Shtemenko records that the post most directly concerned, the Headship of the Operations Directorate, changed hands seven times between its relinquishment by Vasilevsky in June 1942 and the appointment of General A. I. Antonov in December.[15] Antonov proved suitable; he was acceptable to Stalin and to the field commanders, though Rokossovsky, characteristically, is politely critical of him because "in spite of his positive qualities as a master of operational planning, he rarely, if ever, insisted on a point in the face of the Supreme Commander's objections."[16] However that may be, Antonov held the post almost till the end of the war, moving into Vasilevsky's place when he left the General Staff in February 1945.

The daily routine followed by Stalin was not greatly different from Hitler's. Vasilevsky says that there were two daily meetings with Stalin: one at noon, to discuss events of the previous night; and another at nine or ten in the evening, to consider those of the day. At both of these, Vasilevsky presented the reports from the Front, informed Stalin of steps taken by the Army Group commanders, and of their decisions and their requests, and gave the General Staff's judgment on these matters.[17]

Shtemenko, who was a section head in the Operations Directorate in 1942, and Deputy Head of it in 1943, gives a slightly different account, according to which the first daily report was made, usually by telephone, between 10:00 and 11:00 A.M., usually by himself; the second was made between 4:00 and 5:00 P.M. by the Deputy Chief of General Staff; and the third and main one was

14. Of his thirty-four months in office, twenty-two were spent at the front. See Bialer, ed., *Stalin*, p. 638.

15. Shtemenko, *General'nyi shtab*, Vol. I, p. 114.

16. Rokossovsky, *A Soldier's Duty*, pp. 231–232.

17. Aleksandr M. Vasilevsky, "Nezabyvaemye dni" [Part II], *Voienno-Istoricheskii Zhurnal* (Moscow), No. 3 (1966), p. 27; and Bialer, ed., *Stalin*, p. 350.

made in the late evening at the Stavka.[18] It seems likely that the routine varied somewhat according to whether or not Vasilevsky was in Moscow. He was usually there for long periods when a major counteroffensive was being planned, and was away at the Front when it was being executed. Both accounts agree on the importance of the evening meeting, which dealt with and took decisions on the day's events. This practice may well have been more efficient in securing swift decisions than was Hitler's procedure, under which the main meeting took place in the early afternoon, but it undoubtedly imposed very heavy strains on the staff officer. Shtemenko records that Stalin personally allocated rest time to all the leading General Staff officers (for example, Antonov from 5:00 or 6:00 A.M. to noon, Shtemenko himself from 2:00 P.M. till 6:00 or 7:00 in the evening), and that their duties following the evening meeting normally required them to work till 3:00 or 4:00 in the morning. Shtemenko comments: "Several of my comrades subsequently suffered for a long time from nervous exhaustion and heart diseases. Many retired to the reserve immediately after the war, without serving out their normal terms."[19]

Under the system by which Stavka representatives shuttled back and forth between Moscow and the Fronts, while Army Group commanders were frequently summoned to Moscow to give their views, the Army Group generals often resented the feeling that Moscow was constantly looking over their shoulders. This was particularly so when the Stavka representative was not a career soldier. General Tiulenev comments sarcastically that Beria's two-week visit to the Transcaucasus Front in August–September 1942 was "showiness and noise."[20] But the feeling was not confined to "politicals"; Rokossovsky relates how, on taking over command of the Stalingrad Front in September 1942, he dropped a broad hint, which was accepted, that Zhukov should go back to Moscow and leave him to get on with his new job.[21] But however much field commanders may have resented the constant appearances of the somewhat overbearing Zhukov and even of the considerably more diplomatic Vasilevsky, these interactions between GHQ and the

18. Shtemenko, *General'nyi shtab*, Vol. I, p. 175.

19. Ibid., p. 179.

20. Ivan V. Tiulenev, *Through Three Wars* [in Russian] (Moscow: Ministry of Defense Publishing House, 1960), p. 197.

21. Rokossovsky, *A Soldier's Duty*, p. 132.

Front precluded any sense of isolation among the field commanders. There was therefore no crisis of confidence comparable to that
which prompted Manstein and Kluge into unsuccessful efforts to
persuade Hitler to appoint a Commander-in-Chief East.

Next to be considered is how well the Soviet decision-making
apparatus worked in predicting and countering German moves.
Clearly, it worked better overall than the German apparatus, because Soviet setbacks during the Stalingrad crisis did not prove fatal, whereas German ones eventually did. But there were nevertheless considerable shortcomings in the Soviet analytical process,
especially in the early stages, which led to costly errors in decision-
making.

In terms of the Brecher definitions, the periodization of the Stalingrad crisis on the Soviet side is different from that on the German. The pre-crisis period extends from the opening of the German offensive on 28 June 1942 to the crossing of the Don-Volga
"neck" on 17/18 August, which brought German troops to the city.
The period of full crisis extends from then to the opening of the
counteroffensive on 19–20 November. And the post-crisis period
extends from the closing of the encirclement on 22 November to
the temporary end of campaigning brought on by the spring thaw
in March 1943.

In the Soviet pre-crisis period, the main problem in the early
stages was to identify the direction of the main German thrust.
Here interpretation of the significance of Bock's attack on Voronezh
was crucial, and Stalin misread it as designed not merely to secure
Bock's flank but to provide an anchorage point for a northward
thrust aimed at Moscow. Vasilevsky states that the idea that the
main German thrust would be in the central sector of the front, not
in the south, dominated Stalin's thinking right up to July;[22] and
Shtemenko amplifies this by saying that while there was no doubt
in the General Staff that the Germans would be unable in 1942 to
repeat their attempt of 1941 to attack along the whole front, it was
unclear where their actual offensive would come.[23] Soviet attention
was riveted on the Rzhev-Vyazma salient, which was close to Moscow and was in the area of Army Group Center, the largest of the
German Army Groups in Russia. Shtemenko states also that Stalin's

22. Bialer, ed., *Stalin*, p. 404.
23. Shtemenko, *General'nyi shtab*, Vol. I, pp. 56–57.

conviction that Moscow would be the main target derived not merely from this but from the belief that the Germans had not given up hope of seizing it, and that this mistaken view was shared by the other members of Stavka, the General Staff, and the majority of the Army Group commanders. Consequently, Shtemenko writes, Stavka reserves were not concentrated in the south, nor were plans worked out in advance for responding to a change in the situation there.[24] And, in turn, underestimation of the importance of the south led to tolerance of shortcomings in the Southwestern and Southern Army Groups.

This might not have mattered if Shaposhnikov's and Zhukov's advocacy of a strategic defensive had prevailed. But Stalin, while claiming to accept it, argued that in its pure form it was too passive, and that it must be combined with local offensives. His view prevailed over that of Zhukov, who wanted an offensive only against the Rzhev-Vyazma salient,[25] so five offensives were planned: in the Crimea, at Leningrad, at Demyansk, toward Smolensk, and toward Kursk. A sixth offensive, to recapture Kharkov and regain the line of the Dnieper River, was added at the insistence of Marshal Timoshenko, then commanding the three Army Groups of the Southwestern "Direction," over the General Staff's reservations, which were strong enough for Vasilevsky to include, in the plan presented to Stalin on 30 March 1942, a preambular phrase stating clearly that it had been worked out only because Stalin had personally ordered it.[26] Not one of the offensives was especially successful; and two, the Crimean and Kharkov operations, were disastrous failures. In the Crimean case, clear incompetence by the Army Group Commander, General Kozlov, some of his staff, and the Stavka representative, Mekhlis, resulted, as already mentioned, in dismissals and demotions. But the failure of the Kharkov operation was mostly a consequence of its fatal coincidence with the German operation "Fridericus," which was aimed at eliminating the Barvenkovo Salient, from which the Soviet operation was launched. In the initial, apparently successful, stages of the operation, Stalin reproached the General Staff for its previous reservations. When the situation changed drastically for the worse, the only changes in command

24. Ibid., Vol. I, p. 57.
25. Zhukov, *Vospominaniia*, pp. 394–395.
26. Shtemenko, *General'nyi shtab*, Vol. I, p. 60.

apart from the replacement of generals killed in battle were the abolition of the Southwestern "Direction," Timoshenko retaining command of the Southwestern Army Group, the demotion of Golikov in favor of the more optimistic Vatutin, the creation of a new Army Group under Rokossovsky, and the dispatch to Timoshenko of an air support expert, General G. A. Vorozheykin, to improve air force organization. Some additional armored forces were sent south, but Timoshenko's requests for infantry were refused, on the stated grounds that there were none yet ready, but with the unspoken thought that reserves were not to be dissipated, because the General Staff was still expecting an attack on Moscow by Army Group Center.

When, on 20 June 1942, the "Reichel affair" exploded with the capture of German operational plans for the 40th Panzer Corps and the 4th Panzer Army, Timoshenko rightly believed them to be genuine, and again asked for more infantry. Stalin, however, dismissed them as a "plant," and replied sarcastically: "If they were selling divisions in the market, I'd buy five or six for you, but unfortunately they aren't."[27] At the time, not merely reserve divisions but entire Armies were being formed, but Stalin retained them in the center to protect Moscow; and only eight days later, four of these Armies (5th Tank, 6th, 60th, and 63rd) were made available to counter Bock's attack on Voronezh. They were committed for the wrong reason (Bock's intention in capturing the city was to deny it as a focal point for a Soviet counterattack, not to strike toward Moscow), and their operations were unsuccessful, but they made it easier for Timoshenko's forces to escape eastward, contributing to Bock's dismissal in mid-July; so Stalin's decision, taken on General Staff advice, was not in any sense a fatally misguided one.

During the long retreat, first to the Don and then back to the Volga, Stalin issued a number of peremptory orders forbidding retreats, but did not penalize local commanders for their inability to carry them out. He replaced some senior commanders (Kolpakchi, heading 62nd Army, whom he described in a message on 23 July to Gordov, then commanding the Stalingrad Front, as "nervous and impressionable,"[28] was replaced by Lopatin; then Lopatin was replaced by Chuikov; and Gordov was himself replaced by Yere-

27. Ibid., Vol. I, p. 71.
28. Ibid., Vol. I, p. 92.

menko, apparently on grounds of inexperience[29] or inadequacy[30]); but as in the earlier case of Golikov, dismissed generals were given the chance to prove themselves at lower levels of responsibility rather than retire altogether, as tended to happen to those who incurred Hitler's displeasure. While the Stalingrad Front was attempting unsuccessfully to defend the line of the Don bend in late July, Stalin sent very severely worded orders during the night of 25/26 July to the then Front Commander, Gordov, about the need to hold the line, and specified which German penetrations were to be annulled, but he did not, as Hitler often did, specify which units were to be used. That was left to Gordov's discretion, but Vasilevsky was sent to his headquarters to monitor his compliance. Vasilevsky arrived there at 1:00 A.M. on 27 July, and on the same day Stalin ordered the drafting of a particularly sternly worded order, which was especially frank in its references to the likely adverse consequences of further withdrawals: "If we do not stop retreating, we shall be left without bread, without fuel, without metal, without raw materials, without factories, without railways." This, the famous Order No. 227, was issued on 28 July, given wide circulation, and read aloud to all troops.[31] Stalin's willingness to refer to the possibility of defeat and its consequences was to be copied by Goebbels at similar conjunctures for Germany later in the war, with the same object of stiffening the national will, but was never to be given more than indirect and halfhearted endorsement by Hitler. In this respect, the valid comparison of Order No. 227 is not with any utterances of Hitler, but with Churchill's "blood, toil, tears, and sweat" speech of May 1940.

THE COUNTEROFFENSIVE PLAN

On the evening of 12 September 1942, at a meeting with Stalin, Zhukov and Vasilevsky were prompted by him into examining "another solution" other than a mere attempt to pinch out the corridor to the Volga which the Germans had driven between the Stalingrad and Southeastern Fronts. Thus, Stalin provided the impulse, but

29. Andrey I. Yeremenko, *Stalingrad* [in Russian] (Moscow: Ministry of Defense Publishing House, 1961), p. 62.

30. Gordov never subsequently commanded anything larger than an Army.

31. Shtemenko, *General'nyi shtab*, Vol. I, pp. 94–96.

the concept of a massive double encirclement was not his. Zhukov states that he and Vasilevsky assumed, first, that the Germans were no longer capable of capturing Stalingrad or the Caucasus, and, second, that the Soviet strategic reserves, which would be ready for action in October, should be used for a large-scale operation rather than frittered away in small attacks.[32]

The boldness of the concept resembled Zhukov's handling of the campaign against the Japanese in Mongolia in 1939, and the Battle of Moscow in 1941. That an opportunity for encirclement existed was evident from mere scrutiny of the map of the front line.[33] The problems would be entirely connected with execution. The Germans had to be prevented from capturing the city, so that their forces would remain far enough forward to be encircled, and the large Soviet forces needed to encircle them had to be concentrated north and south of the bulge, in open snow-covered country, without the Germans becoming aware of what was planned, its scope, or its timing.

The unified Soviet command structure undoubtedly helped in preserving secrecy. The counteroffensive plan was devised by Zhukov and Vasilevsky during the night of 12/13 September 1942, following a conference with Stalin on the previous evening. Operations officers of the General Staff provided data on the German forces and reserves, but were not told why. After Stalin had approved the basic plan, prepared on a single map, Generals Voronov (Artillery) and Vorozheykin (Air Force) were let into the secret, and they plus its two authors went to Stalingrad with small staffs, to survey the situation on the actual ground, the definitive operations map being completed on 27 September. The Army Group commanders designated to lead the offensive were told of the plan early in October, but were given no indication of the proposed date[34] and were forbidden to tell more than a small number of their staff officers.[35] Commanders of Armies, Corps, and Divisions taking part in the offensive were briefed at conferences held on 3 November by Zhukov (Southwestern and Don Fronts, north of the city)

32. Zhukov, *Vospominaniia*, pp. 413–415.

33. This prompted Yeremenko to claim that he first suggested the idea to Stalin on 1 or 2 August. He may well have done so, but the time was not yet ripe. Yeremenko, *Stalingrad*, pp. 35, 38, and 325.

34. Yeremenko, *Stalingrad*, p. 330; Rokossovsky, *A Soldier's Duty*, p. 138.

35. Rokossovsky, *A Soldier's Duty*, p. 140.

and Vasilevsky (Stalingrad Front, south of it). Of the two Army commanders in the city itself, Shumilov (64th Army) was told "a little later,"[36] because a small counterblow at Kuporosnoye, which he was preparing, fitted into the counteroffensive; and Chuikov (62nd Army), whose Army had no immediate counteroffensive task, was apparently not told what was pending, though he and his staff drew their own conclusions from reductions in their ammunition supplies.[37] Zhukov again visited Stalingrad on 9 November, to check progress, and chaired another conference of Army, Corps, and Division commanders on the 10th at the headquarters of the 57th Army of the Stalingrad Front. The date originally fixed for the offensive had been 9 November north of Stalingrad and 10 November south of it; but at some stage during the preparations, the Front commanders asked for a ten-day postponement, which was granted.[38] Final conferences with Division and Regiment commanders took place two days before the launching, and only then were they given their assignments in full detail.

The curious episode of General Volsky showed Stalin's ability to display magnanimous understanding when he chose to: a Corps Commander so convinced that an imminent operation will end in catastrophe as to bypass all military channels and appeal directly to the Supreme Commander to cancel it could normally expect in most armies to be at the very least relieved of his post. Instead, Stalin spoke to him in a fatherly fashion, to the astonishment of those present. At a higher level, Rokossovsky notes that when he found it necessary to deviate from Stavka orders, he made a practice of appealing directly to Stalin, who "usually endorsed the Front Commander's decision, if he could offer weighty reasons for his action, and stuck to his guns."[39] In short, the relationship which among the German generals was regularly achieved only by Manstein prevailed between Stalin and a sizable group of Soviet generals, including, in the Stalingrad operation, not only Zhukov and Vasilevsky but the three Army Group commanders, as the two who survived the war, Rokossovsky and Yeremenko, have indicated in their memoirs. The relationship was no more totally smooth than

36. Yeremenko, *Stalingrad*, p. 334.
37. Vasily I. Chuikov, *The Beginning of the Road* (London: MacGibbon Kee, 1963), pp. 217 and 235.
38. Rokossovsky, *A Soldier's Duty*, p. 141.
39. Ibid., p. 160.

any other between men of strong personalities undertaking a complex task under severe constraints of time and resources, but clearly lacked the self-destructive elements of that between Hitler and his generals, where a series of dismissals had been undertaken even before the onset of the period of full crisis.

During the preparations for and the conduct of the counteroffensive, Stalin played an important role in prompting others to play and act, rather than in devising plans himself, and in securing the resources needed to implement them. Zhukov specifically states that when he and Vasilevsky were devising the counteroffensive plan mentioned above, they considered all the possible variants and finally recommended to Stalin one only, which he accepted.[40] Zhukov's account of the meeting, which took place at 10:00 P.M. on 13 September, makes it clear that the two generals not only proposed a single plan but gave an approximate date on which it could be mounted: forty-five days from the decision to implement it— that is, about the end of October.[41] While they were with Stalin, Yeremenko telephoned to say that a new German attack was imminent, so Stalin postponed further discussion and ordered Zhukov to telephone instructions about use of the tactical air forces on the next day, and to fly to Stalingrad himself at once. To Vasilevsky he gave specific orders to have a division from Stavka reserve moved across the Volga into the city that night, to see what else could be sent there on the next day, and to go to the Southeastern Front in a few days' time to study the situation south of the city. Then he dismissed them with the admonition that "for the time being, nobody except us three is to know what we discussed here."

Zhukov's account of the meeting at which the plan was adopted is not specific as to the date, except to say that it was "at the end of September,"[42] but it must have been not later than 28 September, because by the 29th he was already back in Stalingrad. At this meeting, not only was the plan discussed, but commanders for it were named. At the time, Yeremenko was still in charge of the two Army Groups, the Stalingrad Army Group and the Southeastern Front. But this situation, tolerable when both were defending the same objective, was clearly inappropriate when both were to be reinforced and launched into a vast encirclement operation from dif-

---

40. Zhukov, *Vospominaniia*, p. 414.
41. Ibid., pp. 416–417.   42. Ibid., pp. 418–419.

ferent directions. It was decided to rename the Stalingrad Army Group the Don Front, and the Southeastern Front the Stalingrad Front, leaving Yeremenko in command of the southern arm of the pincer movement only. Stalin first put forward Gordov's name for consideration as commander of the Don Front, but on the strength of Zhukov's adverse report decided against him. Zhukov and Vasilevsky both supported Rokossovsky's nomination, and that was accepted, while Vatutin was chosen to take charge of the new Army Group, the Southwestern Front, to operate on Rokossovsky's right.

Thus, although Stalin initiated neither the overall plan nor any of the details, he prompted its initiation by others, he gave specific orders for solving the short-term problem of holding Stalingrad in mid-September, and, though he did not choose the executants, he retained the ultimate right of veto over those who were recommended, all of whom were in any case known to him. Then he sent both Zhukov and Vasilevsky back to the front to study again the planned concentration areas, and told Zhukov to take all possible steps to wear the Germans down before the counteroffensive was launched. Only after their return to Moscow was the planning map approved and signed by all three. On 6 October, Vasilevsky discussed the plan "yet again" with Yeremenko at the latter's headquarters; and "as the plan evoked no objections in principle from the Front commander," he reported accordingly to Stalin.[43] On the next day, Rokossovsky received orders to prepare his views on it, on behalf of the Don Front.[44]

During late October and early November, Stavka representatives (Zhukov, Vasilevsky, and leading specialist officers, Voronov for artillery, Fedorenko for armor, and Novikov and Golovanov for the air forces) spent their time inspecting the readiness and plans of individual Armies and their component divisions. Between 1 and 10 November, for example, Zhukov inspected five Armies personally, while Vasilevsky checked on three. They reported regularly to Stalin by cable or radio, and Zhukov's message of 11 November illustrates Stalin's importance at that stage as the chief organizer of the economic base for the offensive.[45] It reads in part:

43. Aleksandr M. Vasilevsky, "Nezabyvaemye dni" [Part I], *Voienno-Istoricheskii Zhurnal* (Moscow), No. 10 (1965), p. 20; and Zhukov, *Vospominaniia*, p. 432.

44. Vasilevsky, "Nezabyvaemye dni" [Part I], p. 20; and Zhukov, *Vospominaniia*, p. 432.

45. Zhukov, *Vospominaniia*, pp. 437–438.

Two rifle divisions (87th and 315th) given by Stavka to Yeremenko have not yet been loaded because up to now they have received no transport or horses. Of the mechanized brigades, only one has arrived so far. Things are going badly with supply, and with ammunition delivery. . . . The operation will not be ready by the appointed date. I have ordered it prepared for 15 Nov. 42.[46]

It is imperative to rush to Yeremenko 100 tons of antifreeze, without which it will be impossible to hurl the mechanized units forward, to dispatch the 87th and 315th rifle divisions as quickly as possible; urgently provide warm uniforms and ammunition for 51st and 57th Armies, to arrive not later than 14 Nov. 42.

Thus, Zhukov had the standing to postpone the launching of the operation, but had to invoke Stalin's authority not only in supply matters but to ensure that two infantry divisions arrived in time.

Further exchanges quoted by Zhukov show Stalin keenly concerned that air support should be adequate: "If Novikov thinks our air forces not at present in a position to fulfill these tasks, then it would be better to postpone the operation for some time and build up more air strength" (12 November 1942).[47] Zhukov and Vasilevsky flew back to Moscow on 13 November 1942, and the plan to launch the counteroffensive on 19 November north and west of Stalingrad and on 20 November south of it received final approval. Rather as an afterthought, Zhukov suggested an attack on the central sector of the front, in the Rzhev-Vyazma area, to pin down German forces that might otherwise be transferred to the south. Stalin replied: "That would be good, but which of you will take it on?" As previously agreed with Vasilevsky, Zhukov volunteered to do it himself, and Stalin accepted, but told him to go back to Stalingrad first to make a final check. Zhukov left Moscow on the next day, and on the day after that (15 November 1942) received a telegram from Stalin which formally gave him discretion to vary the date for the entire operation, or to advance or postpone the start by any of the Fronts involved by one or two days. After discussion with Vasilevsky, Zhukov confirmed the dates of 19–20 November, obtained Stalin's agreement, and returned to Stavka on the 17th to plan the Rzhev-Vyazma diversion. In brief, confidence in the planning was such that both

---

46. This is a postponement from the original dates of 9 November (for the Don and Southwestern Fronts) and 10 November (for the Stalingrad Front). See Rokossovsky, *A Soldier's Duty*, p. 141.

47. Zhukov, *Vospominaniia*, pp. 438–441.

Stalin and his Deputy felt it possible to leave its execution to the three Army Groups, with Vasilevsky coordinating them.

But in fact Stalin made a number of detailed interventions. Late on 23 November, for example, he cabled Rokossovsky, telling him to urge two of his Army commanders to move faster.[48] The reasons for Stalin's urgency are explained by Rokossovsky: he wanted to complete "Operation Uranus" (liquidation of the forces encircled at Stalingrad), to free resources for a drive down the Don ("Big Saturn") into the rear of Army Group A, for neither Stavka nor the local commanders had yet realized that the force they had encircled was several times larger than the 80,000 or so they had expected.[49] Thus, Stalin, Zhukov (who was consulted on 28 November),[50] and Vasilevsky all urged, on forces already depleted by two weeks of constant attacking, an attempt to eliminate the encircled Germans which was beyond their capacity. Repeated protests from Rokossovsky eventually brought reinforcements, in the shape of General R. Y. Malinovsky's full-strength 2nd Guards Army, together with a mechanized corps, so an operation by eight Armies was planned for mid-December and endorsed by Stalin on 9 December.[51] But the opening of Manstein's relief attempt on 12 December caused a difference of opinion when Yeremenko asked for the 2nd Guards Army. Vasilevsky favored granting the request, whereas Rokossovsky advocated going ahead with the planned offensive, so that there would be no German force left for Manstein to relieve. The matter was adjudicated by Stalin over the telephone: he accepted Vasilevsky's view, authorized Rokossovsky to suspend his offensive for the time being, and promised reinforcements. At the same time, he agreed to Zhukov's and Vasilevsky's recommendation to postpone "Big Saturn" and instead mount a "Little Saturn" into the rear of German forces in the northern part of the Don bend, aimed at preventing either a second relief attempt in a West-East direction or the transfer of German troops to the existing attempt at relief from the south.[52]

At a State Defense Committee meeting in late December, Stalin proposed to place the forces encircling the Germans at Stalingrad

48. Ibid., pp. 444–445.
49. Rokossovsky, A Soldier's Duty, p. 147.
50. Zhukov, Vospominaniia, p. 446.
51. Rokossovsky, A Soldier's Duty, p. 152.
52. Zhukov, Vospominaniia, p. 447.

under a single command, to ensure better coordination. According to Zhukov, "someone" proposed Rokossovsky; then Stalin overrode Zhukov's mild reservation that Yeremenko "might feel insulted," appointed Rokossovsky, refused attempts by Yeremenko to telephone his objections, abused Zhukov when he tried, at Yeremenko's request, to raise the matter, and insisted on the prompt issuance of a Stavka directive transferring three of Yeremenko's armies to Rokossovsky. The directive was accordingly issued on 30 December.[53] Yeremenko retained responsibility for frustrating the German relief attempt; and his forces, renamed the Southern Front on 1 January 1943, were instructed to push on down the Don toward Rostov, with the aim of cutting off Army Group A.[54] However, with only three corps-sized Armies at his disposal, all of them under strength and one of them very small, Yeremenko could not advance fast enough to prevent Army Group A's withdrawal; and even had he been able to establish himself across its line of retreat, it is highly unlikely that with those forces he could have prevented a breakthrough. Nor was it likely that he could have been reinforced, as even for the more urgent task of wiping out the Stalingrad pocket, Rokossovsky had been warned not to expect more men or armor;[55] and in any event, removal of the threat to the oil fields was a significant achievement in itself.

Zhukov makes no reference to "Big Saturn" after 28 December, tacitly implying its abandonment. But Shtemenko, who was actively involved in Transcaucasus Front matters from August 1942 until the end of the crisis, was well placed to comment, especially as during Vasilevsky's long absences at Stalingrad, Stalin frequently dealt directly with the Operations Directorate or the "Duty General" at the General Staff, receiving situation reports and dictating orders over the telephone.[56] Shtemenko's account shows that "Big Saturn" was tacitly given up in favor of a joint operation aimed at cutting off Army Group A during January 1943, to be executed not merely by Yeremenko advancing on Rostov from the north, but by an outflanking movement from the south involving three of the four Armies in the so-called "Black Sea Group" of General V. I. Tiulenev's Transcaucasus Front. The decision to launch this Front into an

53. Ibid., pp. 456–457.
54. Yeremenko, *Stalingrad*, p. 473.
55. Rokossovsky, *A Soldier's Duty*, p. 158.
56. Shtemenko, *General'nyi shtab*, Vol. I, p. 124.

offensive was approved by Stavka on New Year's Eve; but while the
Front was preparing its plans, Army Group A began its withdrawal,
and Tiulenev was able to do little more than run after it. Fiercely
critical directives issued by Stalin, one on 4 January and two on the
8th, did nothing to improve the situation, in which Tiulenev's men
could only battle forward against Kleist's rear guards, with no prospect of overtaking, let alone outflanking, his main force. Meanwhile, Yeremenko continued to pursue Hoth's rear guards, narrow-
ing the gap through which Kleist was retreating to less than sixty
miles; and as late as 23 January, Shtemenko felt that the Germans
faced the prospect of a "second Stalingrad." On that day, Stalin
sent a Special Directive to Yeremenko, which returned the main
responsibility for cutting off Army Group A to Southern Front,
stating:

> The enemy in the North Caucasus must be surrounded and de-
> stroyed, as he is surrounded and is being destroyed at Stalingrad.
> The forces of Southern Front must cut the 24 enemy divisions in
> North Caucasus off from Rostov, and those of the Black Sea Group
> of Transcaucasus Front must in their turn close off the exit to the
> Taman Peninsula to these enemy divisions.[57]

But by then almost all of Army Group A was out of danger, while
Yeremenko's tanks had been reduced to a mere handful, and he
himself was within a few days of being ordered to hospital for treatment of the unhealed leg wound he had taken to Stalingrad in
August.[58]

Summing up, then, Stalin did not give up hope of trapping Army
Group A, but clearly gave priority to the destruction of the larger-
than-expected force encircled at Stalingrad over the execution of
"Big Saturn"; and to this end, he deprived Yeremenko of half his
forces by handing over three of his six Armies to Rokossovsky. In so
doing, he falsified Hitler's expectation that he would repeat his advance down the Don of 1920, but not Hitler's assessment of his objective; and he thereby justified Hitler's reluctant acquiescence to
the withdrawal of Army Group A from the Caucasus.

It has already been noted that, during January, Stalin issued
three directives fiercely critical of the Transcaucasus Front's generalship. However, his tendency, already noted, to treat generals less

57. Ibid., pp. 127–137.
58. Yeremenko, *Stalingrad*, pp. 489 and 496.

harshly than Hitler did was apparent here also when, on 24 January, the Northern Group of the Transcaucasus Front was elevated to the status of an Army Group under the title of North Caucasus Front. The officer appointed to command it was the Northern Group commander, General I. I. Maslennikov, who only sixteen days previously had received an angry telegram from Stalin accusing him of having lost contact with his mobile forces, and saying:

> This situation is intolerable. I bind you to restore contact with the mobile units of Northern Group and regularly, twice a day, to report to the General Staff about the state of affairs on your front.[59]

Any comparative assessment of Hitler and Stalin must take account of the fact that no Allied leader was required to demonstrate the same level of competence that Hitler's ambitions imposed on him. Germany, with no large allies except Italy and Japan, virtually attempted to take on the rest of the world. And even after the dramatic German and Japanese successes during 1939–42, the Allies retained a potentially overwhelming superiority in manpower and resources. Which is not to say that they could not have lost the war piecemeal, as they appeared to be doing until well into 1942, but improving their position did not require major gambles, as had every one of Hitler's victories from the reoccupation of the Rhineland in 1936 to the overrunning of Yugoslavia and Greece in 1941. The success of his previous gambles had reinforced his faith in his own omnicompetence, and overridden the professional caution of the German generals to the extent that, in 1941, with the unsubdued British at his back (and, with them, the threat of an eventual Second Front), he undertook the biggest gambles of all by first invading the Soviet Union and then gratuitously declaring war on the United States. From then on, his relations with the military deteriorated, basically because he set them tasks that were beyond the best generalship, and punished them by dismissal for failing to accomplish them.

Stalin, by contrast, learned from his own mistakes not to demand the impossible from the Red Army and its generals. He surrounded himself with a small group of competent advisers, listened to and usually accepted their advice and that of the field commanders, adjudicated between irreconcilable views, prompted the mili-

---

59. Shtemenko, *General'nyi shtab*, Vol. I, p. 133.

tary to broader thinking where necessary, avoided extremes of injustice in rewarding successful and punishing unsuccessful generals, saw that the military's needs were met by industry to the extent possible, and had, by the outset of the Stalingrad crisis, a far more smoothly functioning High Command in the center of Moscow than the divided and increasingly rancorous Führerhauptquartier in its dank East Prussian forest. Stavka did not always have the "right" answers, but it had them often enough; and when it was wrong, it was not irretrievably so.

This relationship between Stalin and his senior military is strikingly at variance not only with that of Hitler but with Stalin's own attitudes toward the senior military before the war and toward his political colleagues at all times. It was clearly a special relationship, born of circumstance, and did not in all cases outlast the circumstances that engendered it. (Zhukov was relegated to semi-oblivion after the war, and achieved his final elevation to Minister of Defense only after Stalin's death. Yeremenko, a four-star general by 1945, achieved Marshal's rank only at Khrushchev's hands, ten years later.) But that it was special and real is shown by the way in which virtually all the senior generals mentioned in this chapter rallied in their memoirs, long after Stalin's death, to refute Khrushchev's wilder allegations about Stalin's war leadership. Most were at pains to demonstrate that, at least from the Battle of Moscow onward, Stalin, though demanding and hot-tempered, was amenable to reasoned arguments and seldom arbitrary in his military judgments, took pains to master the details of the war, and, while keeping a firm hold on powers of ultimate decision, was not reluctant to delegate authority when the situation required it. None of their defenses of Stalin can be applied to Hitler without being severely qualified as to time and place. Hitler's contempt for the "officer class" from 1942 on contrasts with Stalin's enhancement of its status and privileges. And Hitler's occasional flashes of "inspiration," ranging in their effects from the brilliant to the catastrophic, did not compare well in the end with the sustained and methodical teamwork of Stalin's High Command organization.

Appendix

INCLUDED HERE are two reports on the impact of the Stalingrad crisis on German public opinion. They are by: (1) the RSHA, during the first week of February 1943; and (2) the President of the Superior Regional Court, Hamburg, on 6 April 1943.

These reports are included to illustrate the information about German public opinion which was available to the German leadership. The RSHA reports were compiled twice a week, and those from Regional Courts at intervals ranging from once a month to once every three months. There is no evidence that Hitler ever read them, but Goebbels did, and attempted to influence Hitler (with only limited success) to take account of them. The reports indicate that if FHQ tended to fight the war in a vacuum, it did not do so because of a lack of available information about the impact of its activities on the nation as a whole, but because Hitler chose to do it that way.

EXTRACT FROM REPORT OF RSHA (REICH SECURITY MAIN OFFICE), FIRST WEEK OF FEBRUARY 1943*

I. General:

The report of the *end of the battle in Stalingrad* has caused deep shock to the whole people. The speeches on 30 January and the Führer's Proclamation have retreated into the background in the face of this event, and in the serious conversations of the people play a lesser role than a series of questions which are connected with the occurrences in Stalingrad. In the first line is the *scale of the casualties* about which the population is asking. The estimates range in figures between 60,000 and 300,000 men. People consider that the greater part of those who fought in Stalingrad have died. With respect to the troops who have fallen into Russian hands, people waver between two perceptions. Some regard prison as worse

*Bundesarchiv, Koblenz, ref. R58/180/34.

than death, on the grounds that the Bolsheviks will treat those soldiers who have fallen alive into their hands in an inhuman fashion. Others argue that it is fortunate that not all have been killed, so that there is a hope that later some of them will come home. Relatives of Stalingrad fighters are especially troubled by this ambiguity and the uncertainty that arises from it. Among all classes of people, there is further discussion as to *whether the development in Stalingrad was inevitable and whether the monstrous casualties were necessary.* In some cases, people are concerned to know whether the threat at Stalingrad in those days could not have been recognized in time. Air reconnaissance should have established that the Russian Armies that were deployed against Stalingrad were approaching. The question is also being asked on what grounds the city was not evacuated while there was still time. Above all, it is being said that the enemy strength must have been underestimated, otherwise the risk of holding on to Stalingrad even after it had been encircled would not have been undertaken. The people cannot comprehend that relief of Stalingrad was not possible, and some of them, for lack of correct orientation, do not have a correct understanding of the meaning of the battle for the whole development on the southern sector of the Eastern Front. Some express doubt that the defenders of Stalingrad until the last tied up strong enemy forces.

The third point around which the people's discussions focus at this time is the *significance of the Stalingrad battle in the general course of the war.* In general, there is a conviction that *Stalingrad is a turning point* of the war. While to those of a combative nature Stalingrad imposes an obligation for final application of all strength to the front and in the homeland, from which victory may also be expected, the less strong-willed people incline to see in the fall of Stalingrad the beginning of the end. Some people who hold responsible posts, on the basis of which they have a deeper insight into the situation on a certain sector, speak uninhibitedly about the difficulties, and, through their expressions of doubt about the position, incline to infect other people with their pessimism. It has been reported from various parts of the Reich that people who in recent days have been in Berlin for official purposes have noted expressions of low morale in the authorities and departments there.

In other matters, the *attention* of the people is concentrated above all on the *execution of the induction into the work force* of men and women who up to now have not been included. The "soft" and "inconsequential formulation" of the Ordinance of 27 January has been the subject of derogatory remarks. Bluntly, people are waiting tensely to see how this measure is applied, and especially to see whether members of the upper class will really be included. Above all, in the small towns, people speak of certain women whose family situation is known, and are adopting a "wait-and-see attitude" as to how these women will be treated with respect to employment. According to available reports, there is a good deal of skepticism. People believe that the "prominent people," which in a small town includes the wife of the mayor or of the lawyer, will try to find some way to avoid it. Doctors will doubtless be overrun by women who want certificates to show that they are unable to work. In extreme cases, women whom people are "keeping an eye on" may report themselves to the Red Cross, but that will not be seen as full-scale employment. A large part of the people see in the real application of the measures without any loopholes a touchstone for the development of a true communal sense, and for the leadership's resolution to pursue the employment of all without exception. . . .

REPORT OF THE PRESIDENT OF THE SUPERIOR REGIONAL COURT, HAMBURG, TO THE REICH MINISTER OF JUSTICE, DATED 6 APRIL 1943*

Report on the General Situation:

Between my last report and this one lie the events of Stalingrad and the great retreat in Russia. These events have affected the population very deeply. By virtue of statements by all important personages, it had been believed that in this winter not only would a repetition of the defeat of winter 1941/42 be avoided, but that also Russian offensive strength had been finally exhausted. The people were therefore completely unprepared for such a serious setback. In this situation, it can be no surprise that the question is often asked whether it would have been wiser to evaluate Russian strength publicly more carefully than hitherto. There is also a failure to understand why the encirclement at Stalingrad was kept a secret in official reports for so long after it had taken place. The man in the street occupies himself even more critically with the question whether the sacrifices of Stalingrad were necessary, and whether it might not have been possible to save the 6th Army by withdrawal in good time.

However, morale has risen surprisingly quickly again after Stalingrad. Here the soldiers on leave from the front have made a contribution; despite everything, they have preserved the conviction of their superiority in combat, and have expressed this almost unanimously during their visits to the homeland. The report of the retreat from the Caucasus was also accepted much more readily, because the impression prevailed that here it was a case of a withdrawal which to a certain extent was orderly and had been ordered in good time; also the news from Rostov and Kharkov had a less depressing effect. The extraordinary danger that was precipitated from a Soviet thrust via Kharkov in the direction of the Black Sea was apparently not recognized by the majority.

*Bundesarchiv, Koblenz, ref. R22/3366 folio I/108.

The low point of the crisis of confidence had already been passed in general when the thrust toward Izyum and the reconquest of Kharkov brought proof that the German Army has retained its offensive strength. These events have further stiffened morale. The retreat in the center of the Eastern Front was generally judged very soberly and correctly understood as a timely movement of withdrawal which shows that the German Army leadership is consolidating the front without considerations of prestige.

Further developments in the summer of this year will be viewed without great expectations of victory, but without wavering. The main worry is about the third Russian winter. Hardly anybody expects a full defeat of Russia in this summer. One encounters generally the question whether the events of the last two winters in the east will be repeated in a third winter, and whether masses of Russian troops will again attack on such a scale, and whether our reserves can tolerate such wear and tear. This is the main worry expressed by the man in the street today.

Developments in Africa are viewed as skeptically as before. Frequent doubts are expressed as to whether it is possible to hold Tunis for long. However, the danger of a second front in Europe is not yet taken seriously.

The U-boats remain above all the great hope. In them is seen the trump card through which the enemy will be prevented from greater actions, and can finally be made ready to seek peace. The growth of a longing for peace among the people is unmistakable. The effect of the heavy air attacks is growing. Even though Hamburg and Bremen themselves remained undamaged, the catastrophes in other cities, for example in Essen, have an effect. Besides, the damage in the suburbs of Hamburg (Wegel, Rissen, Blankenese) and of Bremen (Blumenthal) was very great.

II

There is considerable criticism among the population, as I already stressed in my last situation report, of the personal life-style of leading men of the Party and State. There are again complaints that in many places the necessary simplicity is lacking. However, in Hamburg this criticism does not extend to the person of the Reichsstatthalter, Karl Kaufmann. It is a really heartening state of affairs, which is certainly not the case in all Districts, that the Gauleiter and Reichsstatthalter find appreciation in all areas. In criticism of the life-style of leading personalities, it is especially the subject of complaint that leading men of the Party, State, and Army make excessive use of motor vehicles. Despite all admonitions in this direction, it is again reported that on official occasions motor vehicles are used even where ample public transport is available. Recently, very many jokes have been circulating again, some of which are malicious in content. . . .

Bibliography

Beesly, Patrick. *Very Special Intelligence*. Revised edition. London: Sphere Books, 1978.

Bekker, Cajus. *The Luftwaffe War Diaries*. Trans. and ed. by Frank Ziegler. London: Corgi Books, 1969.

Bell, Coral. "Crisis Diplomacy." In *Strategic Thought in the Nuclear Age*, ed. by Laurence W. Martin. London: Heinemann, 1979.

Bialer, Seweryn, ed. *Stalin and His Generals*. New York: Pegasus, 1969.

Brecher, Michael. "A Theoretical Approach to International Crisis Behaviour." *The Jerusalem Journal of International Relations* (Hebrew University of Jerusalem), 2:2–3 (1978).

————, with Benjamin Geist. *Decisions in Crisis: Israel, 1967 and 1973*. Berkeley, Los Angeles, and London: University of California Press, 1980.

Bryant, Arthur. *Triumph in the West, 1943–1946*. London: Collins, 1959.

Buchan, Alistair. *Crisis Management*. Boulogne sur Seine: Atlantic Institute, 1966.

Bullock, Alan. *Hitler: A Study in Tyranny*. Harmondsworth: Penguin Books, 1962.

Carell, Paul. *Hitler's War on Russia: The Story of the German Defeat in the East*. London: George G. Harrap, 1964.

————. *Scorched Earth*. London: George G. Harrap, 1970.

Chant, Christopher, et al. *Hitler's Generals and Their Battles*. London: Salamander Books, 1976.

Chuikov, Vasily I. *The Beginning of the Road*. London: MacGibbon Kee, 1963.

Churchill, Winston S. *The Second World War*. 6 vols. London: Cassell, 1948–1954.

Clark, Alan. *Barbarossa: The Russian-German Conflict, 1941–45*. London: Hutchinson, 1965.

Compton, James V. *The Swastika and the Eagle*. London: Bodley Head, 1968.

Deakin, Frederick W. D. *The Brutal Friendship: Mussolini, Hitler and the Fall of Italian Fascism.* London: Weidenfeld and Nicolson, 1962.

Demeter, Karl. *The German Officer Corps in Society and State, 1650–1945.* Trans. by Angus Malcolm. London: Weidenfeld and Nicolson, 1965.

Dönitz, Karl. *Memoirs: Ten Years and Twenty Days.* London: Weidenfeld and Nicolson, 1959.

Erickson, John. *The Road to Stalingrad.* London: Weidenfeld and Nicolson, 1975.

Fest, Joachim C. *Hitler.* New York: Harcourt Brace Jovanovich, 1974.

Gilbert, Felix. *Hitler Directs His War: The Secret Records of His Daily Military Conferences.* Selected and annotated from the manuscript in the University of Pennsylvania Library. New York: Oxford University Press, 1951.

Görlitz, Walter. *Paulus: Stalingrad: Lebensweg und Nachlass des Generalfeldmarschalls.* Frankfurt am Main: Atheneum Verlag, 1969.

————, ed. *The Memoirs of Field-Marshal Keitel.* Trans. by David Irving. London: William Kimber, 1965.

Greiner, Helmuth. *Die Oberste Wehrmachtführung, 1939–45.* Wiesbaden: Limes Verlag, 1951.

Guderian, Heinz. *Panzer Leader.* London: Futura, 1974.

Halder, Franz. *Kriegstagebuch: tägliche Aufzeichnungen des Chefs des Generalstabes des Heeres 1939–1942.* 3 vols. Stuttgart: Kohlhammer Verlag, 1962–1964.

Hegel, Georg W. F. *Lectures on the Philosophy of History.* Trans. by J. Sibree. London: George Bell, 1905.

Heiden, Konrad. *Der Fuehrer.* Boston: Houghton Mifflin, 1944.

Hermann, Charles F. "International Crisis as a Situational Variable." In *International Politics and Foreign Policy,* ed. by James N. Rosenau. New York: Free Press, 1969.

Hillgruber, Andreas. *Staatsmänner und Diplomaten bei Hitler.* 2 vols. Frankfurt am Main: Bernard und Graefe Verlag für Wehrwesen, 1967, 1970.

Hinsley, Francis H., et al. *British Intelligence in the Second World War.* Vol. I. London: Her Majesty's Stationery Office, 1979.

Hitler, Adolf. *Hitler's Table Talk, 1941–1944.* Trans. by Norman Cameron and R. H. Stevens. Introductory essay by Hugh R. Trevor-Roper. London: Weidenfeld and Nicolson, 1953.

————. *Mein Kampf.* London: Hutchinson, no date (late 1930s).

Holsti, Ole R., and Alexander L. George. "The Effects of Stress on Performance of Foreign-Policy Makers." *Political Science Annual,* 6 (1975).

Hubatsch, Walther. *Hitlers Weisungen für die Kriegführung, 1939–1945.* Frankfurt am Main: Bernard und Graefe Verlag für Wehrwesen, 1962.

Istoriia Velikoi Otechestvennoi Voiny Sovetskogo Soiuza [History of the

Great Fatherland War of the Soviet Union]. Moscow: USSR Ministry of Defense Publishing House, 1963.

Jones, Reginald V. *Most Secret War*. London: Hamish Hamilton, 1978.

Jukes, Geoffrey. *The Defense of Moscow*. New York: Ballantine, 1969.

————. *Stalingrad: The Turning Point*. New York: Ballantine, 1968.

Kazakov, Mikhail I. "On the Voronezh Axis in the Summer of 1942" [in Russian]. *Voienno-Istoricheskii Zhurnal* (Moscow), 10 (1964).

Kielmansegg, J. A. Graf. *Der Fritschprozess 1938: Ablauf u. Hintergründe*. Heidelberg: Hoffmann und Campe, 1949.

Kotze, Hildegard von, ed. *Heeresadjutant bei Hitler, 1938–1943: Aufzeichnungen des Major Engel*. Stuttgart: Deutsche Verlags-Anstalt, 1974.

Kriegstagebuch des Oberkommandos der Wehrmacht (Wehrmachtführungsstab). Vol. II (1942), ed. by Andreas Hillgruber; Vol. III (1943), ed. by Walther Hubatsch. Frankfurt am Main: Bernard und Graefe Verlag für Wehrwesen, 1963.

Lavrin, Janko. *Russia, Slavdom and the Western World*. London: Bles, 1969.

Liddell Hart, Basil H. *History of the Second World War*. London: Pan Books, 1973.

————. *The Other Side of the Hill*. London: Panther, 1956.

Lochner, Louis P., ed. *The Goebbels Diaries*. London: Hamish Hamilton, 1948.

Manstein, Erich von. *Lost Victories*. London: Methuen, 1958.

Manvell, Roger, and Heinrich Fraenkel. *The July Plot*. London: Bodley Head, 1964.

Martienssen, Anthony. *Hitler and His Admirals*. London: Secker and Warburg, 1948.

Masterman, John C. *The Double-Cross System in the War of 1939 to 1945*. Canberra: Australian National University Press, 1972.

Mellenthin, Friedrich W. von. *German Generals of World War II*. Norman: University of Oklahoma Press, 1977.

Montague, Ewen. "The Man Who Never Was." In *Courage and Achievement: Three Famous Stories*. London: Evans Brothers, 1968.

Pope, Dudley. "Battle of the Barents Sea." In *History of the Second World War*, ed. by Barrie Pitt. Vol. III. London: Purnell, 1967.

Porten, Edward P. von der. *The German Navy in World War Two*. London: Pan Books, 1972.

Rokossovsky, Konstantin K. *A Soldier's Duty*. Moscow: Progress Publishers, 1970.

Samsonov, Alexander M. "Stalingrad: The Relief." In *History of the Second World War*, ed. by Barrie Pitt. Vol. III. London: Purnell, 1967.

Schlabrendorff, Fabian von. *Offiziere Gegen Hitler*. Zurich: Europa Verlag, 1946.

Schramm, Percy E. *Hitler: The Man and the Military Leader.* Chicago: Quadrangle Books, 1971.

Shirer, William L. *The Rise and Fall of the Third Reich.* London: Pan Books, 1964.

Shtemenko, Sergey M. *General'nyi shtab v gody voiny.* Moscow: Ministry of Defense Publishing House, 1981.

Sinel, Leslie P. *The German Occupation of Jersey.* London: Corgi, 1969.

Speer, Albert. *Inside the Third Reich.* London: Weidenfeld and Nicolson, 1970.

Tiulenev, Ivan V. *Through Three Wars* [in Russian]. Moscow: Ministry of Defense Publishing House, 1960.

Trevor-Roper, Hugh R., ed. *Hitler's War Directives, 1939–1945.* London: Sidgwick and Jackson, 1964.

Vasilevsky, Aleksandr M. *Delo vsei Zhizni.* Moscow: Politizdat, 1974.

———. "Nezabyvaemye dni" [Part I]. *Voienno-Istoricheskii Zhurnal* (Moscow), No. 10 (1965).

———. "Nezabyvaemye dni" [Part II]. *Voienno-Istoricheskii Zhurnal* (Moscow), No. 3 (1966).

Waite, Robert G. L. *The Psychopathic God: Adolf Hitler.* New York: Basic Books, 1977.

Warlimont, Walter. *Inside Hitler's Headquarters, 1939–45.* Trans. by R. H. Barry. London: Weidenfeld and Nicolson, 1964.

Winterbotham, Frederick W. *The Ultra Secret.* London: Weidenfeld and Nicolson, 1974.

Yeremenko, Andrey I. *Stalingrad* [in Russian]. Moscow: Ministry of Defense Publishing House, 1961.

Young, Oran R. *The Intermediaries: Third Parties in International Crises.* Princeton: Princeton University Press, 1967.

Zeller, Eberhard. *The Flame of Freedom.* Trans. by R. P. Heller and D. R. Masters. London: Oswald Wolff, 1967.

Zhukov, Georgy K. *Vospominaniia i razmyshleniia.* Moscow: Novosti Press Agency Publishing House, 1969. See also *The Memoirs of Marshal Zhukov.* London: Jonathan Cape, 1971.

Index

Adriatic, 114
Aegean Sea, 127
Africa, North, 76, 90, 98, 130, 151,
    180; and the Allies, 6, 16, 89, 91,
    96, 102, 176, 210; German offen-
    sive in, 2, 22, 62, 64, 69; and
    Hitler's concern with, 59–60, 61,
    62, 66, 89, 145; loss of, 109–10,
    160, 168, 195, 202; reinforcements
    for, 63, 89, 96, 110, 149, 150, 156,
    168, 195–96, 204, 205; suggested
    abandonment of, 116–17, 144, 147,
    177, 195, 204, 205; supply routes
    to, 96, 98, 116, 136, 159
Africa, West, 79
Afrika Brigade 999, 117, 132
Afrika Korps, 96, 110, 182
Air Fleet I, 163
Air Fleet II, 66, 116, 117, 130
Air Fleet IV, 109, 155
Air Force Field Divisions, 79, 81, 98,
    164; deployment of, 77, 82, 105,
    113, 116, 132, 152
Alam Halfa, 59, 61, 89
Albania, 115
Alexander, General Sir Harold, 89
Alexandria, 6, 59
Algeria, 116
Allies, 96, 204; bombing by, 165, 190;
    in French North Africa, 96, 97,
    143, 208; and invasion fears,
    39–41, 48, 51, 96, 136, 145,
    149–50, 151, 204
Altenfjord, 128
Ambrosio, General V., 160

Ammunition, 134, 139
Anapa, 41
Andöy, 80
Antonescu, Marshal I., 53, 78, 108;
    and Hitler, 105, 118, 135, 136, 149,
    152
Antonescu, Mihai, 68
"Anton" Operation, 101
Antonov, General A. I., 228
Antonyuk, General, 34
Armaments, 121, 122, 163, 190
Armed Forces Command of the
    Ukraine, 131
Army Coast Artillery, 158
Army Equipment, 40
Army Group A., 53, 58, 59, 60, 62,
    66, 112, 146, 148, 170, 184, 201,
    202, 212; command of, 64, 81, 143;
    forces of, 19, 47, 50–51, 54, 98,
    114, 155; formation of, 10, 36; and
    High Caucasus, 54–55, 57, 73; or-
    ders and objectives of, 41–42, 44,
    45, 46, 63–64, 67, 68, 78, 126,
    127, 146; and the Soviet Union, 80,
    88, 130, 142, 214, 239, 240; and
    supplies, 51, 140; withdrawal from
    the Caucasus, 88, 124, 127, 129,
    134, 167, 177, 178, 180, 195, 203,
    206, 207, 241
Army Group Africa, 139, 157
Army Group B, 53, 60, 66, 67, 99,
    105, 145, 170, 178, 184, 201; com-
    mand of, 43; forces of, 19, 47, 57,
    59, 68, 122; formation of, 9–10, 36;
    orders and objectives of, 41–42,

Army Group B (*continued*)
44, 45–46, 126, 146; and the Soviet
Union, 78, 88, 102, 103, 104, 202,
203, 209; and supplies, 55
Army Group Center, 9, 56, 61, 63,
150, 151; forces in, 51, 52, 54, 56,
57, 138; orders and objectives of,
46, 50, 66, 67, 113, 146, 157, 158;
and the Soviet Union, 56, 59, 73,
77, 80, 81, 230, 232; near Sukhinichi, 50, 57, 72, 83; and "Whirlwind" Operation, 51, 52, 54, 72
Army Group Don, 109, 114, 126, 127,
145, 170; formation of, 106, 107,
143, 145; and the Soviet Union, 88,
130; withdrawal of, 146, 220
Army Group North, 9, 46, 53, 78;
forces of, 51–52, 56, 100, 113;
and Leningrad, 44, 51, 55, 57, 58,
59, 62
Army Group South, 9–10, 31–32, 36,
155, 157, 158; at Voronezh, 35, 37
Army Personnel Office (HPA), 49
Arnim, Colonel-General
J. von, 114, 137, 157, 162, 166n35
Assault guns, 148, 151, 156, 162, 165;
and Guderian, 161, 165, 170
Astrakhan, 216
Atlantic, Battle of the, 2, 15, 22, 69,
160n23, 189
"Atlantic Wall," 164
Auchinleck, General Sir Claude, 89
Austria, 74
Austro-Hungarian Empire, 114–15,
177
Azov, Sea of, 26, 41

Bagramyan, General I. K., 34
Balearic Islands, 164
Balkans, 114, 115, 117, 120, 121, 140,
165; fear of invasion of, 113, 127,
136, 151, 168
Baltic States, 137
Barvenkovo Salient, 30–31, 227, 231
Bastico, General, 130
Battle of Britain, 3, 108
Bavaria, 97
Bay of Biscay, 158, 159
Bear Island, Battle of, 7, 128–29, 130,
144, 179, 188

Belgium, 39, 135
Belgorod, 2, 148
Bell, Coral, 17
Belorussia, 151
Benghazi, 100
Berchtesgaden, 12, 107, 116, 125,
176, 209; Hitler at, 97, 103, 143,
144, 208
Berghof. *See* Berchtesgaden
Beria, Lavrenty, 224, 229
Berlin, 76, 161, 198
Berlin Arsenal, 200
Berndt, A. I., 99
"Big Saturn" Operation, 239, 240, 241
Biological warfare, 83, 156
Bismarck, 188
Bizerte, 110, 135
Black Sea, 66, 78, 79
Black Sea Fleet, Soviet, 29, 30, 41, 88
Blockade runners, 98, 138, 158
Blomberg, General W. von, 8, 186,
222
"Blücher" Operation, 44–45
"Blue-1," 31
Blumentritt, Lieutenant-General G.,
67, 151
Bock, Field Marshal Fedor von, 27,
224; dismissal of, 43, 91, 187, 194,
201, 232; and Voronezh, 35–38, 43,
48, 176, 184, 201, 232
Bodenschatz, General K., 161
Bordeaux, 66
Bormann, Martin, 9, 137, 192–
93, 194, 198
"Brandenburg" Forces, 130, 163
Brauchitsch, Field Marshal W. von, 4,
8, 9, 70, 187
Brecher, Michael, 14, 18, 230
Britain, Great, 40, 41, 69, 156, 165,
181; and Europe, 54, 77, 102, 139,
165; and Hitler, 1, 39, 41, 62; and
North Africa, 41, 76, 80, 89, 98,
118, 125, 143, 202
British Air Force, 89
British Government Code and Cypher
School, 2n2, 7
British Navy, 89, 128, 179
Bryansk Front (Soviet), 32, 34
Buchan, Alistair, 16
Budenny, Marshal S. M., 223

Bulgaria, 114, 115, 118, 131, 132, 214;
    arms for, 16, 113, 117, 127, 137,
    165
Bürgerbräukeller, 97, 101
Busch, Field Marshal G. E., 100

Cairo, 6, 59
Campos, General, 163
Canada, 54
Catherine the Great, 173
Caucasus, 52, 63, 75, 201; German
    forces in, 123–24, 126; German of-
    fensive in, 28, 30, 45, 55, 61; Ger-
    man withdrawal from, 88, 112, 118,
    124, 134, 142, 177, 195, 203
Cavallero, Count U., 120
Channel Islands, 64, 76, 77, 80
Cherbourg, 78
Chetniks, 160
Chir River, 43, 117, 118, 120
Christian, Major, 109, 143, 182, 184,
    207, 208
Chuikov, Lieutenant-General V. I.,
    232, 235
Churchill, Winston, 89, 114, 115,
    150n3, 221, 233; as decision-maker,
    186, 187
Ciano, Count G., 101, 102, 105, 113,
    120, 145, 147, 183
Ciphers, 165, 181, 186, 189
Civilians, 39, 60, 61–62, 115, 130, 135
Clausewitz, Karl von, 199
Coal, 93
Commander-in-Chief East: and Ger-
    man generals, 155, 156, 170, 188,
    191, 192, 198, 212; Hitler's refusal
    to appoint, 148–49, 158, 171, 194,
    211
"Committee of Three," 137, 192, 211
Communist Party Central Committee,
    226
Corsica, 81, 102, 159
Council for Military-Political Propa-
    ganda, 48
Crete, 66, 67, 76, 79, 101, 114, 115,
    127; arms for, 78, 80, 101, 118, 159;
    forces for, 51, 64, 105, 107, 209
Crimea, 51, 88, 109, 231; and German
    offensive, 27, 29–30, 31
Crimean Front (Soviet), 30

Croatia, 114, 115, 118, 150, 152, 156;
    and German administration, 130,
    159, 166
Croatian Light Infantry Brigade, 164
Croat Mountain Divisions, 126
Cyrenaica, 101
Czechoslovakia, 74

Dardanelles, 120
Das Reich, 177
Demyansk, 140, 231
Denikin, General A. I., 178n17
Denmark, 137, 138
Dieppe, 54
Dietrich, SS Obergruppenführer
    (General) S., 163
Directive No. 28, 62n26
Directive No. 38, 160
Directive No. 41, 28, 44
Directive No. 42, 132
Directive No. 43, 41, 42, 61
Directive No. 44, 45
Directive No. 45, 45–46
Directive No. 46, 53
Directive No. 47, 62, 127
Dismissals: and German army, 198;
    and Hitler, 33, 75, 90, 91, 184,
    186–87, 188, 194, 223, 233; and
    Stalin, 34, 47, 186, 227, 233. See
    also individual generals
Dnieper River, 153, 159, 231
Donbass, 24, 26, 47, 93, 153
Don Front (Soviet), 85, 86–87, 88,
    237
Dönitz, Grand Admiral Karl, 69, 151,
    162, 165; and the Battle of the At-
    lantic, 2, 160n23; as Commander-
    in-Chief Navy, 129, 132, 140, 144,
    189; and surface warships, 113,
    156–57, 158
Don River: and German offensive, 26,
    27, 35–38, 47; and Soviet
    counteroffensive, 43, 85, 96, 98,
    107

East, Proclamation for the, 159, 161
Eastern Army (German), 64, 65
Eastern Campaign, 21, 23–28, 29–31
Eastern Front (German), 5–6, 10, 53,
    66, 67, 68, 70, 150; and confer-

Eastern Front (German) (*continued*)
ences at FHQ, 11, 72, 77, 144,
184, 192, 194, 211; and decision-
making, 13–14, 92, 93, 96, 97, 104,
106, 110, 111, 124–25, 129, 139,
168–69, 170, 180–81, 214–20;
forces at, 64, 117, 126, 150, 163;
and Hitler, 41–44, 45–46, 90, 118,
122; orders and objectives of, 4, 90,
126–27, 136–37
Egypt, 97, 101, 143
18th Army (German), 58, 116
8th Italian Army, 27
El Alamein, 76, 98–99; First Battle of,
89; Second Battle of, 2, 6, 17, 18,
81, 89, 95–96, 202
11th Air Force Field Division, 133,
162
11th Army (German), 27, 29, 30, 61,
77, 104, 105; and Leningrad, 30,
44, 58; orders and objectives of, 41,
42, 44
11th Panzer Division, 68, 77, 117, 118
Elista, 61, 216
Engel, Major G., 60, 63, 71, 140, 173;
and Hitler, 64, 179; and field generals, 46–47, 52, 81, 155, 156, 157,
170, 184, 224
Europe, 131, 149, 150; fear of invasion
of, 76, 77, 79, 96, 145, 168

Faeckenstedt, Major-General, 71
Fedorenko, General Y. N., 237
Feklenko, General N. V., 34
"Ferdinand" assault gun, 148, 162, 165
FHQ. *See* Führer Headquarters
Fichte, Johann G., 173
Fiebig, General M., 109
5th Panzer Army (German), 114, 131,
158
5th Tank Army (Soviet), 86
Finland, 45, 50, 120, 121, 214; and defenses for, 105, 131, 152, 161, 209
1st Mountain Division, 50–51, 62
1st Panzer Army (German), 27, 79,
113, 118; forces in, 16, 67, 216;
and Soviet forces, 31, 38, 52, 54,
123–24
First World War, 3, 23, 62, 115
Forced labor, 157, 166

Foreign Armies East, 9, 92; and Soviet
intentions, 43, 100, 101, 103n5,
143, 182
Foreign Armies West, 9, 10, 40
Foreign Intelligence Operations, 157
"Fortress Europe," 130
14th Motorized Infantry Division, 52
4th Mountain Division, 50–51
4th Panzer Army (German), 47, 57–
58, 108, 143; addition of forces to,
78, 122, 153; orders and objectives
of, 38, 65; and Stalingrad, 27, 53,
56, 83, 106, 107, 122; at Voronezh,
37, 43, 201, 232
4th Romanian Army, 27, 85, 149
France, 39, 74, 110, 117, 131, 136,
137, 138, 139; defense of, 40, 102,
116, 118, 122, 123, 125, 137, 140,
152; and fear of invasion of, 151,
156, 162, 214; unoccupied, invasion of, 15, 96, 97, 100, 102, 103,
110, 145, 208–9
Frederick Charles, Prince, 198
French Antilles, 131
French Army, 105
French Fleet, 105
French Garde Mobile, 164
French High Command, 103
French North Africa, 15, 18, 41, 100,
101; Allied invasion of, 2, 6, 79, 89,
96, 97, 99, 101–2, 143, 150n3,
202, 208
"Fridericus" Operation, 31, 50, 231
Friedrichshafen, 67
Fritsch, Colonel-General W. von, 8,
186, 222
Fromm, Colonel-General F., 122
Fuchs, Admiral, 69
Führer Conferences, 10–11. *See
also* Eastern Front; Führer Head-
quarters
Führer Directives, 11–12, 14. *See
also* Directives
Führer Headquarters (Führerhaupt-
quartier, FHQ), 9, 71, 90–91, 92,
116; conferences at, 60, 63, 72, 169,
184–85; Hitler's absences from, 12,
97, 153, 176, 184, 185, 206, 208,
210; moves of, 43, 83, 107
Führer Orders, 11, 12

Gallipoli, 115
Gehlen, Colonel R., 43
German agents, 40 n50
German Air Force, 8, 66, 98, 102, 157;
and Britain, 2, 3, 162, 165; and
decision-making, 189–90, 193, 194;
orders and objectives of, 40, 46, 56;
resources of, 59, 68, 82, 131; and
Stalingrad, 43, 58, 78, 145, 182,
202, 207
German Armed Forces Command Staff
(Wehrmachtführungsstab, WFST),
9, 12, 129, 132, 149, 156, 217;
moves of, 103, 107, 208
German Armed Forces High Command (Oberkommando der Wehrmacht, OKW), 9, 10, 23, 78, 91–
92, 97, 99, 153; Chief of General
Staff for, 149, 155, 156, 158; and
the Eastern Front, 77, 170, 184,
211; and Führer conferences, 11,
77, 78, 166, 191; and Hitler, 10, 72,
92, 144, 181, 188, 192, 194, 212;
War Diary of, 7, 13, 14, 71, 89,
129, 144, 166, 170, 217
German Army, 5–6, 82, 157, 167,
198–99, 199–200; and Hitler,
68–69, 179, 194; and manpower
problems, 67–68, 78, 117, 120, 136
German Army General Staff, 9, 27,
40, 44, 179, 231
German Army Headquarters (Oberkommando des Heeres, OKH), 9,
43, 50, 67, 151; and the Eastern
Front, 10, 92, 93; and Führer conferences, 11, 77, 78, 166, 191, 194;
and Hitler, 10, 83, 92, 144, 181,
192, 212, 224; War Diary of, 129,
144
German-Italian Panzer Army (DIPA),
6, 62, 89, 99, 100, 147; resources
of, 115, 132
German Navy, 15, 46, 78, 138, 165;
compared to British Navy, 128,
179; and Hitler, 6, 9, 69, 128–29,
144, 188–89, 193, 194; resources
of, 82, 140, 152, 160
German Officer Corps, 49
German Presidential Secretariat, 10
Gestapo, 101–2

Gibraltar, 99, 100, 101
Giraud, General H., 102
"Gisela" Operation, 110, 132
Glomfjord, 81
Goebbels, Joseph, 116, 163, 165, 168,
197, 233; and Berlin, 161, 198; and
Hitler, 74, 75, 92, 177; and manpower, 161, 163; and Nazi party
officials, 164, 197; and propaganda
in the east, 159, 164; and "total
war" propaganda, 140, 149, 166,
169, 193, 196, 197, 211
Gojlo, 150
Golikov, Lieutenant-General F. I., 32,
34, 232, 233
Golovanov, Lieutenant-General A. E.,
237
Gordov, Colonel-General V. N., 232–
33, 233, 237
Göring, Reichsmarschall Hermann, 8,
23, 58, 79, 128, 159, 190, 193; and
bombing of German cities, 138,
161, 162, 202; and Hitler, 92, 190;
and Mussolini, 113, 145, 161–62;
and Stalingrad airlift, 96, 108, 133,
143, 145, 177, 182, 202–3, 205,
207
"Göring" Brigade, 39, 40, 67
"Göring" Division, 131, 135, 136, 137,
152, 164
Greece, 115, 136, 159, 162, 214, 242
Greiner, Helmut, 13, 60, 122–23, 129
"Grossdeutschland" Division, 63, 67;
deployments of, 46, 52, 54, 56, 57,
58, 59, 127; at Voronezh, 36, 37
Guderian, Colonel-General Heinz,
149, 155, 160, 165, 170
"Gustav" heavy gun, 165
Gylenfeldt, General von, 52, 60

Halder, Colonel-General Franz, 9,
27, 46, 51, 56, 60, 68, 224; and
decision-making, 11, 185, 194, 211;
dismissal of, 13, 60, 68, 73, 188,
191, 211; and Hitler, disagreement
with, on military matters, 44, 48,
49, 53, 54, 55, 57, 75, 176, 181;
and Hitler, relations with, 63, 71,
183–84, 192, 199; and senior
officers, 12, 47, 49, 71, 198; and

Halder, Col.-Gen. Franz (*continued*)
the Soviet Union, 40, 43–44, 67,
85, 174 n6; and Voronezh, 36, 37,
38, 43, 58
Hauffe, General A., 53–54, 108
Hegel, Georg W. F., 173
Heinkel-177, 82
Herder, Johann G. von, 173
Hermann, Charles F., 16–17
Hess, Rudolf, 23
Heusinger, Major-General Adolf,
43–44
Himmler, Reichsleiter H., 105, 131,
150
Hindenburg, Field Marshal P. von, 8
Hipper, 128
Hitler, Adolf, 8, 69, 78, 104, 114–15,
190; absences from FHQ, 12, 68,
97, 153, 161, 210, 224; appearances
in public, 97, 155 n11, 165–66,
197; assassination attempts against,
3, 199, 200; as authority figure, 8,
9, 10, 185–86, 196–200, 212, 218,
221; as decision-maker, 6–7, 8–14,
60, 91–92, 93, 122–23, 135, 144,
148–49, and Chapter Seven; and
defeat, 47, 233; effect of stress on,
103–4, 123, 124, 175–81, 183–85,
200–210, 210–13; and field commanders, 166, 170, 184, 191, 192,
198, 204, 210, 211, 212, 224; and
generals, 3, 5, 43, 67, 151, 222–23,
236, 242; and generals, animosity
toward, 49, 59, 138, 179; and generals, practical contact with, 49,
187–88, 224; and generals, in September 1942, 60, 63–64, 64–65,
69–75, 176 (*see also individual
generals*); and Headquarters Generals, 198, 204, 210; health of, 105,
209–10; and historical experience,
74, 177–80, 210; and interference
in details, 66, 83, 97, 99–100, 125,
139, 166, 192, 216–18; as military
leader and planner, 3, 19, 21, 46,
74–75, 90, 91; and race, 4, 19, 90,
91; and satellite countries, 5, 80,
81, 82, 115, 139, 156 (*see also
individual countries*); and self-
confidence, 74, 75, 102, 105, 182,

183, 188; and the Soviet Union,
misperceptions of, 52, 61, 90, 91,
103 n5, 182; and Stalin, 7, 88, and
Chapter Eight; and underestimation of Allies, 4, 22–23, 96
Hossbach Memorandum, 177
Hostages, 39
Hoth, Colonel-General, H., 37, 38,
118, 125–26, 241
Hungarian Forces, 114, 115, 142, 150,
152; and German command of, 134;
at Stalingrad, 6, 103, 133–34, 134
Hungarian 2nd Army, 27, 80, 132, 138,
166; and German back-up, 51, 56;
reorganization of, 139, 159; and the
Soviet Union, 109, 110, 129, 138

Iberian Peninsula, 151
Iceland-Murmansk-Archangel convoy
route, 24
India, 120
International Crisis Behavior Defini-
tions, 28, 93, 200
International Crisis Behavior Research
Questions, ix, 20, 210–13
Iran, 26 n7
Iraq, 26 n7
Iron ore, 93, 139
Italian Alpini Corps, 57
Italian Army Command, 130
Italian 8th Army, 5, 80, 109, 110,
118–19, 122; and German back-up,
53, 55–56, 57, 66, 81; morale of,
81; reorganization of, 139, 156
Italian Forces, 57, 99; morale of, 115,
159–60, 162; in the Soviet Union,
5, 6, 133–34, 134, 142, 150, 152
Italian Front, 122
Italian Navy, 165
Italy, 96, 101, 117; arms to, 110, 137;
and Corsica, 102; and Croatia, 166;
fear of invasion of, 164, 196, 204;
German lack of consultation with,
78, 89, 131, 140; and Germany, 66,
156, 160, 161–62, 204, 242; and
Tunisia, 102–3, 114, 162–63
Ivanov, V. D., 86

Japan, 2, 22, 26, 242
Japanese Air Force, 24

Japanese Navy, 24
Jeschonnek, Colonel-General H., 56, 122, 162, 190; and Stalingrad airlift, 96, 108, 143, 145, 203, 205
Jews, 161, 163
Jodl, Colonel-General Alfred, 1, 4, 9, 23, 101, 152, 162; and Army Group A, 46, 47, 53, 112, 127, 183, 184, 187, 224; and decision-making, 183, 184, 185, 194, 211; and disagreements with Hitler, 77, 79, 89; and field officers, 12, 157, 198; and Leningrad, 50, 62; in September 1942, 63, 64, 65, 70, 71, 73, 144, 176, 181–82, 192, 208, 210; at the "Small Chancellory," 103, 208; and Stalingrad, 76, 107; and Stalingrad airlift, 96, 207; and withdrawal from Stalingrad, 125, 142, 145, 146, 195, 203
JU-52s, 109
JU-88s, 98
JW-51B convoy, 128

Kalach, 85, 107
Kalitva, 126
Kalmyk Steppe, 122
Kastornoye, 34
Keitel, Field Marshal Wilhelm, 9, 12, 38, 62, 79, 137, 162; and decision-making, 183, 193, 194, 211; and Hitler, 73, 92, 140, 142, 187, 190, 226; and senior officers, 12, 13, 49, 149, 157, 187–88, 193, 194, 198; at "Small Chancellory," 103, 208; and Stalingrad, 195, 203; threats of dismissal against, 61, 65, 70, 184
Keitel, General Bodewin, 49
Kerch, 30, 31
Kerch Peninsula, 29, 30
Kerch Straits, 58, 59, 88, 109; and 11th Army, 41, 42, 44, 61; as supply route, 126, 130, 140
Kesselring, Field Marshal A., 104, 130, 151, 162, 166; and Africa, 135, 136, 157, 160, 164, 196; and replacement of Keitel, 65, 73; and resources for Africa, 132, 150, 151
Kharkov: Hitler's orders to Manstein, 153, 167, 168, 170, 177; Manstein's

counteroffensive at, 2, 148, 161, 180; Soviet counteroffensive at, 31, 231
Khrushchev, Lieutenant-General N., 84, 243
Kiev, 166
Kirov, 61, 82–83
Kleist, Colonel-General Ewald von, 31, 42, 71; and Army Group A, 107, 143, 241
Kluge, Field Marshal H. von, 50, 58, 59, 61, 110, 116; and Headquarters generals, 188, 198; and proposed Commander-in-Chief East, 157, 158, 170, 171, 188, 191, 230; and "Whirlwind" Operation, 54, 55, 72
Kolpakchi, Lieutenant-General V. Y., 232
"Kommandobefehl," 79
Kotelnikovo, 117, 118, 126
Kozlov, Lieutenant-General D. T., 29, 30, 224–25, 231
Krancke, Vice-Admiral T., 128, 179
Krasnoarmeyskoye, 153
Krasnograd, 153
Kremlin, 224, 225
Kshen River, 34
Kuban, 24, 127, 155
Kuban River, 53
Küchler, Field Marshal G. von, 50, 56, 100
Kuibyshev, 224
Kulik, Marshal G. I., 222
Kummetz, Vice-Admiral O., 128
Kuporosnoye, 235
Kursk, 231
Kursk Salient, 167
Kuznetsov, Admiral N. G.: and Stavka, 223, 225, 226

Laconia, 65
Ladoga, Lake, 57, 58, 82, 127
Lammers, Dr. Hans, 10, 137, 193, 194
Latvia, 151, 152
Laval, Pierre, 101, 102–3
Leeb, Field Marshal W. von, 70, 187
Leibstandarte Adolf Hitler (Waffen SS 1st Division), 38–39, 127
Lemnos, 118

Leningrad, 44, 163; German failure at, 223; German offensive against, 5, 27, 45, 46, 51, 93, 134, 140; and "Northern Light" Operation, 50, 72; siege of, 21, 57; and the Soviet Union, 33, 82, 127, 231
Libya: British offensive in, 118, 125; Rommel retreat from, 97, 99
List, Field Marshal W., 36; and Army Group A, 52, 59, 71; dismissal of, 64, 65, 72, 73, 176, 187, 194; relations with Hitler, 60, 63, 64, 71, 176, 184
Lithuania, 151, 152
"Little Saturn" Operation, 88, 239
Löhr, Colonel-General A., 159
Lopatin, General A. I., 232
Lossow, General Otto von, 74
Luftwaffe. *See* German Air Force
Lützow, 128

Main Political Directorate, 48
Malaya, 158
Malenkov, G., 224, 226
Malinovsky, General R. Y., 239
Malta, 76, 98, 101
Mannerheim, Field Marshal K., 152
Manpower, 76, 78, 136, 142, 149, 242; in the civilian sector, 77, 120, 157, 163; drafts for armed forces, 122, 131, 133, 137, 161, 162. *See also* German Air Force; German Army; German Navy
Manstein, Field Marshal Erich von, 6, 30, 68, 146; and Army Group A, 81, 104–5, 106, 143; and Army Group Don, 106, 107, 143, 145; and Army Group South, 155; and February 1943 counteroffensive, 148, 153, 167, 170, 171, 177; freedom of action for, 151, 152, 166, 185, 188; and Hitler, 192, 206; meetings with Hitler, 81, 161; meeting with Hitler, 5–6 February 1943, 150, 171; meeting with Hitler, 17–19 February 1943, 167, 168, 169, 170, 171, 185, 224; and Kharkov, 152, 163; and Leningrad, 30, 51, 55, 62; and proposed Commander-in-Chief East, 156, 170, 171,

188, 191, 230; and relief of Stalingrad, 88, 112, 113, 118, 121, 122, 124, 125, 143, 145, 202, 203; and Stalingrad airlift, 96; and surrender negotiations at Stalingrad, 134, 139; and withdrawal from Stalingrad, 109, 142, 145, 146, 195, 212
"Man Who Never Was," 41 n54
Mareth, 129, 139, 162, 164
Mark III tank, 151, 152 n8
Mark VI (Tiger) tank, 160
Marsala, 159
Marseilles, 131
Marx, Karl, 173
May Day, 1923, 74
Maykop oil field, 41
Mediterranean Sea: Allied superiority in, 89, 114, 117, 121, 195, 196, 204; fear of Allied action in, 76, 81, 96, 97, 157, 162; and German air cover of, 98, 165; German forces in, 41, 116, 125, 131; and Hitler, 66, 110; transport problems in, 89, 117, 136, 138
Mein Kampf, 175, 176, 177, 179
Meissner, Otto, 10
Mekhlis, L. Z., 30, 222, 224–25, 231
Meretskov, Marshal K. A., 223
Mersa Brega, 115, 116, 120
Messe, General G., 81
Middle East, 41, 64, 96
Mihailovich, General D., 160
Mikoyan, A., 223
Milch, Field Marshal E. and Stalingrad airlift, 133, 134, 137, 203, 205, 209
Millerovo, 81
Mius River, 150
Model, General W., 56–57, 65
Molotov, V. M., 120, 121, 223, 224, 226
Mongolia, 234
Montenegro, 160
Montgomery, General Sir Bernard, 89
Morell, Dr. T., 210
Moscow, 21, 33, 70, 74, 230–31, 232
Moscow, Battle of, 23, 174, 234, 243; and Hitler's relations with his generals, 187, 223
Mostar, 156

Mozdok, 113
Munich: Hitler's visit to, 97, 101, 143, 208
Murmansk, 113, 128
Murmansk-Archangel route, 26
Murmansk convoys, 157
Mussolini, Benito, 100, 145, 160, 186; and Hitler, 104, 118; and North Africa, 99, 115, 130, 139, 162–63, 195; and war with the Soviet Union, 112, 115, 120–22, 145, 147, 183

Naples, 136
Naples, Gulf of, 138
Narvik, 139, 155
Naval Coast Artillery, 114
Naval Command (SKL), 99, 100
Nazi Party, 74
Nazi Party Chancellory, 9, 10
Nazism, 174, 178, 185
Nehring, General Walter, 88
Netherlands, 39, 39–40, 166
Neubronn, General, 117
Newspapers, 48
Nickel mines, 45
97th Light Division, 130
9th Army (German), 50, 51, 52, 54, 56, 61
Normandy Peninsula, 62
North Caucasus Front (Soviet), 27–28
Northern Donets: and Manstein's February 1943 counteroffensive, 148, 153, 166, 167, 168, 206
"Northern Light" Operation, 50, 51, 55, 56, 58, 62, 72
Norway, 81, 102, 137, 138, 155, 161; arms for, 118, 150; fear of invasion of, 76, 79–80, 139–40, 162, 168; and German forces, 100, 105, 125, 130, 152, 163, 209; German warships in, 65, 157
Norwegian islands, 80
Novikov, Lieutenant-General A. A., 237, 238
Novorossiysk, 41, 51
Nuremberg, 161

Oil: German supplies of, 26, 42, 93; in Romania, 130; Soviet supplies of, 36, 42–43, 44

Oil fields, 4, 240; Caucasian, 18, 24, 46, 88, 93
OKH. *See* German Army Headquarters
OKW. *See* German Armed Forces High Command
170th Infantry Division, 58
164th Infantry Division, 136
113th Infantry Division, 66
100th Light Division, 68
Orel, 32

Pacific Ocean, 2, 22
Palermo, 136
Panther tanks, 126, 148
Panzer Army Africa (German), 60, 81
Panzer IV tank, 165
Partisans, 53, 131, 150, 156; and Army Group Center, 52, 61; in Croatia, 118; and railways, 98, 167; in Yugoslavia, 152, 160
Paulus, Field Marshal Friedrich, 31, 71, 184; and attempted breakthrough to Stalingrad, 112; and attempted withdrawal from Stalingrad, 122, 125, 139, 142, 145, 195, 202, 203; promotion of, 134, 140, 188, 204; and proposed dismissal of Jodl, 65, 73; and Stalingrad, 107, 108, 133; and Stalingrad airlift, 96; and surrender of Stalingrad, 134, 135, 139, 216; and visit by Engel, 46–47, 224
Pavelic, A., 68
Pavlov, Army General D. G., 222
Peloponnese, 114, 115, 159; forces to, 105, 133, 209
Persian Gulf, 24, 120
Pétain, Marshal P., 163
Peter the Great, 120, 173
Pitomnik, 133, 205, 209
Poland, 157, 222
Porsche, Dr. F., 165
Porsche tanks, 61
Portugal, 110, 149, 151
Poti, 79
Prisoners, 65, 79, 80–81, 133; and German women, 115–16; as manpower, 164; treatment of, 77, 79, 81

Public opinion, 115–16, 140, 164, 196–97, 245–48

Raeder, Grand Admiral Erich, 65, 69, 128; resignation of, 7, 132, 140, 179, 189, 200; and surface warships, 113, 135
Railways, 117, 131, 138, 155, 166; defenses for, 139, 140, 151–52; and Soviet supplies, 24, 26
Rastenburg, 9, 83
Raubal, Geli, 103
Red Army. *See* Soviet Army
Red October Factory, 79
Reichel, Major, 31–33, 35, 232
Reichenau, Field Marshal W. von, 43
Replacement Army, 40
Rhineland, 74, 242
Rhodes, 114, 115, 130, 165
Ribbentrop, J. von, 23
Richthofen, Colonel-General W. von, 58*n*18, 66
"Ring" Operation, 136
Rintelen, von, 99
Rokossovsky, Marshal K. K., 86, 228, 232; Soviet offensive, 237, 239, 240, 241; and Stalin, 226, 227, 235; and Stalin's relations with the military, 225, 226, 229
Romania, 53, 99, 130, 139, 152, 182; arms for, 131, 137; and forces at Stalingrad, 5, 85, 103, 109, 142, 149
Romanian Army, 136
Romanian 4th Army, 5, 107
Romanian oil district, 130
Romanian 3rd Army, 58, 78, 80; at Stalingrad, 5, 105, 106
Romanian 3rd Mountain Division, 58, 59
Rommel Field Marshal E.: and abandonment of North Africa, 116–17, 147, 182, 195–96, 204, 205; at Alam Halfa, 59, 89; and El Alamein, 81, 96, 98–99; and forces in North Africa, 96, 99–100, 136, 157; and Hitler, 70, 76, 89, 143–44, 188; illness of, 158, 162; and Mareth, 129, 139; and Mersa Brega, 115, 116, 120; and North Africa, 97, 109–10, 130, 160

Roosevelt, Franklin D., 186
Rostov, 22, 46, 47, 223; and Army Group A, 88, 129; and German offensive, 27, 42; as a rail center, 24, 126; and the Soviet Union, 203, 240; and threat of Soviet drive on, 82, 83, 126, 130, 142, 178, 180
Rügenwalde, 165
Rügenwalde Artillery School, 133
Rundstedt, Field Marshal G. von, 101; and proposed Commander-in-Chief East, 155, 156, 170, 191; resignation of, 70, 187, 199
Russia. *See* Soviet Union
Russian Academy of Sciences, 173
Russian Army, 173
Russian Front, 81–82
Rzhev, 56–57, 58, 59, 63
Rzhev-Vyazma, 230, 231, 238
Rzhev-Vyazma railroad, 58

SA, 74, 103
Sabotage, 39, 190
Salonica-Athens Railroad, 127, 130
Salzburg, 176, 208
Sardinia, 116, 164; defense of, 149, 159; fear of invasion of, 138, 214
Sark, 77
"Saturn" Operation, 88
Sauckel, F., 163
Scandinavia, 149–50, 152
Scharnhorst, 157
Schelling, Friedrich W., 173
Schmundt, Lieutenant-General, 157, 179, 198
Schott Position, 162, 164
Schramm, Professor Dr. Percy E., 13, 129
Schweinfurt, 67
2nd Army (German), 114
Second Front, 36, 39–41, 120, 242
2nd Guards Army (Soviet), 239
2nd Panzer Army (German), 51, 57, 163
2nd Parachute Division, 152
Second World War, 97
Security Service (SD), 196–97
Seeckt, General H. von, 73
Serafimovich, 26, 59
Sevastopol, 29, 30, 31
715th Division, 164

17th Army (German), 27, 38, 53, 78; and Romanian formations, 81, 149. *See also* 298th Infantry Division
17th Panzer Division, 118
7th Air Division, 40
7th Panzer Division, 114
7th Parachute Division, 62, 62–63
72nd Infantry Division, 52, 54
Shamanin, F. A., 30
Shaposhnikov, Marshal B. M., 35, 223, 225, 227; and planning for Soviet offensive, 33, 231
Shipping, 24, 44, 165
Shtemenko, General S. M., 224, 228–29
Shumilov, Colonel-General M. S., 235
Sicily, 100, 101; defense of, 149, 159
Sirotinskaya, 55
16th Army (German), 100
16th Motorized Division, 36, 55, 122
16th Motorized Infantry Division, 61, 216
6th Army (German), 109, 134, 134–35; alternatives for, at Stalingrad, 202, 212; attacks on, by Soviet Union, 129, 133, 134, 136, 140; attempts to relieve, 116, 117, 118, 121, 122, 124–25, 126–27, 135, 146; defeat of, 133, 134, 136; forces of, 51, 67–68, 98, 108, 114; and "Fridericus," 31; and German offensive, 27, 34, 37, 38, 53, 57, 58; and proposed withdrawal from Stalingrad, 120, 122, 124, 139, 142, 184, 195, 205; at Stalingrad, 66, 83, 96, 98, 105, 107, 108; supplies for, 46, 108, 108–9, 122, 131, 134, 139
6th Panzer Army (German), 143
"Small Chancellory," 103, 107, 208
Smolensk, 77, 231
Social Darwinism, 90, 173, 177, 178
Sodenstern, General G. von, 37, 38
Southeastern Front (Soviet), 84, 85, 107, 233, 236
Southern Army Group (Soviet), 231
Southern Front (Soviet), 31, 240, 241
"Southern Group of Generals," 84
Southwestern Army Group (Soviet), 231
Southwestern "Direction," 227, 232
Southwest Front (Soviet), 27–28, 31,

34, 35; and "Saturn" Operation, 88; and Stalingrad counteroffensive, 85, 86, 86–87, 237
Soviet Air Force, 54, 146, 165, 238
Soviet Army, 41, 48, 73, 80, 90, 138; dismissals from, 34; morale of, 47–48; at Stalingrad, 5, 58, 102, 129, 133; and supplies, 84
Soviet Far Eastern Ports, 24
Soviet General Staff, 223, 228, 230; and decision-making, 186; and fear of attack on Moscow, 231, 232; and the Reichel documents, 32; and the Soviet counteroffensive, 32–33, 226, 234
Soviet High Command, 205, 243
Soviet Navy, 48
Soviet Operations Directorate, 227, 228, 240
Soviet Pacific Ports, 24
Soviet State Defense Committee, 87, 223, 224, 226, 239
Soviet Union, 32–33, 47, 83, 120, 159, 181; and biological warfare, 83, 156; and the Crimean Front, 29, 41, 45–46; and drive down the Don, 142, 146, 203, 206, 208, 214 (*see also* Stalin); German offensives in, 1, 21, 90, 178, 242; German perceptions of, 173–75, 176; and Hitler's misperception of intentions of, 42–43, 48, 51, 82–83, 179–80; and Hitler's underestimation of, 5, 28, 40, 46, 61, 90, 91, 174, 176; and Manstein's counteroffensive, 158, 166, 167, 168, 171; and a Second Front, 40–41; and Stalingrad, 2, 43, 85, 96, 143, 144, 182, 202, 203, 210, 213; and suggested stop to war with, 113, 115, 120–22, 145–46, 147, 183; supplies in, 22, 24, 26, 169, 207; and surrender terms at Stalingrad, 129, 132, 133, 134, 135, 136, 142; tank production in, 55, 181, 183; at Voronezh, 36–38, 58, 201
Spain, 118, 136, 137, 164; arms to, 16, 136, 137, 155, 163; fear of invasion of, 149, 214; and "Gisela" Operation, 110, 132
Speer, Albert, 101, 193; and arms pro-

Speer, Albert (*continued*)
    duction, 122, 161; and Hitler, 75,
    104; and manpower situation, 77,
    120; and war production, 67, 189,
    190
SS Police Division, 133
SS "Reich" Division, 39, 63, 127, 153
SS Totenkopf Division, 126, 133, 138
SS "Wiking" Division, 67, 118, 122,
    123, 124
Stalin, Joseph, 34, 56, 223, 228–29;
    and Army Groups, 224, 235; as
    decision-maker, 7, 186, 187, 221,
    243; and defeat, 47, 233; and dis-
    missals, 34, 87, 231, 233; and drive
    down the Don, 53, 97, 178, 179,
    239, 240, 241 (*see also* Soviet
    Union); and interference in detail,
    233, 239; and Kharkov, 31; and
    planning for 1942, 32–33, 84–88,
    230–31, 233–42; and the Reichel
    documents, 32, 232; relations of,
    with the military, 47–48, 86, 87,
    222–23, 224–25, 226–27, 229–30,
    232–33, 235–36, 241–42, 242–43;
    and a Second Front, 41
Stalingrad, 5, 66; attempts for relief
    of, 127, 177, 204, 205, 209, 210;
    and civilians, 60, 61–62; encircle-
    ment of Germans at, 136, 145, 176,
    180, 201, 203, 205, 234, 239, 241;
    German alternatives at, 144–47,
    200–201, 212; German forces at, 6,
    87, 106, 109, 114, 140; German
    planning for offensive on, 44, 45–
    46, 75; German surrender at, 20,
    148, 167, 168, 179, 181, 210, 216;
    and Hoth's relief attempt, 118,
    125–26; and Manstein's relief at-
    tempt, 112, 113, 118, 121, 143,
    145, 239; and Soviet attacks in Sep-
    tember 1942, 61, 63, 72; and Soviet
    counteroffensive, 96, 105, 129, 133,
    141, 143, 144–45, 178, 202; and
    Soviet counteroffensive planning,
    83–84, 144, 233–41; Soviet forces
    near, 58, 79, 102, 103, 104, 214;
    and Soviet surrender terms, 129,
    132, 133, 134, 135, 136, 142; and
    the Soviet Union, 42–43, 86; So-

viet victory at, 129, 134, 136, 140;
    suggested German withdrawal
    from, 104, 142, 145, 146, 195, 196,
    202–3, 206, 211
Stalingrad airlift: failure of, 121, 125,
    135, 146; Hitler's belief in, 142,
    145, 177, 182, 184, 190, 205; and
    Milch, 133, 134, 137, 209; opposi-
    tion to, 96, 108, 143, 207; possibil-
    ity of, 107, 108
Stalingrad Front (Soviet), 229, 233;
    and planning for Soviet counter-
    offensive, 84, 85, 233, 236, 237;
    and Soviet counteroffensive, 88,
    107
Stary Oskol, 34
State Chancellory, 10
Stavka, 32–33, 203, 223, 231; and
    Army Groups, 224, 225, 229; and
    the Crimea, 29, 30; and planning
    for Soviet counteroffensive, 84, 86,
    87, 225–26, 237, 239, 240, 241
Steel, 45, 140, 160
Strub, 176
Stülpnagel, Colonel-General E. von,
    110
Submarines, 69, 189
Suez Canal, 6, 59, 89, 96
Sukhinichi, 50, 57, 72, 83
Sukhumi, 54, 62
Supplies, 158, 168; Allied superiority
    in, 242; conference on, 162; Ger-
    man shortages of, 55, 137, 146, 159
Swansea, 40
Sweden, 137, 139, 152, 161; action
    feared in, 105, 168, 209
Sychavka, 58

Taman Peninsula, 30, 139; and Army
    Group A, 88, 129, 146; and 11th
    Army, 41, 44
Tanks, 67, 138, 148, 152, 153, 162;
    Mark IIIs, 151; Mark IVs, 160;
    Panthers, 126; Panzer IVs, 165;
    Porsches, 61; Soviet production of,
    55, 181, 183; and the Soviet Union,
    34, 35, 85; Tigers, 59, 113, 114,
    126, 156
Tatsinskaya, 125
10th Panzer Division, 130, 131

Terek River, 53
3rd Mountain Division, 58
3rd Panzer Army (German), 52, 54, 63
3rd Romanian Army, 27, 85, 149
39th Division, 158
Thorn Artillery School, 133
Thrace, 132
328th Infantry Division, 77
327th Infantry Division, 133
Tiger tanks, 59, 113, 114, 126, 148, 156
Tikhaya Sosna River, 37, 38
Timoshenko, Marshal S. K., 223, 224; and planning for Soviet offensive, 227, 231; and Voronezh, 38, 44, 232
Tippelskirch, General K. von, 81
Tirpitz, 157
Tito, 160
Tiulenev, General V. I., 229, 240–41
Todt, Dr. F., 190
"Torch" Operation, 41
Toropets, 78, 105
"Total war" campaign: and Goebbels, 140, 193; and Hitler, 166, 169, 196, 197, 211; and manpower, 149
Toulon, 105, 137
Transcaucasian Front (Soviet), 229, 240, 241
Trans-Siberian Railway, 24
Trapani, 159
Tripoli, 100
Tripolitania, 101, 139
"Triton" German U-boat cipher, 2, 7
Taupse, 68, 71
Tunis: arms for, 110, 136; and French forces at, 103, 110; reinforcements for, 114, 116, 117
Tunisia, 114, 129, 131, 137, 157; forces in, 102, 122, 132, 136, 147, 149; and "Göring" division, 135, 136, 137; and Italians, 102, 130–31, 162–63
Turkey, 30, 115, 117; and the Allies, 113, 127, 131–32, 168; and the Balkans, 136, 151; and Bulgaria, 114, 214
"Turkish Ditch," 30
12th Panzer Division, 52, 53, 57
20th Mountain Army (German), 45, 131

24th Panzer Division, 36, 37
29th Motorized Infantry Division, 98
22nd Airborne Division, 63, 107
22nd Panzer Division, 53, 55, 57, 59, 66
27th Panzer Division, 67
23rd Infantry Division, 39
23rd Panzer Division, 32, 36
256th Infantry Division, 52
298th Infantry Division, 53, 54

U-boats, 131, 136, 138, 151, 152; and the Battle of the Atlantic, 2, 160
Udet, Colonel-General E., 190
U506, 65
Ukraine, 23, 24, 137, 157, 166
United States of America, 22, 24, 131, 242; and biological warfare, 156; Hitler's underestimation of, 4, 22–23; and North Africa, 41, 102
U156, 65
"Uranus" Operation, 85, 88, 239

Vasilevsky, Marshal A. M., 87, 223, 227, 228–29; as Chief of the General Staff, 35, 227; and decision-making, 186, 225; and Soviet counteroffensive, 33, 84, 85, 86, 233–40; and Stalin's contact with Army Groups, 224, 229, 233
Vatutin, General N. F., 34, 223, 232, 237
Vehicles: requisitioning of, 137, 139, 159
Velikiye Luki, 77, 113, 116
Vienna, 164–65
Vinnitsa, 9, 43, 49, 83
Vladivostok, 24
Volga River, 27, 31, 45, 107, 201; as supply route, 24, 44
Volkhov Front (German), 58
Volovo, 34
Volsky, Lieutenant-General V. T., 87–88, 235
Voronezh, 35, 76; and Bock, 43, 48, 91, 174; German offensive at, 26, 28, 34, 114; and Hitler, 35–38, 65, 67, 201; and the Soviet Union, 35, 38, 58, 230, 232
Voronezh Front (Soviet), 34, 88

Voronov, Chief Marshal of Artillery
    N. N., 86, 105, 223, 234, 237
Voroshilov, Marshal K. E., 223, 224
Vorozheykin, General G. A., 232, 234
Voznesensky, N. A., 223

War-gaming, 86–87
Warlimont, General Walter, 13, 23,
    52, 80; dismissal of, 99, 187; and
    Hitler, 60–61, 74–75, 184
Warships: decision to scrap, 113, 130,
    143, 156, 158, 179, 210; in Norway,
    65, 157; Raeder's memorandum on,
    135
Wartenburg, General Count Yorck
    von, 199
Weather conditions: effect on Hitler,
    55 n14, 61, 64, 72–73; in High
    Caucasus, 54–55, 57, 73; at Vin-
    nitsa, 49
Weber, Max, 173
Weichs, Colonel-General M. von, 43,
    145, 184, 187; and forces near Sta-
    lingrad, 67, 71, 138; visited by En-
    gel, 46–47, 224; at Voronezh, 36,
    65; and withdrawal from Stalingrad,
    195, 202
"Werewolf," 9, 43
Western Front (Soviet), 32
Weygand, General M., 101
Wfst. See German Armed Forces
    Command Staff
"Whirlwind" Operation, 50, 51, 52,
    54, 55, 72
Winter, Colonel August, 47, 71
Wolf's Lair, 9

Yeremenko, Colonel-General A. I.,
    232–33, 235, 243; and planning for
    Soviet counteroffensive, 86, 236,
    237, 240, 241
Young, Oran, R., 16
Yugoslavia: and Bulgaria, 131, 152,
    160, 242

Zaporozh'ye, 153
Zeitzler, Colonel-General Kurt, 9, 67,
    81, 83, 109, 144; and Army Group
    A, 78, 112, 127; and decision-
    making, 183, 192, 194, 211; and
    disagreements with Hitler, 76, 130,
    131, 138; and discussions on the
    Eastern Front, 11, 13–14, 72, 92,
    129, 170; and Hitler's relations
    with field generals, 198, 224; and
    Hitler's reluctance to make deci-
    sions, 97, 104, 177, 209; relations
    with OKW, 77, 78, 191; and Sta-
    lingrad airlift, 96, 108, 145, 207;
    and surrender negotiations at Sta-
    lingrad, 134, 139; and withdrawal
    from Stalingrad, 122, 125, 142,
    146, 195, 196, 211
Zhdanov, A. A., 223
Zhukov, Field Marshal G. K., 32,
    223, 225, 227, 243; and decision-
    making, 186; and planning for So-
    viet counteroffensive, 33, 84, 85,
    86, 87, 231, 233–40; and Stalin's
    contact with Army Groups, 224,
    229
Zubtsov, 59

Compositor: G & S Typesetters, Inc.
Text: Caledonia
Display: Caledonia
Printer: McNaughton & Gunn
Binder: John H. Dekker & Sons